EYES AS BIG AS CANTALOUPES

An Irreverent Look at TV

by

Don Freeman

With a Preface by Bob Hope

Joyce Press, Inc.
San Diego, California
1978

Much of the material in this book appeared originally in different forms in The San Diego Union and various newspapers subscribing to Copley News Service. Special gratitude is expressed to the Union-Tribune Publishing Company and to Gerald L. Warren, editor of The San Diego Union, for permission to reprint it.

"Portrait of a Genius" Reprinted with permission from THE SATURDAY EVENING POST © 1977

"Bing" reprinted with permission from TV GUIDE® Magazine. Copyright © 1978 by Triangle Publications, Inc., Radnor, Pennsylvania.

"Television is proof that people would rather look at anything than at each other."

— Pat Buttram

To my mother and father.

Preface by Bob Hope

Don Freeman knew he was safe in asking me to write the preface to his book. If I didn't do it, you'd have seen me referred to in one of his future columns as the "plump, balding, seldom-funny comedian."

Listen, it pays to stay on the right side of the press in general and television critics in particular. With an act like mine, I can't be too careful.

Not that I have anything against television critics. They have their problems and they review mine. There's really a lot of tough critics in America and they have their audience ... my canary gets to read all their columns! But one of the reasons for my success is that I have a very short name and the columnists find it easier to type.

I once asked a critic how he liked my show and he said: "I really can't say — I'm a very heavy sleeper."

But I don't argue with the press. Once I said something the Christian Science Monitor didn't like and the next morning their editorial read: "THERE IS NO BOB HOPE."

And that was nice compared to a columnist who wrote that "Bob Hope is a boy who came up from nothing and brought it all with him." Another said that my career "symbolizes the triumph of stubbornness over talent." And when I got a medal from President John F. Kennedy, one paper had it on the front page under "Today's Chuckle." And when I was hired by Timex, one TV columnist wrote in the headline on his page: "Watch company tries new torture test." And when I wrote my first book, one critic wrote: "The kindest thing I can say about Bob Hope's book is that he's as good a writer as he is an actor."

I've always welcomed criticism — and then I started getting some. My severest critic, however, is my wife Dolores. Fortunately, she doesn't know what I do for a living — she thinks I'm a pilot for Pan-Am.

But my advice to all critics is, if you want your paper to be more widely read, there's one important thing you can do ... teach the delivery boys to throw straighter.

Face it — critics are a necessary evil ... like dentists and loan sharks. And their job is a tough one. It isn't easy to think up all those different ways to say "LOUSY."

Seriously, though, I hold great admiration for the television reviewers throughout the country. They are the ones who help establish the public's criteria for good entertainment. With television being such a major part of our society, of our daily existence, we need guidelines with which we can make the most productive and rewarding use of our time. The Don Freemans of this world provide those guidelines — for the viewer and for the entertainer as well.

Bob Hope

Foreword

When television was emerging in the post-World War II era, the star performers who had graced radio sought to bridge the electronic gap as the actors in silent movies had, many years earlier, ventured into talkies. For some, such as Jack Benny, Red Skelton, Bob Hope, George Burns and Gracie Allen, the transition was accomplished with ease.

Others encountered bitterness and failure. One star of radio comedy who never found his niche in TV was the beloved wit, Fred Allen.

In his last years, Allen was reduced to the demeaning role of panelist on the occupational guessing game, "What's My Line?" Television and Fred Allen were ill-matched, which was a loss both for us and television. Before his death in 1956, Allen was a disenchanted man, heavy with disdainful wrath for this new inhospitable medium. But his wry, ironic, New England wit never left him.

Someone asked Fred Allen to issue a prediction on the impact of television. He grimaced. "The next generation," Allen said in his distinctively nasal fashion, "will have eyes as big as cantaloupes — and no brains at all."

It is from that throwaway remark that I have chosen the title for this book. As it turned out, Allen may have been right about the disappearance of our brains. As for the eyes of that next generation, they do seem to be slightly distended. I know that after 20-odd years of professional viewing, my own eyes have expanded now to the shape of vaguely reddish kumquats.

In that time, I have been writing a nationally syndicated column for The San Diego Union and the Copley News Service. On the whole, it almost beats working. As I have construed the general outlines of my job, it has produced in me and many of my colleagues a curious, new conglomerate breed of journalistic cat, being part critic and part columnist.

In the first capacity, one comes to grips — esthetically, subjectively and preferably with humor — with what transpires on the TV screen and occasionally off of it as well. A critique is an uncommonly good place to vent one's gripes and prejudices and these, often as not, are gripes and prejudices shared by other viewers — namely, the readers.

As all teachers, preachers and patients of psychiatrists will attest, having a personal forum can be great fun. Except for the doubtful joy of staring at a blank piece of paper and waiting for those "tiny drops of blood to fall from the forehead" (as the sports columnist Red Smith once observed), I have enjoyed every other minute of it.

In the second capacity, as columnist, one ventures with a less Olympian approach into the province of people, interviews, associations and friendships. And this can be great fun, too. And often illuminating.

I doubt, for instance, that in any other line of work I would have had the opportunity to lunch with William F. Buckley Jr., television's keeper of the keys of conservatism, at his Manhattan townhouse. That luncheon I remember well because it was followed by an unusual adventure. The time had whizzed by, as it does when one is listening to Bill Buckley, and it was necessary now for me to leave for the theater and a matinee performance.

"Hop on the Honda," Buckley urged, indicating the motorbike parked in his hallway.

And so we zipped down Park Avenue, Buckley at the throttle, hair flying in the breeze, snaking in and out of traffic — always to the right, of course. A few weeks later, when Buckley dispatched a copy of his newly published book, "The Unmaking of a Mayor," his inscription read: "From your chauffeur, Bill Buckley."

In the capacity of a TV critic-columnist, one's education is unarguably furthered. I found myself in London once when the BBC was presenting a show filmed in a nudist colony. The next day, Mary Malone, the critic for the Daily Mirror, observed in her review: "The perils of going about starkers are a revelation. Keeping a wary eye out for nettles and thistles is obvious enough. But who would have dreamed that the most dangerous job a nudist can do is to fry sausages?"

There are fewer perils, but they exist nonetheless, in a television critic-columnist going about saying publicly that he actually likes television. Once, on Tom Snyder's "Tomorrow Show," on NBC, I was among four TV columnists assembled to discuss the season. At one point, I mentioned casually that I liked television. Snyder was amused, my colleagues shocked. One of them glowered and said he "hated" television.

8

Had I said something so outrageous? A drama critic is presumed to love the theater, a music critic is daft about music, a writer on politics delights in the excitement of a political race. I like television but I see its warts plain: it is a medium of mendacity governed by the ratings that bring in the millions, but the people in it — the performers, the producers, the directors, the publicists, the executives at the networks and the local stations, even the fellow who repairs my set — are generally a likable lot, colorful and quotable.

And I would use similar phrases in describing my fellow television editors on newspapers across the land, a convivial group whose individual views, even when differing from mine, I respect. In our periodic meetings, these editors give the lie to a statement made by David Eisenhower, Ike's grandson, who worked on a Philadelphia newspaper one summer and was later asked for his overall impression.

Young Eisenhower gave the matter solemn thought and then he declared: "Newspaper people aren't as interesting as they think they are." Put them at a hospitality suite bar and they are.

What I like about television is what I watch on it for my own pleasure. As this is written, I can cast my gaze in one week on "M*A*S*H" and "Barney Miller" and "60 Minutes," on the "Today Show" or "Good Morning, America" or the local equivalent called "Sunup," on Johnny Carson late at night, on a "Police Story," the network and local newscasts, reruns of the "Andy Griffith Show" (which I guess is my favorite vintage series), an old movie or two, at least one sports event, a Dick Cavett interview, a "Masterpiece Theater," a panel discussion, a "docudrama" of moment, certainly a few talk shows, plays when they come around.

Now all of the foregoing would add up to at least 20 to 25 hours in front of the set, which is still below the national average estimated at around 27 or more hours. How much television are we supposed to watch, anyway? Once, in that regard, I asked a fellow named Tom Fournier, who is my barber, why he didn't have a TV set in his shop.

"For a good reason," Fournier replied. "A lot of my customers, businessmen, tell me that they're hooked on soap operas. I'm here in the shop all day. *I don't want to get hooked on soap operas!*"

Well, at least I don't watch soap operas. And I don't watch television while my hair is being cut.

When the thought of putting together a book first took hold, there was loose talk of setting down a rounded, exhaustive history of television, a worthy if dreary project to contemplate. Instead, I elected on the happier notion of passing along more of those gripes and prejudices, some seriously, some frivolously, mostly from television but others from the vast and inviting world beyond the 21-inch screen.

The history I will leave to the historians. I am, strictly speaking, a newspaperman and, like so many of us, I was inspired to the profession by the Ben Hecht-Charles MacArthur play, "The Front Page." We wanted to be newspapermen — not journalists, which by one definition is a newspaperman who carries a walking stick. We wanted to be Hildy Johnson out of "The Front Page" and yell into a phone: "Stop the presses! I got a scoop that'll set this town on its ear!"

I never did become Hildy Johnson. Instead, I became a TV critic-columnist and perhaps, eventually, if I keep at it, Fred Allen's ominous prophesy will bear fruit as I continue to stare at the set, watching with eyes as big as cantaloupes ...

Don Freeman

TV and the Intellectuals

"Video is hideo." — Ogden Nash

One Sunday afternoon in the early 1960s, when Brendan Behan was on one of his periodic visits to the United States, I accompanied this brawling boyo of an Irish playwright to his first bullfight. We ventured down to Tijuana, Mexico, a half-hour's drive south of San Diego. Behan, then at the height of his fame, had lived for a time in Spain — most of the other time he was either writing plays or languishing in jail for his rebellious activities with the Irish Republican Army — but he could never afford the luxury of a ticket to the *corrida*.

The bullfight in Tijuana that day turned out poorly. The bulls were pacifists, lacking in combative zest, the matadors were inexpert and at the conclusion the spectators registered their disapproval by noisily hurling seat cushions into the arena.

Ducking under the flying seat cushions, I turned to Behan. "Well, Brendan," I said, "your first bullfight — what did you think of it?"

He sighed, glumly. Then, in his lilting Irish brogue, Behan replied: "It could have been worse — it could have been folk singing!"

And so it is with television. It could have been worse. It could have been Cher singing "Blue Tail Fly." Still, if there is one singular fact about this curious medium, it is — and always has been — its incomparable diversity. In contrast to the movies and theater and literature and journalism, all of which it embraces in one vast umbrella, television defies any but the most superficial of judgments on its totality.

But this has never prevented such utterances as: "Television is rotten. How can you stand to watch it?" What is generally meant by

11

this is that a succession of dull programs had led to, in Marya Mannes' phrase, the "11 o'clock letdown."

And yet, if a Broadway season were to include an original comedy-drama starring Laurence Olivier and Katharine Hepburn, at the height of their game, breathing great humor and fire into "Love Among the Ruins," *and* a riveting production of Eugene O'Neill's "A Moon for the Misbegotten," with Jason Robards and Collen Dewhurst at the top of *their* game, it would be hailed as a truly rewarding if not glorious season indeed. "The theater is terrific," it would be said. In one recent television season, these two programs were offered and as yet nobody has been heard proclaiming the glories of the medium in its entirety. Nor should they, not if they had also been witness to "Let's Make a Deal" and the "Gong Show" and so on. "All I want from life is truth and beauty and money," said H. Allen Smith, who was one of the most snappish of American humorists. It is that way with the three major television networks. All they want from life is truth and beauty and money, with the order slightly reversed, leaving beauty and truth about ten laps behind the winner — and Olivier and O'Neill are not, on TV, synonymous with money. The belly dancers always outdraw Ibsen.

Parenthetically (or perhaps significantly), in the mid '70s, one of the networks promoted an executive with great hurrah into a prime position of authority over its programming. It was commonly known that this fellow had for some time been seeing a psychiatrist. Having reached an exalted pinnacle in the business of communications, he was consulting a shrink about his basic problem — his inability to communicate with people. It is one of the many ironies about this most ironic of mediums.

Begin with the first irony — an image based on tiny dots beyond count on a 21-inch screen has a startling effect when observed in real, or non-television life. Ogden Nash, the late poet, was once a panelist on the old "Masquerade Party" show and his face suddenly became a part of the TV viewers' experience. "When a New York cabbie knows you from TV and calls you by name, your tip status automatically jumps," Nash told me once. "I used to tip a quarter. Now I have to make it fifty cents. If you're a public personality you cannot, after all, be a public cheapskate."

Once, sitting in a convertible on the Coronado ferry boat of old crossing the bay from San Diego, James Arness of "Gunsmoke," wearing his frontier costume as Marshal Matt Dillon, was spotted by a woman in the next car. She moved in for a closer look.

"Matt Dillon!" she shrieked. Then she shook her head in disbelief. "Why, you look exactly the way you are!"

The unchallengeable truth is that nobody on television ever looks exactly the way he or she is — on American television, that is. The picture image on the TV screen in this country is one of the world's worst. In technical jargon, the faulty image stems from the number of "lines" projected by the image-orthicon tube onto the screen. France is far ahead of us in quality of TV image, followed by England, Russia and Spain.

As Alistair Cooke once observed, "The question of whether we should have better shows on TV pales before whether we'll ever get a TV image capable of making a human face appear not to be made of cement. Viewers in this country accept the fact that on TV a man's eyes will look like two raisins and his mouth like a gash across his face. Most of us on TV look like gangsters and the women on TV have torsos distorted beyond description."

Alistair Cooke's donnish good looks and his soothingly non-specific English accent have graced television for many years, going back to the celebrated "Omnibus" series and, more recently, as the host of the BBC import, "Masterpiece Theater." Although he has resided on our shores since the 1940s and has, in fact, renounced his British citizenship, Cooke possesses the most British voice regularly heard on American television.

Once I asked Cooke about his voice and how, conversely, the British take to any of the subtle changes in its locutions over the years.

"Oddly enough, the British accept my voice now as typically American," Cooke replied. "There's a story about accents. According to the American view, the British started out in life talking like regular fellows — in other words, like Americans — but ended up putting on the dog. But the British view is that the Americans started out talking nicely — in other words, like the British — but ended up talking like juvenile delinquents."

Bob Hope once offered this pointed definition — "A snob," said Hope, "is a guy who turns on his television set and if he doesn't see Alistair Cooke, he turns it off." The ripple of truth in Hope's line came to mind when the Saturday Review, a magazine of earnest pretensions, came out with a cover that heralded its lead article, as follows: "The Intellectual in Videoland."

The writer was Douglass Cater, identified as an author and political correspondent and director of the Aspen Institute's Program on Communications and Society. "No doubt about it," Cater wrote, "television is a booming presence in American life, even though most of us hardly know what to make of the medium."

He expanded on the swiftness of television's emergence. In January, 1949, Cater wrote, only 2.3 percent of American homes had the box with the cathode-ray tube then known as video. Five years later, TV had penetrated more than half of our homes and that, further, by 1975 fully 97 percent of American homes had one or more sets — "a distribution roughly matching that of indoor plumbing." Or, for a less dramatic but just as valid comparison, kitchens.

Cater quoted from "the prescient Mr. Marconi," who predicted long ago that telecommunications would become part of the "almost unnoticed working equipment of civilization," a most apt phrase to come from an inventor.

"Why unnoticed?" wrote Cater. "What has prevented thinking people from applying their critical faculties to this medium, which reaches greater masses than do all the other mass mediums combined?"

Cater's answer followed: "Scientific evidence suggests that thinking people — at least those over 25 — are left-brained in development. That is, they rely mainly on the left hemisphere, which controls sequential, analytical tasks based on the use of propositional thought. But TV . . . appeals mainly to the right hemisphere of the brain, which controls appositional — that is, non-sequential, non-analytic thought."

And you are at liberty to accept that line of reasoning if you wish. "The Intellectual in Videoland," indeed.

The "intellectual" who wanders into "videoland" simply doesn't know the territory. The intellectual — a weary and imprecise term that escapes definition — doesn't watch television, or pretends not to.

In that regard, a cartoon in the New Yorker pictured a man watching a western on TV. His wife has the phone in her hand and the man is yelling: "I know I'm watching 'Gunsmoke' but tell them we're looking at Channel 13."

Channel 13 in New York is the old educational television channel and now there is no more "educational" television, which was an intellectual's phrase and clearly an ill-advised one. Now we have in its stead Public Television, which offers enough in the way of program nourishment to satisfy any intellectual — if he could be lured away from surreptitious viewing of "Let's Make a Deal."

One of the few men of intellect ever to step gingerly into video's treacherous waters was Dr. Marshall McLuhan, a Canadian professor with a flair for an occasional insight, a slick turn of phrase and a gift for obfuscation in the thunderous turgidity of his prose. But for a time, in the late '60s and early '70s, McLuhan commanded attention for his seemingly learned pronouncements, an Andy Warhol of the campus telling us what we already know in a form of language that Casey Stengel would envy.

From the scholarly Dr. McLuhan, in all of his volumes and lectures, our knowledge was enriched by such statements as TV is a "cool" medium, and print and radio are "hot" mediums. It is a thesis that Steve Allen, the comedian-author, expressed just as well when he theorized: "The people who will last on television are the ones who talk softly. TV is not a medium for yelling." Archie Bunker proved him only slightly off-target.

From Dr. McLuhan we learned that "the medium is the message," a catch-phrase as tricky as it was self-evident. A more cogent if less quotable statement came from Ted Geisel, the children's writer known as Dr. Seuss, who explained one of his TV animations with: "The statement is the picture."

☆ ☆ ☆

Television is the biggest, the grandest, the most stupefyingly vast mixed bag ever conceived. Television is life reflected in all of its hues and textures, a catch-all as evasive as mercury. "Of all the so-called wonders of our time, television may well be the most momentous," wrote Malcolm Muggeridge, the waspish former editor of Punch, when TV was just beginning. "Nothing since the invention of printing has so drastically affected the way human beings live, think and generally react to their circumstances."

Muggeridge was indisputably on the button. Television *is* the most revolutionary spin of the wheel of civilization since the Chinese invented ink, 1,200 years before Christ. Television is, in its present form, more than anyone could have reasonably foreseen when, in the late 1940s, what was visible on that novelty of a tiny screen was only the blurred movement of the wrestlers and the roller derby. There was also, in those days, a cool performer named Dave Garroway, as cool as the medium was cool, who needed no McLuhanesque phraseology to steer him to his rightful place on television. The presence of a Garroway — and Burr Tillstrom's puppet show, "Kukla, Fran and Ollie" — should have served as clue that TV would not for long be so easily classifiable by the intellectuals or the rest of us.

Television *is* all of us, all of our experiences, fantasies, fears and dreams, the best and worst in the human character, with all of the shadings in between. Television is Lucy and Rhoda and Howard Cosell and Bob Cromie's "Book Beat" and Merv and Mike, Dinah and Johnny (Griffin, Douglas, Shore and Carson for the non-talk show viewers) and Archie Bunker and Lawrence Welk and Cronkite and Cher and Barbara Walters and "Hollywood Squares" and "Roots" and "Kojak" and "Wall Street Week" and on and endlessly on, an incredibly diverse and inextricably tangled blend of reality and illusion.

To the old saw about politics being too important for the politicians and war too important for the generals, it might be added that television is, quite simply, too complex for the intellectuals.

Intellectuals should read TV Guide but it is unlikely that they do — and perhaps it is good that they don't, for then the editors might curry to this new-found interest with tomes as dreary as those to be found in doctoral theses on any campus — all written, of course, by certified intellectuals. However, if the intellectuals did read TV Guide, they might have encountered the following from Eric Sevareid, former national correspondent and commentator for CBS, written in December,

15

1967: "There is, and always has been, a broad swatch of professional intellectuals who fear and detest anything new, particularly if it is adaptable to the pleasure of the great mass of ordinary people. This particular type of intellectual neither knows nor likes ordinary people. This is why they write about 'humanity' and not about persons ... Of course, they hate TV, which is simply the latest and most universal symbol of a culture of universality ...

"We need a little less hypocrisy, and a lot more common sense in our evaluations of an all-pervasive (if not all-persuasive) medium for amusement, information, enlightenment, inspiration, boredom, irritation and anxiety — one that is already imbedded within the warp and woof of America, is going to be with us permanently, often reflects the mediocre in our society, rarely the worst and sometimes the finest."

The finest of television has come from many sources, including in only two instances — and that is appallingly small — men recruited from the halls of *academe*. First, in the mid-1950's, there was Dr. Frank C. Baxter, who enlivened the airwaves and the viewers' storehouse of appreciation with his "Shakespeare on TV." It was generally believed that he would be the forerunner of many other educators on the medium. Surely, from colleges across the land, there would be enlisted into TV's ranks other lively professors, more Dr. Baxters. John Crosby, then the TV columnist for the New York Herald Tribune, suggested that "professors will be coming out of the woodwork, swarming happily into television."

This never came to pass. Dr. Baxter, then a shining light in the English department of the University of Southern California, was that conspicuous rarity, a learned professor who could talk, entertainingly and compellingly, on a popular level. Others signed on for brief auditions but were rejected, with sound reason, by the viewers. Not for nearly twenty years would there be another Dr. Baxter and he was spawned on the BBC, a Polish immigrant who had migrated to England. He was Dr. Jacob Bronowski, who died in the summer of 1974, shortly before his BBC production, "The Ascent of Man," was visible on American television. At the time of his death, Dr. Bronowski was a senior fellow at the Salk Institute in La Jolla, Cal. "Bronowski was a small man, not very handsome but when he walked into a room, he seemed ten feet tall and blazingly attractive," observed George Steedman of the BBC, who knew Bronowski throughout his career in radio and TV in London.

The host and interviewer for the American version of "The Ascent of Man" was Anthony Hopkins, an English actor of the top rank. Earlier Hopkins had seen a BBC program called "Brains Trust," on which three prominent scientists grappled with weighty questions phoned in by the viewers. On this particular show, someone asked, "Does a chicken know it's a chicken?"

As Hopkins recalls, "The question was given to Julian Huxley, who spent what seemed like hours in arriving at some vague answer. Then another panelist tied himself in knots on the pure philosophy of existence. Finally, they came to Jacob Bronowski, who said, 'I don't know if a chicken knows it's a chicken. I've never been a chicken. Who cares, anyway? What's the next question?' "

Hopkins immediately became an avid Bronowski fan. A few years later, after seeing "The Ascent of Man" on the BBC, Hopkins wrote a fan letter to Bronowski. Typically, Bronowski, who was known to London cabbies affectionately as "Bruno," always answered his own fan mail. He wrote back: "Are you Anthony Hopkins the actor? If so . . . thank YOU very much."

Only two months after this exchange of letters, Bronowski died. But his widow remembered and asked Hopkins to host the series when it was distributed to the Public Broadcasting Service in America. "The Ascent of Man," a high watermark of profound thought and a distillation of one man's assessment of the peak moments in the million years of cultural evolution, is Jacob Bronowski's legacy on film. But where, one asks with plaintive insistence, were the other professors, the other intellectuals, from the campus or elsewhere, who could have contributed to the substance of television?

Occasionally, television does go to the campus for guidance. For example, in the early 1970s, NBC had in readiness the notion for a Saturday morning children's show called "Land of the Lost." In it, Rick Marshall, a forest ranger, and his teenage son and daughter, Will and Holly, are floating down a river on a raft. Then an earthquake hits and they are transported by a treacherous waterfall into a prehistoric world lost somewhere in the vast corridors of time.

There they are confronted with strange reptiles, dinosaurs, flying animals and the native monkey-men, known as the Pakuni tribe — and, as every right-thinking viewer soon learned, the tribe speaks flawless Paku.

Paku is a real, made-up television language, a linguistic first and, possibly, a last. When the show was conceived high in the corporate headquarters of the National Broadcasting Co., a vice president named Joe Taritero reasoned: "What I don't want in this show is the monkey-men going around saying 'umgawa.' I want their sounds to be a real language. Maybe *a whole new language!*"

Taritero, seeking a whole new language, was referred to Dr. Victoria Fromkin, a renowned scholar and head of the Department of Linguistics at UCLA.

"Need-um new language," Taritero said, more or less.

"You got it," said Dr. Fromkin, not in those exact words.

The creation of Paku emerged as a fascinating and scholarly project. This is by no means a form of pig latin. Paku is — to use a phrase not yet found in Paku — the real McCoy. Although her colleagues were amused by Dr. Fromkin's association with children's television, known to readers of Variety as "kid-vid," she went at her work with dedicated fervor. She devised the Paku language according to the strict international rules of syntax. Plurals, for example, were formed not by adding "s," as in English, but by adding "ni" (pronounced knee). Thus, the Paku word for child is "abu" — for children it's "abuni."

In the very first "Land of the Lost" script that she received, there were indications that two Pakuni were swearing. Accordingly, she made up some Paku obscenities. NBC, naturally, censored them out.

They are a busy lot, the network censors, and their principal concern in the 1970s has been the proliferation of violence on television. It's a subject that has been analyzed and pawed over and gnawed at with tiresome and inconclusive results. When a young U.S. boy, about 12, killed his next-door neighbors, his defense was based on the supposition that watching violence on TV had instigated his own acts of violence.

Despite his lawyer's eloquence, the case was lost but a precedent was clearly set in the defense of other, similar murders. And television may not be entirely blameless. When the violence on TV shows is wanton and purposeless ("Starsky and Hutch" and "Baretta" are prime examples), it does us no good. Our sensibilities are bruised, our collective shells hardened. Excessive violence on television chips away at our humanity; it diminishes us in indefinable ways beyond measure.

On this issue, the behavioral scientists are at odds mainly because they disagree over the roots of human aggression which in turn lead to violence — and then to violence portrayed and observed on television.

There are those from the ranks of science who say that our aggressiveness is so deeply ingrained in our nature that it is all we can do to hold it in check. Others proclaim that aggressions, in common with other behavior, are largely learned. Erich Fromm theorizes that modern society, with its stresses and frustrations and deprivations of the human spirit, is the major wellspring of aggression.

How will these experts resolve their differences? Who can say? Maybe they'll fight.

The fear of violence persistently intrudes our consciousness and this is obviously reflected in what we see on television. It is the fear of being mugged, for example, that underlies the TV commercials in which Karl Malden, star of the now defunct "Streets of San Francisco" series, does his pitch for American Express. So long as the traveler carries American Express checks instead of cash, Malden informs the viewers, one can feel trouble-free.

To see Malden on the TV screen, speaking with gruff confidence in his product, is a ticket to intimations of security. Wearing his snap-brim fedora and the same resolute, well-remembered expression that enhanced his police lieutenant's role in the television series, Malden delivers the commercial with the crackling authority granted him by more than 40 years of acting experience.

On a visit to San Francisco, I met Malden one day. Proudly, I whipped out a sheaf bearing the American Express imprint.

Malden shrugged. "Forget it," he said. "The bastards will steal them, too."

He was right. They did.

Some Brickbats

How, I have been asked with numbing frequency, can you watch all that junk on the television night after night? And I reply that the junk is the source of columns that are, I have to admit, maliciously enjoyable to write. Show me a columnist who doesn't rub his hands with anticipation while watching a rotten show and I'll show you someone who's been rendered diabetic from watching too much Donny and Marie.

"I love criticism," Noel Coward once wrote, "so long as it's total praise." Nobody loves criticism that is total bombardment except for those who write it and those who read it. Nielsen maintains no such surveys but I would suspect that the readers delight as much in a stabbing critique as the writer who pours his sweet venom into the typewriter, which is at least a more acceptable release than kicking the dog and belting the kids.

In the last few years, I think the worst show to befall these weary eyes (a phrase that Alexander Woollcott conceived even before there was such a thing as television) was an NBC "Big Event" so dreadful, so witless and ill-conceived that I found myself almost hypnotically entranced. I couldn't wait to spring to a typewriter. A recitation of that "Big Event" follows, along with some other items that provided almost as much pure diabolical pleasure at the typewriter.

Star-Studded Parties

Scholars of television history, a small but enormously erudite if bug-eyed bunch of fair-minded observers, will never forget Sept. 26, 1976. As it dawned clear, somehow in the very air you could detect the odor of history about to be made, which is an acrid smell if you've never noticed. This was the day that witnessed the debut of "The Big Event" on NBC, thus instantly taking rank among historic dates somewhere between the fall of the Bastille and the cancellation of "My Mother, the Car."

When NBC first announced the concept to be known as "The Big Event," nobody at the network had an answer for the burning question: what is a "Big Event," exactly? Now we know what it is. "The Big Event" is an earthquake followed by a bomb.

To commemorate the opening "Big Event," NBC brought us first the television premiere of "Earthquake." This is a movie of 1974 vintage starring Charlton Heston, Ava Gardner, Lorne Greene, Richard Roundtree and a cast of thousands of falling buildings as a city undergoes total collapse. Of course it was only Los Angeles.

Thereafter, NBC fleshed out "The Big Event" with something called "The Big Party." This consisted of — and I quote here from a network communique — "live coverage of three star-studded parties being held in New York City to celebrate the start of a new season in motion pictures, the theatrical arts and sports."

What emerged was a Titanic of television, a disaster of such monumental proportions that Charlton Heston himself would have thrown up his hands. (In a gesture of mercy rivaling the best of Florence Nightingale, one local station chose to take a pass on "The Big Party." Rarely has the public interest been so judiciously served.)

The executive in charge of "The Big Event," Alvin Cooperman, had predicted that his series "will include the kind of outstanding television events that will become the topic of conversation on Monday morning." Undoubtedly, "The Big Event" was the topic of lively, morning-after discussion in the network's upper echelons, much of it conducted between clenched teeth.

Anyway, the thing began with Dick Cavett as the host of the sports portion of the show. "You could say," Cavett said, "that this is a tribute to every fighter who ever stepped into a ring, to every kid who ever wanted to compete in the Olympics. You could say it." Pause. "It would be corny but you could say it."

Moving right along, and none too soon, the cameras turned to Leonard Nimoy greeting the stars entering a theater. "It's raining in New York," Nimoy declared, "but the stars are out."

Unfortunately, Nimoy had divested himself of his pointy ears from "Star Trek" and, being unrecognized, was compelled to introduce himself to the stars before he interviewed them.

Back now to Cavett who stood at "ringside" for a weigh-in by Ali and Norton. "The scale," Cavett explained, "was made by the Cosa Nostra Honest Weight Co. in New Jersey."

Ali hollered menacingly at Norton: "I will destroy you! You talk too much!"

Only someone with the gifts and the space of a Charles Dickens could adequately describe the confusion that followed. At one point Ethel Merman walked down Shubert Alley, carrying an umbrella against the rain and singing "Everything's Coming Up Roses."

Safely inside Sardi's restaurant, Merman sang a few songs accompanied at the piano by Marvin Hamlisch, who is very good at composing and showing off for company. Later, they conducted a community sing at the piano. I have no idea why they did this.

This incomprehensible onslaught of delicious idiocy continued with Lauren Bacall interviewing such people as Dustin Hoffman about his new flick, "The Marathon Man," which also stars Laurence Olivier.

"Many in our business," she said, "think Olivier is the greatest actor in the world."

"He must have the greatest taste of any actor," Hoffman said. "That's why he's not here tonight."

It was about then that a thought crossed my mind. I began to suspect that this incredible jumble was not the result of ineptness. Thinking the best of everyone, I prefer to believe that NBC, proudly and deliberately, chose to lighten our burden in these grim times with a production so awful that it would bestir great hilarity across the land. I know I was helplessly captivated and I suspect I wasn't alone.

Now back to Dick Cavett at ringside. "I'm absolutely humiliated," Cavett announced. He held a flower in his hand. "A lady at ringside threw me a flower," he explained. "I wish it had been a life preserver ... I suggest we all get a good night's sleep."

Good night, Dick. Good night, "Big Event."

The Liberace Phenomenon

It isn't true, as an embittered colleague of mine once suggested, that Liberace's entire repertoire consists of playing "Lady of Spain" over and over again. He has lots of other numbers, most of them Rachmaninoff's "Prelude" in C sharp minor and "Beer Barrel Polka," all played heavily with theatrical trills and flourishes, usually ending with one finger daintily scampering the length of the keyboard.

There is a further theory about Liberace, that the elephantine delicacy of his touch on the keys could be traced to all those ponderous rings that graced his fingers — four or five rings in all, sapphires and diamonds and I don't know what all else.

Twinkling and dimpling like the angel that he is, Liberace chirped: "I can hear you saying, how does he play the piano with those rings on his fingers? The answer is, 'Very well!'"

Giggle, giggle. Smirk, smirk. And he wore a watch, too. "An' here's my watch," Liberace went on. "You press the two diamonds and the lid opens and you can tell the time." He peered intently at this dazzling Tiffany's window of a watch. You want to know what time it was? "I got 24 rubies after nine diamonds," Liberace proclaimed in that breathless voice of his, which can't be the way everybody from Milwaukee talks.

I'm not making any of this up. No kidding. All of the foregoing transpired on a 1978 special called "Leapin' Lizards, It's Liberace." The show came to us with dancing waters, candelabra and flashing lights, from the Hilton in Vegas, from where, presumably, Liberace does his laughing all the way to a bank. Or several banks.

You've got to say this for Liberace — he doesn't withhold anything from his adoring audience (plus, I'll bet, a number of ordinary people listed among the helplessly incredulous). Taking off his mink coat to reveal his sequined outfit, Liberace said confidentially: "Don't be afraid to ask to see anything. If I got it, I'll show it."

Still twinkling and dimpling, Liberace went on revealing all of his secrets: "I used to have a swimming pool shaped like a piano, but I had to get rid of it. The piano tuner damn near drowned."

And, preening vigorously: "You like the coat? You know what it's made of? Virgin mink. Took forever to get the pelts."

Pause for laughter, plus a few shocked gasps. Then: "Take a quick look. I'm taking it off. It's hotter'n hell."

It was about then — my notes here seem to have turned into a sullen scrawl — that Debbie Reynolds turned up, full of verve and energy. She has a lot of explosive talent, that Debbie does, but whenever she bounces onstage I always expect to be led in cheers for the gallant lads on the gridiron. Instead, she stood by the piano, ready to burst into song.

But first, from Debbie: "I have the most expensive accompanist in show business."

"Not really," Liberace said, wittily. "I work for the government, on a percentage basis."

Wink, giggle, smirk. And much flashing of teeth, those miraculous teeth, one of the wonders of the dental world despite a slight discoloration of a lower bicuspid.

Did I tell you how this thing began? You really want to hear how we encountered this Liberace in colorful pajamas with a sequin here and there, leaping from his bed, then being assisted into a sequined robe and then — have I ever lied to you? — we see Liberace in a bubble bath, playing an imaginary piano. Lots of coy winks here.

Then, and not a minute too soon, he is dressed and adorned in a mink coat of some length and driven (by his piano-playing protege, one Vince Cardell) in a Rolls Royce right onto the stage of the Hilton. And then Mr. Showmanship, as I believe he is called, pranced out of the Rolls and posed for his cheering fans.

"Well, look me over," Mr. Showmanship announced. "I didn't get dressed like this for any old special."

There are some people who think of such sappy simpering as shamelessly vulgar. They get no rebuttal from me.

'Pinocchio' With Changes

I think disenchantment set in just about the time that Pinocchio was uttering his first words as a very English puppet born of the efforts of this Italian word-carver named Gepetto. Of course there's no reason why Gepetto's wooden creation shouldn't talk as though he were part of the Carnaby Street generation or, for that matter, like Herman of Herman and his Hermits, who is as English as the Union Jack. I mean, he wouldn't necessarily have to sound like the son of Sergio Franchio, would he?

As a matter of fact, Herman himself — also known as Peter Noone — turned up as Pinocchio in this "Hall of Fame" musical adaptation of Carlo Collodi's classic little tale. Now I'm as ready to suspend disbelief as anyone in the room but ol' Herman, with his English accent and gangling ways, was rather hard to swallow as the wooden marionette who longs to be a real boy.

Maybe he was just too big to be a puppet. Maybe it was that odd accent of his which sounded suspiciously like Tammy Grimes imitating one of the Beatles. Come to think of it, Noone closely resembled Tammy Grimes. It's possible. I've never seen them together.

Or maybe I'm being grumpy and out of sorts. Perhaps I should have simply sat back and viewed this 90-minute musical through a child's eyes instead of through my own beady, cynical ones. But who finds that possible, really? In the immortal words of the jazz musician, Johnny Hodges: "Can a moose crochet?"

"Pinocchio," it seems to me in my jaded state, never made up its mind whether it wanted to be a straight kids' story with the element of magic that entails, or whether it wanted to spoof kids' stories. The enterprise, in short, suffered from what I can only describe as a disparity of purpose.

This is a terrible state of affairs. Because if you can't entirely suspend disbelief, you suddenly find yourself thinking terribly mundane thoughts — you say to yourself, "Hey, here's the guy from Herman and his Hermits dressed like the creation of an Italian puppet maker played by Burl Ives, who is really a folk singer from the prairies of Illinois."

And yet this production did have its charm and some pleasantly inoffensive songs by Walter Marks. One tune in particular, "Too Soon," was sung by the master, Burl Ives, who can give any song an added dimension.

Another tune, this one sung by Peter Noone in his best Herman and his Hermits manner, had a wry twist in one line that went: "Nobody's perfect. Even a saint ain't."

A touch of light cynicism, in fact, ran through the yarn. Someone says to Pinocchio: "Gold can't make you a success."

"No," replies Pinocchio, wise beyond his years, "but it can make you a rich failure."

Educators and psychologists took their raps, incidentally, in a deliciously irreverent sequence wherein Pinocchio is tested to determine his IQ. They consider him an "under-achiever."

"Ever had any disturbing dreams?" he is asked.

"No, I've never been asleep," says Pinocchio.

"Mmmmm — no psychology at all."

Pinocchio agrees. "I'm very shoddy workmanship," he admits. "They don't make marionettes the way they used to. I think my personality is splitting."

Despite my caviling, it's still a potent story when it dwells on that very human predicament of the boy who can't live up to his father's ideal. He wants the kid to be "magnificent." But even puppets are only human.

Characters From the Comics

With pen in hand, I have just witnessed "The Funny Papers," a television special unaccountably billed as a "CBS Family Presentation." My notebook seems to be blank, however, except for a few vagrant scrawls — items such as "awful" and "unbelievable" and, "At last, a show worthy of the Gilligan's Island Award for witlessness."

It was the conceit of the producers here to bring comic strip characters to life — Orphan Annie and Daddy Warbucks, for instance, portrayed by Raquel Welch and Carroll O'Connor. Can you picture it? Raquel Welch, symbol of sensuality, playing a little girl who's worn the same dress for the last 50 years.

Impelled by a sense of duty, I stayed with this ode to pop culture all the way. I happen to be a fan of the funny papers. Nothing better than starting the day with Blondie and Mike Nomad and the Wizard of Id.

Ah, the comics! I learned to read picking out the words in the "Katzenjammer Kids." I grew up with Skeezix. Dick Tracy was my hero. I rooted for Joe Palooka in every fight. Why, I remember when Mary Worth was called Apple Mary — she sold apples then, long before she started sticking her nose in everyone's affairs.

It's a marvelous dream world, the world of the comics, but with few exceptions its people should be permitted to remain there, curiously immortal. Radio was, of course, a more hospitable medium. Orphan Annie, in the long ago, flourished on radio, the theater of the

182146

mind where, as Hans Conried once observed, the diamonds could be as large as your imagination willed them.

Recreated on television, seen plain, the world of comic strip people withers into a literal distortion. Instead of gaining life, they lose their own special reality. Their voices alone are never precisely how you had imagined them to be.

Anyway, they were all there, on this show — Steve Canyon, Brenda Starr, Beetle Bailey, Major Hoople and the rest, in lumpy, would-be satiric sketches. I will say that one bit wrenched a small chuckle from me as a girl says to good old Mary Worth: "We don't know how to thank you for all your help."

"Of course you don't," sniffs Mary Worth, with a weary sigh.

Sonny and Cher — A Special Taste

Frankly, I wasn't too crazy about Sonny and Cher even when they were together. But that may well be a character flaw on my part, for they enjoyed an enormous success. Still, they were hugely derivative, Sonny and Cher, as they borrowed a stance and attitude unblushingly from Louis Prima and Keely Smith, who invented the Italian fellow plus the deadpan girl singer routine.

What's more, Louis and Keely did it better — they were more sophisticated, more professional, more talented, more interesting and a lot funnier. But, alas, they didn't endure and neither, as a team, did Sonny and Cher.

Together or apart, Sonny and Cher are, I suppose, a special taste — like olives. And I guess there are any number of persons around who dig olives. Why have I always been gripped with the notion that they aren't what they seem to be? Why did I always think that Sonny was the fellow who had just delivered the pizza and Cher was really a tango instructor at Arthur Murray's?

Anyway, at the start of the 1976 season, there was Sonny without Cher. Then it was Cher without Sonny. For all of you folks who have been away, they are quite easy to tell apart. Cher is the one who wears — or, occasionally, almost wears — all those spectacular gowns that the designer didn't have enough material left to finish.

In fact, at one point in the premiere of her new variety series on CBS, Cher saw fit to talk about the bugle beads that adorned her gown. "If this show stays on three years," Cher confided, "I'll have enough beads to buy back Manhattan Island."

If it's wit that you're looking for on the Cher show, I'm afraid that's about as much as there was in evidence. Contrarily, there might be those who howled with glee when Cher, as Laverne the shop girl, continually belted Raquel Welch on the back and called her "Rackle."

At the very outset, that cute kid from "Paper Moon" — the movie, that is, not the TV series — came aboard to announce: "My name's

Tatum O'Neal. When I grow five inches and lose 10 pounds, Cher's gonna be in big trouble!"

Cute? No, I don't think so. How old is Tatum O'Neal, anyway — 11 or 12? And am I alone in my belief that kids shouldn't be compelled to utter lines with grownup allusions? Kids should be kids, I say.

In another bit, the kid did a lampoon of Catherine Deneuve, the French actress, in her semi-sultry perfume commercial. I fervently hope the level of taste in this series rises a notch. If it doesn't, Cher will never acquire enough beads to even buy Staten Island.

As nearly as I can determine, the personality that Cher has chosen for herself (or that Sonny originally imposed on her) is the glamor gal with the heart of gold. "Today," and I quote here from a publicity communique about Cher, "she is recognized as the personality who has the most influence on the dressing style of the young women in America, and her frequent appearances in high fashion magazines have made her name synonymous with elegance."

So that's what "elegance" is, eh? And here I was, fool that I am about such matters, secure in the misguided belief that elegance was Mary Tyler Moore or Dinah Shore or, when she's out of uniform, Angie Dickinson.

In the vocal department, Cher pours a ton of undeniable sensuality into her singing. She sings quite well but her songs all sound the same. My theory is, she just sings one tune and wears different gowns.

Romance of the Century

Watching "The Woman I Love" march its stately, predetermined course toward its final resolution, filled me with nagging annoyances. Mainly, I wondered how this dramatization of the romance of the century could emerge with such stodgy dullness.

Here was the love story that rocked an empire. A king — Edward VIII of England — gives up his throne to marry the twice-divorced American, Wallis Simpson. Here is an epic, real-life story that Shakespeare might have conceived, molded into proper dramatic structure and it would have thrilled audiences for centuries.

Somehow, in this production, in the acting, in the overall concept, it was a story reduced in size and scope. Where, I kept asking myself, was the passion, the excitement? Where was the grandeur?

Where was the tension of the conflict of wills between the king and his prime minister, Baldwin? It was touched on, poked at, toyed with, hinted at and then dismissed in one foreshortened scene that should have produced fireworks but came off, instead, as largely tentative and defused.

It was all so careful and underplayed and — a terrible thing to say about a romantic yarn — so bloodless. Even the king's abdication speech, as romantic a document as you're likely to hear anywhere, came off as strangely flat, lacking in human juices. As it was originally spoken, in 1936, over BBC radio, this splendidly written speech had a thunderous impact. But not, alas, when the words were uttered by Richard Chamberlain, playing the king as though, as they say, he expected someone else to play the ace.

And therein lies the rub. Although Richard Chamberlain has grown as an actor since he was patrolling the hospital corridors as TV's Dr. Kildare, he was simply an unfortunate choice as the king. To begin with, he doesn't have the years. At one point, the king describes himself as "40ish." Chamberlain doesn't look 40ish. He looks, instead, like young Dr. Kildare trying to portray someone who is 40ish.

There's an English movie called "The Ruling Class" in which Peter O'Toole characterizes the lofty air, the superior demeanor, the speech patterns and the distinctive stride of the British peerage. O'Toole, a fine actor, nailed down every nuance. Chamberlain, contrarily, was reaching for all of these touches but they were beyond him.

Why, then, didn't they get O'Toole for the part? Beats me. He would have been perfect.

If Chamberlain (who did handle the English accent well, I must admit) was stiff and uncomfortably wrong as well as too young for the part, Faye Dunaway certainly struck sparks as Wally Simpson. I wouldn't have believed this was the same actress who played the living whey out of her role as Bonnie in "Bonnie and Clyde."

It is the claim of Adela Rogers St. Johns, the writer, that the irresistable attraction of the woman who would later become the Duchess of Windsor was a mystery visible only to the king. Whatever the merits of that observation, Miss Dunaway, with her warmth and her wit and her great beauty, made us see this woman clearly as through the king's eyes.

If her portrait of Wally Simpson was otherwise inaccurate, it is a small matter. How the king saw her — there is the nub of the tale. That is what mattered. It is what always matters.

Where Did Mystery Show Mystery Go?

Joe E. Lewis, the comic, knew a man who was gripped with a sudden case of melancholia. A friend asked, "How did that happen?" Lewis shrugged. "Oh," he explained, "he was sitting around moping and he got it."

Well, there I was, sitting around moping on a midsummer's vacation and when melancholia set in I naturally turned to the television set. (Doesn't everybody?) And thereon unfolded one of the more curious epics in NBC's "Mystery Show" series.

"Trial by Fury" was the title impaled on the particular mystery I saw, its plot being concerned with a lawyer who defends himself against a charge of murder. The lawyer (played grimly by Warren Stevens) is no Perry Mason — as who is nowadays? — but with a writ here and a *noncompos mentis* there he gets himself acquitted.

But then he must face a kangaroo court arranged by the victim's wife, played very southern and dripping with calumny by Agnes Moorehead. She is not only very southern and strong willed, she also has a grown son who is weak, weak, weak.

Mmmmmmmm, a strong southern mother and a spineless son — and a father they all call Big Daddy. No, not really. I just made that last part up. There was no Big Daddy, but, somehow, I couldn't avoid the nagging suspicion that this script breathed a certain — how shall I phrase it? — familiarity.

I envision the scriptwriter, suddenly this summer, being under the influence of Erle Stanley Gardner frightened by Tennessee Williams. There was a wonderful confrontation scene at the end where, owing to a slight case of fingerprints on the murder weapon, it looks bad for Big Mama. Heroically, she points the finger of guilt at her weak son.

"Ah'm callin' you a liar, Mama," says the son, named Randolph Macon Marshall. He might have had another middle name, such as Lee or Calhoun, but I guess the writer didn't want to make him sound southern.

"Oh, Randolph," she cries. Then she confesses and is taken away, gently, with full respect for her past glories, by a nice policeman.

I, of course, immediately burst into a song that had been swelling up within me. Goes like this: "I've got those when the streetcar named Desire is rented out for hire, I'll be coming home to you, Blanche DuBois, blues." And back came my melancholia.

A Potpourri

Now you take ice, for example. Ice is admirably functional inside of a glass or for hockey games but a televised ice show, with all the hoopla and production and dancing girls skating to Wagnerian opera, wins my nomination as the biggest bore going.

They are rather a special taste, at that, ice shows, even when presented by the redoubtable Ice-capades people on NBC's "Summer on Ice." Not that I'm altogether anti-ice show. Actually, I'm as bug-eyed as anyone else when Ron Robertson spins around the ice at incredible speeds and I lead the applause when Wagner and Paul, the Canadian Olympic aces, strut their stuff.

But why, I kept asking myself, are ice shows so all-fired elaborate? It's getting to be a rarity when you see skating — just plain, old-fashioned skating — on an ice show and that, I thought, is why the darned things were dreamed up in the first place.

☆　☆　☆

If the Age of Candor didn't begin with Morley Safer's undeniably personal inquiry of Betty Ford a couple of years ago, then it was certainly given a good shove in that direction. "If your daughter came to you one day," Safer asked in a voice of innocence, "and said she was having an affair, what would you do?"

I remember watching that interview, on "60 Minutes," and wondering, first, why it was the usually ingratiating Mr. Safer instead of the tart-tongued Mike Wallace who was asking such a blunt, trendy-kicky question. And, second, why Betty Ford didn't say in response to Safer: "It's none of your damned business, friend. And close the door when you leave."

The Age of Candor probably reached its full flower — or am I being optimistic? — when Barbara Walters asked Jimmy Carter, then the President-elect, and Rosalynn Carter about their sleeping arrangements in the White House. "Separate bedrooms?" she asked. Absolutely not was the answer. And Jimmy Carter smiled, but there was no humor in his eyes.

Whatever the redeeming values in "Helter Skelter," the two-night, four-hour 1976 dramatization of the mass murders committed by the Manson Family and subsequent trial, the persistently nagging questions remain. Would the showing of the film, a depiction of repugnant and debasing horror, have been more appropriate in a movie theater?

Should this account of unspeakable reality — and therefore a far remove from the fantasy-fiction of "Kojak" or "Columbo" — have been granted availability on prime-time television? Should the film have been shown in our homes? CBS clearly shared these doubts. The network inserted cautionary disclaimers, citing the crimes as "heinous" and warning that elements of the program "may be too mature for younger and more sensitive viewers."

Too mature? A curiously inexact choice of phrase for a theme of such singularly obscene depravity. Even in its press releases, CBS felt compelled to add the following sentence, boxed for emphasis, at the bottom of the page — "Advisory: Due to Mature Theme, Viewer Discretion Advised."

Discretion, one must ask, for whom? For the editors glancing casually at the page? For the viewers who might just possibly, for reasons of prurience as well as curiosity, be attracted to rather than repelled by the "mature" theme? Is discretion advised for the unattended children at their TV sets at 9 at night, in the wake of what the networks choose to call the "family hour?" Discretion for impressionable teenagers?

In the opening episode, two of the characters are physically sickened, one as he identifies the victims slaughtered by Charles Manson's followers (and is then shown in the act of retching), the other as she hears the events described in grand jury proceedings. Surely, this must have given a clue to the network that a movie theater, not our air waves, was the place for such a graphic film.

I think if I have any least-favorite special of all, it would be the 1976 version of "Peter Pan" with Mia Farrow — which wasn't very special. This particular show was — and I'm choosing my words here with the utmost care and precision — simply awful. Still, I'm afraid that's a terribly accurate summation. The only thing it omits is that it took two hours, which is an awfully long time for a revival of doubtful merit.

"Peter Pan" is, of course, a children's classic, one of the most disarming and improbable treasures of the American theater. It was written by Sir James M. Barrie, who was once considered a sugar-coated Shaw, a master of gentle, whimsical humor in pre-World War I England.

I suspect that Sir James would have been dismayed with this version wherein Mia Farrow portrayed the high-flying lad who won't grow up to Danny Kaye's sword-wielding pirate nemesis, Captain Hook ("vain and egotistic and a bit sadistic"). Visually, Mia Farrow is quite appealing, with an endearing kind of petulance.

But where, I kept asking myself, was the sheer joy and exuberance that Mary Martin brought to the role? Where was the winning charm, the fanciful air, the impudent energy?

"The most unique event in television," proclaimed Howard Cosell, referring to ABC's "Battle of the Network Stars." Most unique, eh?

At the risk of missing Farrah Fawcett-Majors or Adrienne Barbeau demonstrating proper form in the 40-yard dash, I scurried to the bookcase and pulled out "The Elements of Style," by William Strunk Jr., and E. B. White, which is as sound a guide to the language as I know. Under "Unique" is listed the following: "Means 'without like or equal.' Hence, there can be no degrees of uniqueness.' "

Perhaps, on reflection, Howard Cosell, the Phi Beta Kappa and author on constitutional law and all-round scholar, was simply trying to talk like common folks. He does that occasionally, you know, as Bill Buckley will now and again shatter the airwaves with a deliberately uttered double negative.

"The Battle of the Network Stars" is an idea whose time, alas, had come to grace the '76-'77 season. This thing is an outgrowth of "Superstars," wherein top athletes compete in events other than their own specialty. In "Network Stars," the participants don't seem to have any specialty, unless you count Robert Conrad's rather nasty competitive zeal. He was out for blood, that Conrad, protesting decisions and carrying on.

The show was filmed at Pepperdine University up at Malibu hard by, in Cosell's phrase, "the majesty of the mountains and the awesome beauty of the Pacific." They raced and jumped and swam, with a team of stars representing each network. And Dr. Joyce Brothers explained — using the word loosely here — the psychological significance of it all without once mentioning the ratings or the wondrous sight of Lynda ("Wonder Woman") Carter on a diving board.

Polite Disdain of Royalty

Oscar Levant, that acerbic fellow, once said he couldn't watch Dinah Shore because of his diabetes. I wondered, watching that 90-minute epic about Grace Kelly — Her Serene Highness, Princess Grace of Monaco — just what Oscar would have said about this one.

"The Story of Princess Grace ... Once Upon a Time Is Now" is the title they affixed on this NBC special, a gushing soporific which surely violated the proposed ban on saccharine. NBC, moreover, chose to call it a "Big Event," which is a way of saying that inflation has thoroughly overtaken the language.

For reasons best known to the network and its producers, Lee Grant, a sterling actress usually seen in portraits of neurotic anguish, was tapped as host-interviewer on a show about an actress celebrated for her cool, beauteous serenity — and for marrying a prince of a fellow named Rainier.

"Tell me," said Lee Grant, sitting with Prince Rainier and the former Grace Kelly, "when you proposed, how did it happen?"

"That's a very original question," the prince said.

In journalistic circles, such a reply is known as a conversation-stopper. The prince issued a wan forgiving smile, however, and said: "It was in New York on New Year's Eve."

To which Princess Grace countered with: "I thought it was Philadelphia."

I was hoping for a full chorus right there of "I Remember It Well" as it was once done so memorably by Maurice Chevalier and Hermione Gingold in "Gigi." Instead of song, we were treated to more wan, tolerant smiles from the prince, who gave the distinct impression that he wished he were elsewhere — reviewing the troops, perhaps.

Undeterred by the polite disdain of royalty, Lee Grant, ever the persistent interviewer, pushed forward with her hard-hitting inquiries. She's a regular Mike Wallace, she is.

"What was your first impression of Princess Grace?" she asked Rainier.

"That's a silly question, isn't it?" said the prince with princely charm and the unmistakable look of an untipped waiter.

"Uh, yes," Lee agreed.

"It's fairly obvious, isn't it?" said the prince.

The later interviews with lowly commoners proved more fruitful. Alfred Hitchcock, who directed several of the early Grace Kelly movies, for instance, said in his distinctive manner: "The subtlety of her sex appeals to me . . . She had such an outside purity. Isn't that a phrase — outside purity?"

And Stanley Kramer, the producer, was asked: "Why did you cast Grace Kelly in 'High Noon' opposite Gary Cooper?"

"Genuine arrogance," said Kramer. He meant his arrogance, not hers. "I just decided Grace Kelly was a girl who was going to be in the picture. But she was miscast. She was too young. Coop was a pebble-kicker and she was shy, but somehow it worked for her."

Early in her career, Grace Kelly made a big score as a model, working mostly in ads and commercials for cigarettes and beer. Lee Grant asked her if she smoked. No, she replied.

"Do you drink beer?"

"Yes, that I do," said Princess Grace.

Good for her. You've got to like a princess who drinks beer. Maybe she'll hoist one some day with Billy Carter.

Near the conclusion, she recalled the wedding reception and how she and the prince entered the lobby of a Monaco hotel and a photographer said, "Hiya, Gracie." The prince said: "Who is he?" She said she didn't know. And the prince said: "But he called you by your Christian name and you say you don't know him?"

The prince doesn't know much about photographers, either, does he?

And Some Bouquets

Gilbert and Sullivan never dreamed of expressing the thought in song but the critic's job, like the policeman's, is not a happy one. Benjamin Disraeli, that master of the stiletto phrase, testily defined critics as "men who have failed in literature and art." Lord Byron observed: "A man must serve his time to every trade save censure — critics are all ready made."

But then, as Richard Maney, the late theatrical publicist (once irreverently described as "the most literate press agent since St. Paul") suggested long ago: "Critic baiting is as old a sport as falconry."

And a very popular sport, too. Nietzsche, whose thoughts were generally occupied with more profound matters, compared critics to "insects which sting us not because they want our pain but because they need our blood to live."

The British humorist and playwright P. G. Wodehouse asked querilously: "Has anybody ever seen a critic in the daytime? Of course not. They come out after dark up to no good."

It is axiomatic among those who deal in criticism that dishing out praise is no easy matter. For one thing, the complimentary review is much more than a string of warming adjectives. For another, and herein lies the main difficulty, the critic must tap his own emotions and discover exactly, in precise detail, why he viewed a performance favorably. The following are some performances, on and off the air, individual and collective, that I viewed with great pleasure.

At the Heart of M*A*S*H

The essence of "M*A*S*H," which is set in the Korea of the early

1950s, lies in its delicate counterpoint of war's absurdity and, in Alan Alda's apt phrase, "humor that is both funny and felt." It is Alda, moreover, who provides the wellspring, the generating force behind this extraordinary television series and its shifting moods.

His performance as Hawkeye, the freewheeling Army surgeon, is so natural he seems hardly to be acting at all, which is undoubtedly the best kind of acting there is. Alda, through some curious and mysterious alchemy, can register emotions that cut to the marrow of human experience. It is his gift, a peculiar genius that goes beyond the demands of craft, to transport an audience as he articulates utter despair and compassion and monstrous fatigue and the wildest, most rarefied kind of humor.

This is accomplished with surpassing honesty, which is also the hallmark of the show itself. It remains one of the essential ingredients, this honesty, as the show entered its sixth season in September, 1977 — with Alda's irreplaceable Hawkeye as one of the few major figures that have endured. And, just possibly, it is Alda who is at the core of the show's success.

The original cast was depleted first when McLean Stevenson, who created the role of Col. Blake and played it masterfully, left for supposedly greener pastures. Then Wayne Rogers, good buddy to Hawkeye as Trapper John, departed for his own greener pastures of expanding his career.

Harry Morgan smoothly entered the scene as the new commander, a career colonel with a fondness for horses. And Mike Farrell, an actor blessed with immediate likability, became the successor to Rogers. And now, as the new season begins, Maj. Frank Burns (played with mumbling thick-headedness by Larry Linville, also moved on to greener pastures) has gone bonkers over Hotlips Houlihan's marriage to another.

How does one describe Frank Burns? Hawkeye did it best a season or two earlier in a yarn wherein he and Radar liberate a general's Jeep in Seoul and provide a lift back to the 4077th for a new surgeon, fresh from stateside.

The newcomer inquires about Frank Burns: "Is he a good surgeon?"

Hawkeye nods. "With the same light touch as a German jazz band," he says.

Beautiful, and typically Hawkeye who, in another episode, returned to the base one night a shambling wreck, his eyes narrow slits. "I have the Mt. Rushmore of hangovers," Hawkeye declares. "Six aspirin companies are bidding for my head."

He turns to Radar. "Did you ever have cotton in your mouth?" he asks, mournfully.

"No," Radar says. "We were vegetarians."

Anyway, Frank Burns is off on a tear in Tokyo and he is picked up by the MPs. One of them calls the colonel. "Do you have a Major Burns? Medium build, beady eyes, weak chin?"

"That's him," the colonel says.

Frank Burns is gone — permanently, it turns out — and the collective IQ of the 4077th immediately soars. Played with a grand, imperious manner by David Ogden Stiers, Burns' replacement is also his mental opposite, one Maj. Charles Emerson Winchester.

"Where are you from, Charlie?" Hawkeye asks.

"Charles," says the other, loftily.

"Oh," says Hawkeye.

In this particular "M*A*S*H," as in its predecessors, a time and place are faithfully recaptured, with odd, haunting echoes. And yet, in a most curious way, the past assumes an undeniably contemporary flavor. The dialogue in the opening script, written by Jim Fritzell and Everett Greenbaum, was reflective of both the '50s, in the intimations and connotations, and the rhythms, the wit and crackle of the '70s.

"In this camp," Maj. Winchester sniffs, "cleanliness is next to — impossible."

For all of his hauteur, the major from Harvard Medical School and Massachussetts General is one helluva surgeon. "The whole family has gifted hands," he explains. "Mother's a concert pianist."

Hawkeye comes back with: "My dad can get an olive out of a jar with one finger."

The major looks askance: "Frontline humor, I suppose — crude and boorish."

"Crude and Boorish, an old vaudeville team," Hawkeye cries.

Otherwise, things go apace at the 4077th. Hotlips the nurse, back two days early from a honeymoon, is still as officious as she is good-looking. Radar, the company clerk, is still prescient. Klinger is still trying desperately for his Section 8 discharge by wearing frocks and flowery bonnets. And the colonel, overseeing the madness, is still grumpily sardonic.

One of the patients brought in is himself a doctor. What, the colonel is asked, should we do with him? The colonel's reply: "Sew his fingers together and make him a psychiatrist."

'Long Day's Journey'

When Laurence Olivier elects to act on television, it is clearly an event to herald, to witness and absorb and then to contemplate. For by any yardstick, Sir Larry — he's a full-fledged Lord now but still addressed with easy familiarity — reigns as the world's foremost actor, the most honored by critics and audiences, the one most hailed by his fellow players.

It has been said of Olivier that the needle of his compass will lead him directly to the heart of a role. And so it was, on ABC-TV, in his incomparably complete portrayal of James Tyrone, heading a first-rate National Theater of Great Britain company in Eugene O'Neill's "Long Day's Journey Into Night," which was adapted for television with care and vast professionalism.

Many times, in a career ranging over four decades, Olivier has shaken hands with greatness (to borrow Kenneth Tynan's apt phrase), taking a playwright's words and kneading them, ripening them into monumental statements, lit by lightning flashes of insight. Once again, Olivier delivered a performance of depth and grandeur.

The marvel of an Olivier performance lies partly in the sheer, risk-taking technique, the mastery of every nuance of his craft, in that matchless full symphony voice in which each word, each syllable, has its own distinct measure. Above all, there are those unusual eyes, with their mystery and power.

Olivier uses his eyes better than any actor alive. In TV, with its closeups, this is a great asset for an actor and for an audience an incalculable dividend. In Olivier's eyes, one reads the full range of human emotion, an illumination of fury and joy and the heart-cry of an insurmountable anguish. They are eyes that reflect character, an intuitive intelligence and his own iron precision, weary but majestic.

It began, this extraordinary television experience, with Olivier setting the tone with an introduction and a touch of understated English courtesy. He pointed out that a predominantly English cast was attempting the work of an American playwright.

"This is done, believe me, in no sense of know-how, in no sense of show-how," Olivier said in his crisp, rolling diction. "It is done in a sense of tribute to a great American dramatist."

He explained, simply and with the clarity that is his hallmark as an actor, the wellspring of "Long Day's Journey," an unflinching autobiographical drama in which O'Neill used only a thin gauze of fiction. In this searing family portrait, O'Neill wrote of a miserly father, a morphine-addicted mother, a drunken brother, and himself, a young man home from the seas and racked with consumption, a family held together as much by hate as by love.

It is the greatest work by the greatest of American playwrights, an unforgettable concerto of tragedy and soul-shaking revelations, an expiation with no residual rancor. If, as Tennessee Williams wrote about one of his own works, "The play is memory," this play of O'Neill's is memory enlarged into an act of forgiveness.

When O'Neill finished "Long Day's Journey," he presented it to his wife, Carlotta, on their 12th anniversary. With it was a letter which began: "I give you the original script of this play of old sorrow written in tears and blood . . ."

Tears and blood. And no moralizing and no sentimentalizing and no assessment of guilt.

As he has his mother explain in a line of searching poignance:

"None of us can help the things life has done to us. They're done before you realize it, and once they're done they make you do other things until at last everything comes between you and what you'd like to be, and you've lost your true self forever."

Throughout the play, compressed to three hours of television, O'Neill's people touch bottom, each conversation leading inexorably to an utterance of aching self-revelation — by the sons, skillfully played by Denis Quilley and Ronald Pickup, and the mother, brilliantly enacted by Constance Cummings. And by the father, in the dominating presence, and the galvanic, surpassing eloquence of Laurence Olivier.

The Last of a Breed

"The Blue Knight" is a superlative television mini-series — uncompromisingly realistic, touching, frightening, raw, a searching, often compassionate look at a cop who has been, for 20 years minus three days, seduced by his beat. He is Bumper Morgan, the last of a breed.

And it is those final days of his career in blue, the resolution of a lifetime lived entirely on the brink, that was the substance of Joseph Wambaugh's extraordinary novel and this absolutely top-cork TV adaptation.

We follow Bumper Morgan as the days spill out of his cup until all that he has left is a small piece of Friday when he is to pull the pin, which is the police way of saying he will opt for retirement.

Initially, being the total perfectionist, Joe Wambaugh harbored reservations about William Holden being tapped for Bumper. But Holden's portrayal, a masterpiece of sustained reality, brought Wambaugh second and more positive thoughts.

"I suppose at first I wasn't looking past the physical differences," Wambaugh says. "Bumper in the book weighs at least 275 pounds, with the belly. Holden weighs about 175. But what a performance! He really captured the essence of Bumper Morgan. I was very pleased."

My sole complaint, and it is a minor one, is that some of Bumper's size was necessarily reduced, some of his heroic, massively larger than life, almost legendary stature, his overwhelming presence.

Small matter. Holden's Bumper is, quite possibly, more human, less gargantuan. And his size is expressed in other, more revealing ways.

"Somehow," says a bookie about to be rousted, his narrow eyes summing up Bumper Morgan, "I figured you'd be a bigger man."

"I am," says Bumper.

Bumper is 50 and weary of the self-deception that he is 30. His eyes — and here is where Holden's acting job reveals such uncommon depths — tell of disillusion, street-wise eyes grown very old. They are the most world-weary eyes imaginable and they reflect what he has seen on the street, on his beat in downtown Los Angeles.

They are a grim and resigned reflection of the hustlers, the snitches, the bums, the winos, the pimps, the total underbelly of his beat. And they reflect, those ancient and tortured eyes, the essential fact of a man alone. His badge is cynicism.

"Don't you cops ever believe anybody?" someone asks Bumper.

"We keep trying," Bumper replies, sadly.

And there is a new breed of cop, fresh from the academy, that Bumper keeps trying to understand. He watches a rookie facing a mirror in the locker-room, flashing on the hair spray.

"Who invented that stuff?" Bumper demands in disgust.

"I dunno, Bumper — why?" the rookie says.

"I'd like to bust him," Bumper grunts.

Thus the world of Bumper Morgan, and it is told here with candor and fury in scene after scene that must cling fiercely to the memory — the anguish of a dead prostitute's father, the agony of Bumper trying to explain his own perjury, the banter and tenderness of the love scenes with Lee Remick. It is all here, the story of a cop and his search for — for what? For what only the beat can give him.

A Series Retrospective

It is difficult to realize that it was as recent as 1970, with the unfolding of "All in the Family," that Archie Bunker entered the language. Almost from the very outset, the name of Archie Bunker was as much a symbol of a type as other enduring descriptive names in literature, such as Scrooge and Mrs. Malaprop and Babbitt and Quixote, names that are their own badge of allusion.

Appropriately, on the occasion of the 100th airing of "All in the Family," producer Norman Lear elected to put on an hourlong special, with 71 clips from 41 past episodes. It was, in a sense, the best of "All in the Family" and a mighty unusual slice of television.

Never before in my memory had a hit series paused in the midst of its run to pause, look back and reflect on the reasons for its success. They had Henry Fonda as the host-narrator, setting the scene and providing a narrative continuity, and it all worked beautifully.

Aside from Fonda's obvious qualifications to do anything in front of a camera, he was, it seems to me, an interesting choice. Here's the Nebraska-born actor who once played Lincoln and who was summed up, in a magazine profile, as the "archetypal American." Here was this product of the prairies, in his bemused flatlands tones, acknowledging yet another archetype — the hard-hat philosopher, Archie Bunker, from the streets of New York and the mainstream of bigotry.

"One of the most acclaimed and controversial shows in television history," Fonda noted, in truth, at the start of the hour that included some great examples of biting humor, occasional poignant moments and the constant tang of reality.

As I remember the thunderclap that was the beginning of "All in the Family," I harbored some reservations.

Carroll O'Connor, an absolutely top-cork actor in the role of his lifetime, had his reservations, too.

"The minute I saw the script," O'Connor said later, "I knew that Archie Bunker would be a marvelous character to play on the Broadway stage. But television?"

But Norman Lear, it turned out, had his finger on the pulse of the nation. And, what's more important, he had the backing of Bob Wood, who was then president of CBS, one of the few network people with faith in the project. "Audiences simply want a true picture of what the United States in the 1970s is all about," says Lear. And of course he was right.

As Lear points out: "People watch 'All in the Family' on a gut level. It's a visceral experience. Liberals laugh. Conservatives laugh. So we all inter-connect."

Lear had used his own father at least partly as a model for Archie Bunker and, when I interviewed him, he summoned up the phrase, "lovable bigot." The choice of words created a furore. Many objections were promptly voiced, topped by novelist Laura Z. Hobson's nagging diatribe in the New York Times. How, she demanded, with lofty self-righteousness, can a bigot be "lovable?"

The answer was as simple as it was obvious. Lear clearly meant that it wasn't Archie Bunker's bigotry that was lovable but that Archie did have his own virtues, among them a capacity for affection. Part caricature he may be, but Archie Bunker is, above all, a figure of dimension.

He is universal and he is real. And therein lies the source of the show's longevity — the reality of its people as they transcend the limits of comedy, probing emotions and permitting us, beyond the laughter, to see ourselves with unremitting clarity and perception.

Hepburn's 'Menagerie'

"The play gives every one of the four characters that it presents a glowing, rich opportunity, genuine emotional motivations, a rhythm of situations that are alive, and speech that is fresh, living, abundant, and free of stale theater diction."

Thus wrote Stark Young, a leading critic of the day, when Tennessee Williams' fragile drama, "The Glass Menagerie," made its first imprint. That one sentence still says it all, an evaluation whose accuracy and insight have been upheld, both by the years and with the first television adaptation, presented as an ABC special.

In its television form, with Katherine Hepburn at the top of her game "The Glass Menagerie" emerged as one of those rare combinations of superior writing, first-class acting and direction and production and, moreover, an eloquent blend of tone and flavor all in tune with Williams' intent.

Many times in the past, Katharine Hepburn had been asked to take her turn at "The Glass Menagerie." And always she had refused with the most reasonable of explanations. She had seen Laurette Taylor, a theater legend, in the original production and one shouldn't attempt to improve on perfection, on a characterization so fully realized.

What a fortunate spin of events that Miss Hepburn was persuaded to accept the role, her first on television, by the gifted Englishman, Anthony Harvey, who staged this production. For she was, to sum it up in a word, magnificent, her performance a thunderously instructive essay in the nuances of her craft for all the neophytes and a treat beyond measure for the audience.

Until now, it would be difficult to conceive of Katharine Hepburn, sturdy Kate, with her crisp Connecticut speech patterns and her angular self-sufficiency, as a prototype Tennessee Williams woman. She had seemed too — too northern, too resolutely New England. Where was the plantation lilt? Where was the faded magnolia manner?

But there it was, unfolding magically on the screen, in scene after unforgettable scene, a portrayal of stunning dominance and unquenchable character and affecting vulnerability.

What a fortunate turn of the calendar it is that Katharine Hepburn, by her own declaration, had reached a point in her life where it is important, perhaps wholly necessary, to accept challenges. And there is, by any yardstick, challenge in nailing down the full flavor, the essence of imposing strength coupled with illusions of a romanticized past, in Amanda Wingfield, a Tennessee Williams woman to the bone. For Miss Hepburn, an actress with a sure grasp on the subtleties of desperation, it was a thorough-going triumph.

In terms of story, "Glass Menagerie" really isn't much — a "memory play," Williams called it, as opposed to, in the author's phrase, "the straight realistic play with its genuine Frigidaire and authentic ice cubes."

There is Amanda, the mother, described by Williams as "a little woman of great but confused vitality, clinging frantically to another time and place."

And there's her daughter (very well played by Joanna Miles), gentle, terribly shy, a collector of glass figurines in a menagerie that reflects the fragility of her life. And there's her son, (Sam Waterston) an extension of the playwright himself, crying out for escape. Finally, there's The Gentleman Caller (Michael Moriarty), who upsets their lives as the play resolves into a haze of tormented futility.

It is a modern American classic, "The Glass Menagerie," and now, with this simply presented and very moving television adaptation, its reputation is even more secure.

'J. W.' on the Small Screen

When a movie takes on some mileage and pops up on the TV screen, by the rules of the game it thereby falls into my purview. And a good thing it is, too, when the movie is a first-rate item such as Cliff Robertson's "J. W. Coop," a film of 1972 vintage which became an ABC entry five years later.

"J. W. Coop" was written, directed and produced by Cliff Robertson and he essayed the title role as well. In short, this was an intensely personal statement by an extraordinary and, it seems to me, vastly underrated actor.

Robertson's first quadruple effort had the distinction of putting all of his diverse talents on display. It also had the distinction of packing an awful wallop and setting a pace for anyone else invading the same turf of the lost cowboy and the metaphor of the rodeo, his arena for fulfillment.

As Coop, taciturn and a self-admitted loner, Robertson nailed down more than the externals — the slightly bowed cowboy stride, the suspicious, squinty eyes, the speech rhythms of the Southwest. With great subtlety, he caught the essence and flavor of the man. His words — the entire dialogue, in fact — seem less to have been written than overheard. Both author and actor — and of course they are one — collaborated here to create a genuinely moving and real person.

At the outset, for instance, Coop is being released from prison after 10 years served for bad penmanship on a check, among other offenses, and he is halted at the gate by the warden. Coop had brought honor to the prison rodeo team and the warden is solicitous.

"Anything else you want, cowboy?" he says.

With more resignation than rancor, J. W. Coop replies: "All I want is some 'gone' between me and here."

As the scriptwriter, Robertson went to great lengths to keep his story plausible and unsentimental (especially his foredoomed love story); there is throughout an unerring smack of authenticity. Even if you had never been near the men of the rodeo, you knew that in "J. W. Coop" the words they uttered had the right body and color.

Seeing his old rodeo buddies, J. W. says: "You boys look like you've been rode hard and hung up wet."

"How'd they treat you there in jail?" someone asks.

"Oh, it warn't no county fair."

And why is J. W. going back to the rodeo? "I'm too lazy to work and too nervous to steal," he says with a grin.

But the old rodeo hands are grieved by the heightened commercialism with its taint of big money from the big city. "Rodeoin's changed, I'll guaran-dam-tee-ya," one of them is saying. "All them cowboys and their endorsements."

"Endorsements!" another says with disdain. "Nobody's ever paid me for drinkin' someone's coffee or wearin' someone's purty underwear."

The symbol of today's rodeo is the flamboyant figure of Billy Hawkins, who may be modeled after the all-round champion Larry Mahan (who plays himself in a scene or two). Billy Hawkins flies his own plane from one rodeo to the next, fending off the groupies at every stop. He is one tough-riding cowboy but he sure doesn't talk like one.

"Anything I can do for you, Billy?"

"Yeah," Billy says. "Call my broker. Tell him I'll take his advice on those mutual funds."

I have just seen what may be, quite possibly, the funniest single episode of any comedy series in all of television's history. Does that sound excessive? Nonetheless, I suspect I'm not alone in my judgment of the monkeyshines on "The Trial of Harry Speakup," a segment of the old Phil Silvers show, known familiarly as "Sgt. Bilko."

They showed it again on the rerun of those great old Bilko shows and the response throughout, speaking personally, was helpless laughter, 30 minutes of boffo time.

This is the yarn wherein an Army captain, full of eager industry, devises a plan to reduce by half the time required to process inductees. The platoon thus turns into an assembly line that includes, through a preposterous comedy of errors, a chimpanzee dubbed "Harry Speakup."

Was there ever a funnier half-hour on the tube? Several contenders come to mind — Dick Van Dyke in his first series, Jackie Gleason and Art Carney on "The Honeymooners," Lucy and Desi in "I Love Lucy," Andy Griffith and Don Knotts in their Mayberry days.

Episodes of more recent vintage, from "M*A*S*H" or "Sanford and Son" or "Mary Tyler Moore" or "All in the Family" or "Barney Miller," might rate a call. But none of the foregoing has been tested by time. Contrarily, this one Bilko show has been repeated more than any other single comedy episode, wrenching protracted guffaws each time out of the chute.

Mary Hartman's Troubles

Mary Hartman has more troubles than Lockheed as she faces life bravely, chin up, mouth agape, eyes vague, her expression persistently dim and lugubrious. Mary is, of course, the harassed matriarch of "Mary Hartman, Mary Hartman," the split-level comic soap opera which is such a funny show they had to name it twice.

Watching "Mary Hartman, Mary Hartman," one thinks of how Dickens used to poke around London in search of the misfortunes that provided him with plots for his novels. Today, Dickens might well conduct his research into protracted agony by witnessing "Mary Hartman, Mary Hartman."

I haven't encountered such a stately progression of misery since the days of "Queen for a Day" when Jack Bailey presided jovially over his bedraggled group of unfortunates. On that show of cherished memory, an out-of-work waitress would gulp out her sad tale — her husband had deserted her and the kids, then the kids came down with measles and the babysitter ran off with a saxophone player.

So, she had to stay home and take care of her children, which cost her the job at the beanery — but it did win her the title of "Queen for a Day."

Next to the travail of "Mary Hartman, Mary Hartman," such complaints are right out of the "Donny and Marie Show." What, you ask, has befallen poor Mary Hartman, her friends and family thus far?

Aside from the waxy buildup on Mary's floors, here are only a few of the calamitous incidents — a mass murder, an illicit affair or two, indecent exposure charges against Mary's Grandpa Larkin, known as the "Fernwood Flasher," Mary's sister began work at a massage parlor equipped with rubber hoses, and her neighbor, Loretta, who wants to be a country singer in Nashville, is paralyzed as a result of her car being struck by a station wagon full of nuns.

Through all of this (and much more), as life becomes complicated beyond comprehension, Mary remains a font of optimism. "After this is over," she says, cheerfully, "we'll all go to the International House of Pancakes."

Mary's neighbor, Loretta Haggars, the flower of singing southern womanhood, has enough hair for two Dolly Partons and she has her measure of optimism as well. Moreover, she is entranced by Dorelda Doremus, the television faith healer.

"A couple of weeks ago," Loretta is telling Mary, "there was a woman on her show with a shriveled hand? No fingers? Well, Dorelda Doremus just prayed over her and right on the TV that woman grew fingers like a bunch of bananas growing on a tree."

"Maybe it was a trick," says Mary with mild skepticism. "You know — sleight of hand."

"It was a miracle," Loretta insists. "Faith makes miracles. I wish you and Tom would develop faith. I think it's awful how you never go to church or anything."

"I used to," says Mary, "but Tom made me stop when Rev. Stanfast wanted me to come out for choir practice."

"What was wrong with that?"

"Tom thought it was strange," says Mary, "when the Reverend said my breath control would be better for singing if I didn't wear a bra."

The foregoing is uttered in flat, even, unchanging tones, which is the standard speech for the locale of these curious happenings, the mythical town of Fernwood, Ohio. It's a swell little town, this Fernwood, a wacky Peyton Place and, just possibly, the world capital of platitudes.

Occasionally, sprouting through the delicious madness there are oddly touching moments. Why, for instance, has 83-year-old Grandpa Larkin become the "Fernwood Flasher"? Loneliness is the reason, the purposeless rhythm of his life. As Grandpa complains: "They've invented all these drugs to make us live so long, but we haven't got anything to do ... The hardest decision I have to make today is whether to play checkers in the park or go down to the Safeway and watch them unload melons."

Indomitable Child of Slavery

Perhaps it is the characters of fiction who are most often truly alive. In "The Autobiography of Miss Jane Pittman," Ernest J. Gaines wrote a spare but richly detailed novel about a black woman whose life spans 110 years, from her childhood as a slave on a Louisiana plantation to the first simmerings of the civil rights movement in the early 1960s.

First, in reading the novel and then being witness to the superb, two-hour television adaptation on CBS, one encounters a curious resistance to accepting Jane Pittman as merely fictional, a character spawned out of a typewriter. Quite possibly, this is the ultimate praise.

In Miss Jane Pittman, Gaines was able to create a figure of fiction as true, as real, with as much of life's inhale and exhale as, for example, Mark Twain's Huckleberry Finn, who was also a child of the river, sharing with Miss Jane Pittman the same earth wisdom of the ages.

This sharp smack of reality was enhanced further by Cecily Tyson's dazzlingly expert performance. With all of the human juices and aspirations intact, her Jane Pittman, an indomitable child of slavery, springs to full-blooded life in all her triumphs and defeats and, in her last act of defiance, with surpassing courage and strength of spirit.

Cecily Tyson is a brilliant actress, nominated for an Academy Award for her work in the movie, "Sounder." As Jane Pittman, she goes beyond that performance, acting all the way with great lucidity and warmth and a marvelously endearing simplicity of line.

Throughout the two hours, with episodic flashbacks sorting out the past, Miss Tyson is pictured in the various stages of an extraordinary life.

Although the art of the makeup man is an asset, the concept emerges here as much more than gimmickry. For it is by no means the device of makeup that brings such authenticity to Miss Tyson's characterization. It wasn't the makeup that did the acting. It was all Cecily Tyson, in the honesty of her performance, with its bare-boned economy of style and delivered with the most surefooted professionalism.

In its adaptation, Tracy Keenan Wynn borrowed a device from the novel wherein Jane Pittman recalls the years into a tape recorder. The television version has a magazine writer calling on the aged woman, tape recorder in hand, knowing little of her past.

"I understand you were a slave," he says to Jane Pittman, taking her ease in the Louisiana sunshine.

"Lots of people were slaves," she replies.

"Yes, but you're still alive."

"Just about," she says, wearily.

He is intrigued, his writer's curiosity nudged, along with his sense of history. But he approaches his subject with uncertainty. He is deferential but wary.

"You're 110 years old," he says to Jane Pittman.

"So they tell me," she says.

"How far back do you remember?" he inquires.

There is a faint, almost imperceptible flicker of a smile. She looks up as she pauses before issuing the trump card of age.

"How far back do you want to go?"

Thereafter, as a very old woman might do, she relives the past in her own way, leaving great gaps, selecting and omitting, her focus always coming down on the events that are for her intensely personal.

It is a remarkable tale, a string of bittersweet remembrances told with forbearance against a backdrop of black history. But the producers wisely avoided turning "Jane Pittman" into a tract.

Always it remains a personal document, an eventful diary — the Civil War era (with Jane Pittman played expertly by young Valerie O'Dell), the plantation days during the Reconstruction, her marriage to a bronco-buster and the move to a ranch in East Texas, the return to the Delta, the scene-by-scene rollcall of the years of subsequent poverty, violence and despair, a century in a blur of memory.

Reality in Minneapolis

Not long after the "Mary Tyler Moore Show" began in 1970, Goodman Ace did a piece in the Saturday Review. Goody Ace is an old comedy writer himself and he views television through the narrow eyes of the professional. Goody Ace, in other words, is not your average viewer swept easily into a suspension of disbelief.

All the same, Goody Ace confided wistfully that he would like to hop out to Minneapolis and drop into the WJM studios and say hello to Mary Richards, have a belt with Lou Grant, swap ironies with Murray Slaughter and josh with Ted Baxter, that vainglorious peacock of an anchorman whose deepest fantasy was that, just possibly, he might be the illegitimate son of Eric Sevareid.

Goody Ace spoke for all of us in wanting those fictional people in that fictional studio to be real — and, of course, in the best sense, they are real and they are warm and they are funny.

There was an odd sense of finality, in knowing that the last episode of "Mary Tyler Moore" was set to film. Only members of the MTM "family" were present, 350 of them, and producer-writer David Lloyd informed the assemblage: "Let's not sit here sniffling during the show. You'll get Mary crying and her eyes will puff up. Besides, this is a comedy show."

But there were tears when Mary Richards gives her final, touching speech to Lou Grant, and there were tears at the party afterward. But Mary Tyler Moore had a grand idea. At each table, she had placed pocket-sized packages of Kleenex.

"This is a comedy show," David Lloyd had reminded the audience, a good thought to remember. From the outset, when Alan Burns and Jim Brooks conceived the show and assumed the producers' reins, Mary Richards emerged as — to borrow from the jargon of the psychologists — a "role model" for the contemporary young woman, and those are rare.

She was unmarried, unengaged and independent, and, if she were home on Saturday night, it was because she wanted to be. With the years, she changed and she grew. More than a survivor, she thrived, she coped, she won respect. But all of this was essentially a bonus, this fulfillment of a woman of the '70s named Mary Richards played by an extraordinary actress named Mary Tyler Moore with matchless style and grace and, above all, a delicious comic spirit.

When I think back on the seven years of "Mary Tyler Moore," my thoughts dwell less, however, on the issues that concern Gloria Steinem (as significant as they may be) than on the humor, the laughter that came out of this reality.

She changed, all right, Mary Richards did. In one episode, she has become a "big sister" to a prostitute, who sums her up all too accurately with: "Sure, I know you, Goody Two Shoes. I bet you were a cheerleader. Straight A's in school. Went with the captain of the football team."

"Uh, no," Mary gulps, "he was just a halfback."

From this confession of galloping blandness, she would in later episodes learn to snap off zingers. In one story, for instance, Murray has written a speech for Ted Baxter and Ted is saying: "I've got to memorize my address."

"Good, Ted," Mary says, "and if you master that, maybe you can memorize your phone number."

Minor catastrophe was often the stuff of humor on this show and I think back to the lampoon of the perfection that is Mary Richards. This was the night of the Teddy Awards dinner and Mary has had a rotten day — she has sprained her ankle, she has a cold and, for a topper to all calamities, her hair wouldn't curl. She is, in short, a mess.

And then her name is announced as a winner and she accepts the award, standing morosely at the podium and she's blubbering. "I'm sorry. I usually don't look like this ... I have a much nicer dress." A great scene and very funny — and so real.

Another line clings to the memory. They are talking, Mary and Murray, about this new Mexican restaurant they discovered in Minneapolis. Ted Baxter strolls in and then, hearing the words, he halts in mid-strut.

"New Mexican restaurant?" he says brightly. "I went to a New Mexican restaurant once in Albuquerque."

Caricature of Empty Lives

It has been said that only an Irishman living in France could have concocted the deliciously bizarre and oddly serious joke that is "Waiting for Godot." For more than 20 years now, critics and audiences in varying degrees of bafflement have tried to unravel Samuel Beckett's play which exists, by all the commonly accepted criteria, in a dramatic vacuum.

What's it all about, Alfie? Damned if I know, really. But, as someone once observed, "Waiting for Godot" is basically a means of spending two hours in the dark without being bored. And on PBS the Los Angeles Actors Theater put on a corking good production starring Dana Elcar, Donald Moffat and Ralph Waite, and TV's intimacy became a surefire asset. And, just possibly, the setting on the tube offered a clue into the allegory that Beckett created in this stunning piece of absurdist theater.

My theory is as good as any, I think, and there sure have been a lot of them articulated. This unseen person that Beckett's two quirky hoboes are waiting for, this Godot — he stands for God, doesn't he? Or does he?

Does Godot refer to man's eternal hope in the face of rotten destiny? Is Godot some kind of spiritual signpost? Is Godot a symbol of man's frustration? Man's need for dreams and symbols?

Into the bubbling stew I toss my own theory, to wit: "Waiting for Godot" is the ultimate lampoon of the TV talk show. It's the essence of Carson-Griffin-Douglas-Donahue-Shore, a crazy-quilt distillation of comedy and verbosity (purposeful and satiric verbosity in Beckett's case), an endless flow of human speech.

And they're waiting for Godot, too, on those talk shows. Godot is the commercial. But, you say, Godot never did come around ever in

Beckett's play? And to that I say, sure, but what did Beckett know about television? I rest my case.

Ideally, Laurel and Hardy should have costarred as Vladimir and Estragon, the two tramps who engage in an extended music hall turn, aimlessly bickering and aimlessly making up, two metaphysical Micawbers waiting for the mysterious Godot. Dana Elcar (he's the vindictive commanding officer in "Baa Baa Black Sheep") and Donald Moffatt (costar on TV's "Logan's Run" series) give the tramps here a warm and endearing and compassionate lunacy.

"I'm so unhappy," one of them says.

"Since when?" says the other.

"I've forgotten," says the first.

It's pure Lewis Carroll — "Alice in Wonderland" with darker, more grave and introspective impulses. Carroll's Alice had said: "Dear, dear! How queer everything is today! And yesterday things went on just as usual. I wonder if I've been changed in the night."

And Beckett's Vladimir puts it this way: "Was I sleeping while the others suffered? Am I sleeping now? Tomorrow, when I awake, or think I do, what shall I say of today?"

They breathe such an amiably bemused frustration, those two, as they act out a wild caricature of empty lives with their staggeringly cosmic and elusive conundrums.

"Let's go," says one.

"We can't."

"Why not?"

"We're waiting for Godot."

"Ah," says the first, understanding nothing. Another fine mess. I'd given a lot to have seen Stan Laurel and Ollie Hardy do the foregoing with appropriate gestures. They never did, of course, and that's a pity.

Anyway, the two tramps engage in their clowning and their quarreling for a very sound reason. They do it, as one of them says, "to give the impression that we exist." Is there a better reason?

Into the bleak nothingness of the stage, with its one droopy tree, enters Ralph Waite, the whip-cracking Pozzo, and his woebegone man-servant (Bruce French), stoop-shouldered and subservient and ironically called Lucky.

Isn't that Ralph Waite, the father from "The Waltons?" One and the same. And what does he symbolize, him with that whip? The rating services, I think. And the servile, unresisting man-servant is — what else? — television.

'Gunsmoke' at Full Gallop

Raw-boned and leathery, features burnished by the winds of the prairie, their faces might well have sprung to life out of the paintings of Remington or that other cowboy artist in whom greatness dwelled, Charley Russell from Montana. These were men with names like Will and Doak and Quincy and they were the central figures in a western that was, I guess, just about as good as any I've ever seen on television.

And it was, as you might expect, an episode of a series that Frederic Remington, who was too fat to get astride a horse, and ol' Charley Russell, who was born to the saddle, would surely have taken to — "Gunsmoke," of course.

It is by no means the "Gunsmoke" of old. Certainly the Longbranch saloon in Dodge isn't the same without Kitty serving up a cold beer and saying, "Be careful, Matt."

Matt Dillon himself, played with towering strength by James Arness, has fleshed out a bit. Doc (Milburn Stone) doesn't make so many house calls and his good buddy, Chester, has been gone now for at least 10 years, replaced in kind by the drawling Festus (Ken Curtis).

But the quality remains. In this particular episode, written by Jim Byrnes and called "Thirty a Month and Found," all of the "Gunsmoke" elements were present, with an extra measure of compassion and, perhaps, a deeper, more intense feeling of melancholy in the face of inevitable change in which the Old West would recede forever into the most enduring of American myths. First came the barbed wire and then the train and the West would never be the same.

"The glory days are gone," someone says, "and I'm afraid they ain't coming back."

Not too many years ago, Kirk Douglas starred in a movie he considers his best. It was called "Lonely Are the Brave" and in it he played a contemporary cowboy, a product of the Southwest, who is roped in by the encroachments of civilization and progress. And that was when? Somewhere in the 1960s, I suppose, and it was extraordinarily effective and memorable.

In a "Gunsmoke" episode the time is roughly a century earlier but the theme, a seedling then in historical terms, is no less profound, or emotionally stirring.

Simply put, "Thirty a Month and Found" (which is the cowhand's pay, plus board) is the story of an aging ramrod of the trail drive, a younger cowpoke and a still younger one, described as being "all cowlick and Adam's apple but he'll do." Historically, the issue is between the cattlemen and the railroaders over shipping the herds but here the conflict narrows to a barroom brawl in the Longbranch.

The next day, in the town jail, Marshal Dillon asks, "Why do you always start it with railroad men?"

"Railroad's come to stick in my craw," says ol' Will. "Used to be drivers didn't have to share the town with railroaders ... Herdin' cows into box cars instead of 'cross grass. Don't make sense."

"Country changes, Will," says Matt Dillon. "Called progress."

There follows the development of a powerful story line as sure and swift as a Greek tragedy, with classic inevitability, a drama fully realized. Over a $12 misunderstanding, the cowhands become outlaws, an ironic parable of their impending doom as they are caught up in history's sweep.

Ol' Blue Eyes and Ol' Four Eyes

With great buoyancy and the musicianship that is the envy of a generation of singers, Sinatra poured it on, creating a distinctive and mesmerizingly fluid blend of melody, lyric, style and that indefinable Sinatra excitement. Listening to Sinatra now, one couldn't help but think of Dizzy Dean in the waning days of his pitching career, his arm gone but working still with guile and cunning and, by all means, style.

It is an autumn night in 1976 and Frank Sinatra's voice is far from gone, but the parallel is nonetheless apt — the vocal machinery has turned heavier, the old floaty ease less apparent. Now the voice has its husky overtones, the high notes are elusive and taunting. Now there is a curious wintry melancholy to go with the autumnal mellowness.

He is more performer than the singer of old, an actor with lyrics as his dialogue — an actor who has created his own character, his own mythology, an artist persistently aware of his own capabilities. An artist who has never lost an ounce of pride, he is still the disciplined master of nuance and timing and the most finely honed, most intensely concentrated simplicity there is — at once very simple and very complex.

By the fundamental act of lifting his voice in song, which may be the most basic of poetic expressions by all sublunary beings, Sinatra creates his own celebration of a special art — the interpretation of the popular song. This he does — as he has done for more than three decades — with extraordinary felicity, evoking from the romantic platitudes a dream that turns into sudden, sharp reality.

A professional in an age of amateurs, his absorption in his craft is total and yet one feels in Sinatra's presence something beyond mere song — there is an odd sense of danger, of unpredictability. He is a performer ruled by instinct, stoked by his own intuitive fires, moody, complex, turbulent.

This is one quality which those who would imitate his singing can never achieve. It is the essence of the man that is inimitable.

It is an opening night of a nightclub act at Harrah's, at Lake Tahoe, that is a continuation of a TV special and he is in exuberant spirits, sleekly barbered, conservatively tailored in a tuxedo, which is the traditional uniform of the saloon singer. Where are the floppy ties of yesteryear? Where are those wide collars and the extravagantly padded shoulders and the bushel of untamed hair? Where are the squealing bobby-soxers? Did it all happen so long ago?

"There's nothing more old-fashioned than being up-to-date," Noel Coward once proclaimed. However the years have shaped Frank Sinatra, he can never be old-fashioned. He is timeless, as Duke Ellington was timeless. Fashion is perishable, style endures.

On the stage now Sinatra has finished his own turn and he is joined by John Denver, one of the best of the new breed of song-writing singers. It is a uniting of opposites, of Coca-Cola and cognac, Rocky Mountain high and the streets of Hoboken. But they work uncommonly well together, "Ol' Blue Eyes and Ol' Four Eyes," in Denver's phrase.

Sinatra has seniority here and the songs they do first are the Sinatra songs. Among them, sung individually or in duet, are "Witchcraft" and "Come Fly With Me" and "Nancy With the Laughing Face" delivered with great good humor and that rarity on any stage, a non-competitive, joyously harmonious professionalism shared by the performers — and shared with the audience.

Then, from a smiling John Denver: "How about doing some of my songs?"

"All right," Sinatra agrees. "I'll go get my cow."

Mostly, the Denver songs speak of the outdoors; they are artfully crafted, full-bodied and contemporary. Denver sings his lyrics right on the button. Sinatra, contrarily, makes his own personal statement with his phrasing — each word, each consonant enunciated with precision and clarity, each thought fully rounded in a rich and highly individual musical flow.

It is typical of Sinatra that he still dares to walk on the precipice. Working alone (abetted by 40 musicians, including the masterful guitarist Al Viola), he sang the Gershwins' "Embraceable You" at a very, very slow tempo. For a singer, this is an Evel Knievel leap — but throughout this high-risk performance Sinatra's intonation remained miraculously firm, impeccably musical.

On this night, his repertoire embraced the old and the new — from Neil Diamond's "Stargazer" to Cole Porter's "Night and Day." But it was, particularly, in Barry Manilow's "I Sing the Songs" that all of the years were wrapped in a moment of wonder, the Sinatra voice a coupling of strength and delicacy, so wistful and warm, touching the far recesses of our deepest emotions.

A Worldly Innocent Returns

Remember Jack Paar? You remember Jack Paar, mercurial, complicated, impulsive, emotional, whimsical, given to an occasional tear, a man with an intense curiosity, a searching and often very funny man propelled by a cluster of impish inner demons.

You remember ol' Jack, whose personality some people — me, for instance — often likened to a prickly pear, as abrasive as it is endearing; a man, in short, who bounced off the screen as a many-sided human being, warts and all, and who was never just another plastic smile.

And he still isn't. He was back, Paar was, on the "Merv Griffin Show," in November, 1977, and in that all-too-brief, 10-minute interview, the old Paar excitement, the electricity and magic, was a part of the air, and I must say it was invigorating to experience.

This particular occasion was a celebrity tennis tournament in Monte Carlo, the last place in the world I would expect to attract Paar. But Merv is a rabid tennis buff and he had corraled all of the celebrity players, such as Charlton Heston, who would rather score an ace than part the Red Sea, for this fancy tournament in the land of Her Serene Highness and they had a style show and other festivities.

And somehow Jack Paar was there and one afternoon, with Carl Reiner also at the table, Paar was interviewed by Merv. It happened during the day, I know, because Carl Reiner was devoid of his hair piece, or doily. Carl has always insisted that it is "bad taste" to wear one's hair before sundown.

Anyway, Paar was in tremendous form, unfailingly interesting as always, slightly edgy but charming, his voice cracking, his observations bemused, still the worldly innocent. And the emotions never stray far from the surface.

"I keep having this dream," Paar related, "that the band is playing the theme and I'm walking out in front of the cameras, and Hugh Downs says, 'Here's Jack,' and I stare out at the studio audience and I freeze, WITH NOTHING TO SAY. The dream occurs twice a week."

I wouldn't be surprised at the implication of the dream, at the terrible anxiety that is probably its wellspring. I would be surprised only at Jack Paar having nothing to say.

He was the best there ever was, certainly, at stirring up the juices as a talk-show host (and a brilliant reporter-narrator on his specials from such places as East Africa), viewing the oddments of life from a sharply original tilt. He was the hottest article on the tube in the late '50s and through the '60s, and he talked about those days with a certain detachment.

"There's something about this present era that doesn't create the same kind of people we had on the show," Paar said. "Like Oscar Levant — with Oscar, you were seeing one of the real neurotics of all time. The people we'd have on the show — we had James Thurber, George S. Kaufman, Alexander King, Peter Ustinov, Randolph Churchill, Winston's son, who had such trouble living under his father's fame.

"Malcolm Muggeridge once said that Randolph could have been the greatest of all the Churchills. There was greatness in him. Such a pity."

So there was Jack Paar talking about the British and for me it summoned up memories of Paar's first show in England when he almost single-handedly revived the War of 1812.

Paar was facing a London studio audience that was reserved and wholly undemonstrative and very, very cool. They weren't sure about this Yank. For openers, Paar cracked: "We'll take so many things away from your country — like pneumonia."

To that sally the response was grim-lipped silence. Paar rolled on: "I think you British speak very nicely, for a people who drink warm beer and drive on the wrong side of the street."

The silence tightened. Then Paar, with his acute ear for audience reaction, paused and cried, plaintively: "We must have some rapport here, eventually." Finally, they did establish first a truce and then an understanding and in time the British grew very fond of our Jack.

Now Paar was saying to Griffin: "Somebody asked me once if I could walk across water. 'I'm not sure,' I said. 'Once I went to the edge of the Hudson River and I realized if I walked across the Hudson, I'd only get to Newark. Why get the bottom of my socks wet for that?'"

With the exception of a brief, abortive foray into TV a few years earlier, Paar has been largely out of view, which is a shame. He is a man of immense style and professionalism who is sorely missed. And I kid you not.

Bicentennial Recalled

There they were, passing in review once again in New York harbor, a stately procession of grand ships, all those full-sailed square-riggers from out of the past, all the schooners and the ketches and the sloops and the barks. "It looks," said Walter Cronkite, in tones of awe, "like the battle of Trafalgar."

Here was a retrospective on July 4, 1977, summoning to memory an event dating back only a year — to "Our Happiest Birthday," which was the apt title of this Fourth of July special that graced CBS. Now we are 201 years old, not very long in the tooth as the world's civilizations are measured, but it seemed an excellent idea, nonetheless, to remember for one hour how it was then, on July 4, 1976.

It was one terrific day for television and Cronkite observed the celebration, with great good humor and his reporter's interpretative eye, sitting in the CBS booth from 8 in the morning until after midnight. And you still ask why Walter is known to his colleagues as Old Iron Butt?

Elsewhere on the dial, you could see James Whitmore doing his Will Rogers, who was assuredly the most American of our funnymen. Or you could see the movie version of Meredith Willson's "The Music Man," unarguably the most American of our musicals. And then there was Walter Cronkite. That's quite a red-white-and-blue parlay for this Fouth of July.

"Where were you when America celebrated the Bicentennial Fourth of July?" Walter Cronkite said at one point in the hour. Well, many of us can remember celebrating with Walter himself, witnessing that perfect blend of technology and event, a kaleidoscopic view of a country and its people in the best of moods.

"Oh, it was an exhilarating day," Walter said. "Its sights and sounds will remain in our memory . . ."

And then we had another flashback to 1976 and the tall ships in the tall city. Some of those ships, as Walter noted, bore some fine names, such as Voyager and Pioneer, Spirit of '76, and Restless, Hope, Freedom and the Spirit of America.

Cronkite gave to the reading of each name a very special tone, at once crisp and warm. It was almost musical, the way he articulated the names, as proud as Jimmy Cagney, in his George M. Cohan role, chirping out "It's a Grand Old Flag."

On this Bicentennial Fourth of July, America seemed to be marching to the same drummer — but with an extraordinary diversity, all of it recorded by the cameras across the land. They were fiddlin' and pickin' at a Folklore Festival in Washington, D.C., and they were calling the hogs in Polk County, Iowa. In the skies over St. Louis, a wingwalker took a calculated stroll aboard his biplane, and one thought of another, less sophisticated time.

At an annual powwow in Carnegie, Okla., an Indian woman told an interviewer, with no trace of irony: "I feel this is our country as well as your country."

They played jazz in New Orleans. They had a mass swearing-in of new citizens in Chicago. And in a small town in Pennsylvania, its name forever engraved in a nation's memory, they reenacted the battle of Gettysburg.

And in Boston, a quarter of a million people listened to Arthur Fiedler and the Boston Pops in a rousing "Stars and Stripes Forever." What a happy sight! What happy sounds! What a birthday!

"We're 200 years old," said Walter Conkite. "It's a milestone that makes us wonder what will become of us as a nation. We're not sure of the future . . . We don't know what's behind the doors that we must open. We only know that the keys we have, keys cut in Independence Hall, became our ideals: Liberty, justice, equality . . .

"We have not fulfilled our ideals even after 200 years. Correcting wrongs will be a part of our future. It will demand courage, but correcting wrongs has been a dramatic part of our history . . . We'll be all right if we keep in our hearts the story of America. If we do, well, then a hundred years from now our country's hearts will be host to these ideals that we gave the world on July Fourth, 1776."

Some Random Views

A columnist is, among other things, an essayist and often the subject matter for the essay seems unrelated to television itself. In one essay that follows, for instance, the subject was cats. I am not too keen on cats. I think I might like cats but cats don't like me. They know I like dogs and horses — this they know instinctively.

Is a television column the proper avenue for one to exhibit his distaste for a domesticated animal that slinks around the house? That acts sneaky? That is too independent? That, to get to the nub of the matter, doesn't like me?

A television column may not be the proper platform for such personal animosities, but then a television column is all I've got. The result of this particular essay was not surprising — the cat-lovers reacted like a she-moose protecting its young. The letters were predictably abusive. For reasons that I have yet to unravel, people sent me photographs of their pet cats, some with paw prints. I showed them to my dog. He growled. I trust my dog's instincts.

A Man Barks At Cats

Henry Morgan, who breathes good will and philanthropy on the "I've Got a Secret" panel, has come out unequivocally against cats, a stand I firmly applaud.

Show me a man who likes cats and I'll show you a man who hates dogs. Or, more to the point, a man who is hated by dogs — in short, a man who can't be trusted, if I'm any judge of character. Have you ever known a spy who wasn't instinctively hated by dogs? Or a jewel thief? Or a city editor? Well, I think I have proved my point.

Anyhow, writing in the Saturday Review, Mr. Morgan says: "At someone's house the other day, the cat sneaked into my lap. 'Why,' said the hostess, 'she likes you.'

"Well, I don't like cats," continues Mr. Morgan, in his customary sweet tones, "and if cats don't know that they're even dumber than I thought. They sit on laps because it's warm there. They couldn't care less if it's you or a radiator.

"A cat likes me. Me? Here's an animal that can't read, has never been anywhere but on the fire escape, lives on free milk and garbage and this bum has an opinion," writes Mr. Morgan, later adding this cutting thrust. "People with insufficient personalities are fond of cats. I suppose that when the lady said her cat liked me, she meant to pay me a compliment. I still don't like cats."

Henry, you are my kind of guy — perceptive, bold, fair. Frankly, I don't like cats, either, and, as a critic of the performing arts, my principal reason is not emotional but logical: Cats have no talent.

You see other animals bursting with talent all over the dial. If not dogs or monkeys or seals performing tricks on a variety show, then there are dogs and horses acting magnificently — and heroically — on the dramatic shows.

Cats can't act magnificently — or heroically — because cats can't act at all. Out chasing helpless mice all day, they are, or playing wastefully with balls of thread. Meanwhile, the dogs study their lines and learn their craft.

With solemn pride, I point to Lassie, for instance, a real trouper, show biz to the bone and in his (or her) soft-spoken way, brave and virtuous. Come to think of it, there's never been a TV show yet named for any cat.

And look at Rin Tin Tin, who also was the proud possessor of his own show, who ranks right up there in gallantry. Has there ever been a cat in history that saved a cavalry regiment from the Indians?

Don't talk to me about cats. A cat would be off smuggling rifles to the Indians.

Cats have no prestige. But dogs reflect their own innate goodness. Jimmy Cannon, the sportswriter, did a piece once about a drunken loafer who beat his wife and kids. However, in the neighborhood he was treated with great respect simply because he owned a dog.

"He can't be all bad," Cannon heard one woman inform another as the guy lurched by, with a load on and the faithful mutt at his side. "He loves that dog."

Can you imagine a man thus in his cups walking with a cat? Those women would have averted their eyes in disgust. And there you have a highly revelatory difference between cat and dog.

Besides being unblessed with talent, the cat is icy, forbidding, deceitful and reflective of man's darkest instincts. (Catty, feline, a cat's paw — all terms bereft of compliment and no accident, either.)

The cat is a wastrel, howling on back fences all night. But the dog fulfills humanitarian functions — pulling sleds for Mounties, transporting brandy to thirsty mountain climbers, protecting Little Orphan Annie. (Do you think Daddy Warbucks would have entrusted his Annie with some cat? Don't be silly.)

One recalls the old vaudeville team of Weber and Fields. Weber used to say to Fields: "This dog is worth $5,000." To which Fields would say: "My, I never heard of a dog who saved that much money."

That's another thing. Cats never save their money. Shiftless, no-account beasts, all of them.

Return of 'The Godfather'

"'The Godfather' Returns With a Bang," said the headline in TV Guide for Nov. 12, 1977. And this time I want to tell you I was prepared — I sent out for a pizza beforehand. For what I remember most vividly about "The Godfather" is unrestrained hunger. They were always eating in that movie and a fellow, watching all that serious eating, gets hungry.

Well do I remember seeing "The Godfather" in a theater and being filled with visions of Veal Parmigiana and Chicken Cacciatore (who is not, contrary to rumor, the cowardly member of the Family).

And I wasn't alone in that regard. At intermission, I remember, there was a determined rush to the refreshment stand. The patrons clamored for popcorn and there were those, strongly influenced by what they had witnessed on the screen, who lamented that it was butter that was poured over the popcorn, instead of red clam sauce.

And I remember drinking a Pepsi and imagining that it was a wryly sardonic Bardolino or the amusingly unpretentious if laconic Valpolicella.

For all of the fascination of the story line, based on Mario Puzo's powerhouse novel, and the intriguing quality of Marlon Brando's performance, my own thoughts throughout the film dwelled mainly on food. They never stopped eating in that movie. Well, hardly ever. It takes time to reload.

I think of Clemenza (played by Richard Castellano with great zest and sterling appetite) standing by the stove and he is saying: "Some day you might have to cook for 20 guys. Watch me. First, you put in a little olive oil and then the onions." And on he goes, putting together the meat sauce for the pasta. I watched and my mouth watered, my own appetite tantalizingly whetted.

This Clemenza is a serious eater, an artist with a knife and fork. Do you remember that scene where Clemenza is leaving his home to attend to the unpleasant detail of having Pauly, the turncoat bodyguard, erased?

"Don't forget the cannoli," Mrs. Clemenza says.

"Yeah, yeah," Clemenza says.

Here is a man, Clemenza, who is clearly preoccupied. But he is, as I say, a serious eater, and with all that is weighing so heavily on his mind, he does not forget the cannoli.

And there was the wedding party for Connie and Carlo and all those lofty mountains of lasagna, the pizza grande, the tasty capuzelli, the tangy antipasto, the gloriously steaming pasta. What a scene to stir up the taste buds!

I think of Sonny (James Caan) who is the hot-headed Corleone brother, always plotting reprisals, forever on the run, but he has time always to stop and dip a chunk of crusty bread into the meat sauce simmering invitingly on the stove.

And there's Michael (Al Pacino) saying to Kay (Diane Keaton): "You like your lasagna?"

Of course she likes her lasagna. It's terrific lasagna. The best. Are you kidding? You think anyone would dare serve up a bad lasagna to the future Mrs. Corleone?

And even before he gets hit in Louis' restaurant in The Bronx, Sterling Hayden as Police Capt. Wolf McCluskey has put away a substantial portion of what Sollozzo (another unfortunate victim) had told him was the best veal in the city.

Both Sollozzo and McCluskey are forced to stop eating by circumstances which Don Vito Corleone would probably have called "regretable." I thought it was sad, too. They never did get to taste the spumoni.

I think of another scene where another of the Corleone brothers, Fredo, is sitting in the dining room and he is sulking. "What's the matter with you?" his wife says.

"Shut up and set the table," he orders. In the Corleone family, it's first things first.

In scene after scene, as contracts were let on various persons who would have to learn to swim in concrete suits in the Hudson River, my thoughts remained fixed on the splendid food that had been consumed and on what would be served next.

Let me put it this way. The food in the movie was a continuing offer that I couldn't refuse. With pristine clarity, I can remember the exact moment that I realized how thoroughly the food eaten and displayed had distracted me from the story. Marlon Brando and Al Pacino were talking — I think they may have been munching pasta fazool at the time — and suddenly, instead of seeing the two stars on the screen, Brando and Pacino, I saw two George Pernicanos. (George serves the best Italian food in San Diego.)

What is most significant, I think, is that in the transferring of "The Godfather" parts one and two, to television, NBC sacrificed not one morsel of food to the censor's scissors.

Buon appetito.

Not Ready for Prime Time

What's Jimmy Carter doing perched aboard that famous statue of Andrew Jackson astride his horse on Canal Street in New Orleans? Wait a minute. That's not Jimmy Carter. It's Danny Ackroyd of NBC's "Saturday Night" troupe and his Carter impression is, as always, right on the button. You can almost sniff the peanuts and taste the Dr. Pepper. And, of course, he's wearing a sweater.

Why is he there, in New Orleans? What he's doing is telling us about the fun to be had at Mardi Gras, to wit: "We must work — those of us who have work — to have fun."

And: "I promise always to carry my own garment bag and to carry my brother, Billy, when he's unable to walk by himself ... He ain't heavy. He's my brother."

Usually, Ackroyd is seen along with the rest of the iconoclastic Not Ready for Prime Time Players at 11:30 on Saturday nights. Perhaps as a test for their readiness, the show was scheduled as one of NBC's Big Events on a Sunday evening out of New Orleans — and, just possibly, they aren't ready for prime time, at that.

Perhaps the late-night frolics assume an inexplicable weightiness at an earlier hour or, perhaps, our mood shifts into freewheeling around midnight. Whatever the cause, uneven is the word one might charitably apply to this particular outing. But then, consistency has never been a virtue on "Saturday Night," wherein the material can run to the tastelessly juvenile, which is a notch below sophomoric.

For example, on a show only two days after the murder of an entertainer known as Prof. Backwards, they explained why nobody came to his rescue. Prof. Backwards, the line went, kept yelling: "Pleh, pleh!"

At its best, however, the "Saturday Night" troupe has evoked memories of the Sid Caesar-Imogene Coca era with its inspired lunacy and crackling irreverence. I remember with special fondness an explosively funny — and angry — parody of "Star Trek" with John Belushi as Capt. Kirk. He's a brilliant comic, this Belushi, my favorite of the lot.

Down in New Orleans, in the madness of Mardi Gras, Belushi contributed his share of nonsense. In one sketch, Belushi was a terrific Brando getting off the streetcar named — what else? — Desire and hollering for — who else? — Stella.

And there was Buck Henry and Jane Curtin serving nobly as commentators on the festive Mardi Gras activity below their announcers' booth. The routine emerged as a delicious lampoon on all such events, including the familiar gushing commentaries that affront us each year at the Tournament of Roses parade.

"This is a beautiful city," Jane said.

"I don't think I've ever seen a more beautiful city," Buck agreed, "except for Havasu City."

It was swell of Jane and Buck, I thought, to pass along the historical derivation of the celebration called Mardi Gras. "Thousands of people used to meet for no reason, lining Canal Street," Jane said. "After years of the crowds going home disappointed, the city put a parade in the middle of the street."

And by all means there was Baba Wawa (Gilda Radner) interviewing Henry (The Fonz) Winkler, who has a position of honor in this Mardi Gras. Baba Wawa, who may or may not resemble a network newscaster known to millions, does have a slight difficulty pronouncing certain letters, namely "r" and "w." A phrase such as "proper perspective" does not exactly fall trippingly off her tongue. Neither, come to think of it, does "Harry Reasoner."

You might well ask if such humor is indelicately malicious and I guess it is, falling somewhere along the border line of taste — in short, a shock laugh.

But then, it is the nature of laughter that it is composed, at least partly, of shock. It is the unexpectedness of a line that wrenches the laugh out of you, and the lines on this show are never pasteurized.

When you pasteurize humor, when enough people handle it and inspect it to be sure it doesn't offend the sponsor or the network or even some of the viewers, then the shock is taken out of it and you have to bring in the laugh track to do the laughing for you.

TV Glimpses

Red Skelton was taking his ease on the "Dinah Shore Show," Red at his ingratiatingly flamboyant best, telling a hilarious tale about how he once liberated a $5,000 piano from the MGM studios. It was a typical Skelton performance, a yarn related with all of his comedic powers at full-blast, his pliable clown's face reflecting every detail as he wrenched a continuous outpouring of laughter from Dinah and her studio audience.

Then Red was saying that he had brought a circus friend of his along, a midget sword-swallower. "Why," said Red, "he can swallow a six-foot sword. Just a little midget, too."

"That's certainly amazing," Dinah said. "Where is he?"

"He's backstage rehearsing his act," Skelton said.

At once, a horrible scream was heard from the backstage area. Skelton shook his head. "I told that guy not to take bows," he said, sadly.

☆ ☆ ☆

Mark Twain, whose fertile imagination knew few bounds, found great delight in inventing gadgets, such as a self-pasting scrapbook and an elastic vest-strap, both unsuccessful. And he invested — and lost — a sizable amount on someone else's invention of a newfangled kind of typesetting machine. As a man of his time, Mark Twain witnessed with keen interest the innovations that sprouted all around him — the telegraph, the typewriter, the electric light, the telephone.

And what, you may well ask, about television? Could the old boy, prescient as he was, have foreseen TV?

He might have, at that. Lightly cynical, pointedly irreverent, Twain insisted that not great genius but accident was the greatest of the inventors.

"A man invents a thing which could revolutionize the arts, produce mountains of money, and bless the earth and who will bother with it or show any interest in it?" Twain once wrote. "But you invent some worthless thing to amuse yourself with, and would throw it away if let alone, and all of a sudden the whole world makes a snatch for it and out crops a fortune."

Television, for instance?

There is a story, perhaps apocryphal, about the early days of television. Several executives, Ivy Leaguers all, were assembled around a conference table. One of them suggested a program he thought would be perfect for Sunday afternoon.

"Sunday afternoon!" the president of the network cried. "Nobody watches television on Sunday afternoon — they're all out playing polo!"

On a talk show, Buddy Hackett passed along his advice for visitors to Las Vegas. "You arrive with $1,000," Buddy says, "and immediately you send home $500 of that amount. Then if you gamble and lose $500, you can return home, open the envelope with your other $500, and you feel that you broke even."

Do you remember the comedy team known as Wayne and Shuster? A pair of Canadians, Johnny Wayne and Frank Shuster enjoyed a considerable vogue in the mid-'60s with countless appearances on the "Ed Sullivan Show." Once, a New York agent visited Johnny Wayne in his palatial Toronto home and implored him to move to the States.

Sitting on the patio overlooking his swimming pool, Wayne puffed on his outsized cigar. "Why should I move to the States?" he said. "I'm happy here."

Exasperated, the agent cried: "But, Johnny, happiness isn't everything!"

☆ ☆ ☆

"Why is it," the woman out there in televisionland wrote Phil Donahue, "that all your talk-show hosts are Irish? You and Merv Griffin and Mike Douglas — you're all Irish. Why is that, anyway?"

As he pondered the question, Phil Donahue, who is indeed a product of the Ould Sod, agreed that it is an intriguing coincidence. "Probably a wide segment of American women who watch TV like the shaggy-haired, round-faced look," he mused. "And maybe it has something to do with the old blarney."

☆ ☆ ☆

Well, it was a nice wedding, complete with tears and laughter and "Lady of the Spain" on the accordion. Finally, on the hit television show in which she is the title character, Rhoda committed herself to marriage on the night of Oct. 28, 1974, in a special one-hour session that was warm and beguiling and, I wouldn't be surprised, the most popular episode of any series in the season.

Perhaps that is the kind of season it was. Besides, television has long been ripe for the type of event in which the folks out front could participate along with their viewing. Actually, they are a rarity, this kind of happening that becomes, in a curious way, a part of our lives — the birth of Little Ricky on "I Love Lucy," many years ago, was one. The finale when David Janssen stopped running on "The Fugitive" was another.

How many others were there in television's brief history? Not many. And I don't suppose one can think of a better tribute than this strange blurring of reality and fiction. Of course it happens every day on the soap operas. But in prime time — well, it's different in prime time. With nightfall our capacity for suspension of disbelief is obviously lessened.

Anyway, there was this marriage of Rhoda and Joe on the TV and somewhere that mystic line was crossed and the smack of reality achieved. People across the land responded — and spontaneously, at that — with wedding parties of their own, some with formal invitations.

Viewers, happily crossing the line of make-believe, sent presents for Rhoda to CBS. Others dispatched cards and letters, all presumably approving of the union.

Slightly Pasteurized 'Soap'

I have just devoted about three hours to watching an awful lot of "Soap," which is the new ABC comedy series and, by all means, the most hotly controversial show of the 1977-'78 season. Although, I was witness to tapes of the first three episodes, including both the original and the revised — and only slightly pasteurized — version of the opening yarn that put some segments of the populace into mild shock.

And I saw snippets and pieces of ensuing episodes, among them a particular scene that stirred up several church groups. In the spring of '77, in Newsweek, Harry F. Waters wrote about the show on, it seems to me now, a note of hysteria. That one scene, moreover, he summed up — errantly, it turns out — as follows: "Jessica's promiscuous daughter will try to seduce a Jesuit priest in church."

Those words alone instigated a sea storm of protest which might have had more substance if Waters' description had been closer to the mark. It is hardly a seduction scene, either in the original or in the version slightly revised. In the confessional booth, the teenage girl, not known for her shyness, says to the young priest: "I could tell when you kissed me that you loved me." To which the priest replies: "But that was when we were five years old." And that's about as seductive as it gets.

In theme and intent and general texture, "Soap" is the comedy of "Mary Hartman, Mary Hartman," of "All That Glitters" and, perhaps, "Maude" and the early "All in the Family" and, by all means, NBC's "Saturday Night." It is absurdly outrageous, pointedly irreverent, and it is also undeniably funny. It is, in short, the comedy of the 1970s.

Is the show, as charged, "offensive?" Some moments I would prefer to see excised as sniggering and sophomoric. There are attitudes that fail to win my approval and there are untidy excesses beyond the fence of good taste (which is to say, my version of this intensely personal judgment and that may or may not be yours).

The writing occasionally embraces the subtle flavor of a barracks joke and the acting — not all but some of it in this cast of newcomers — ranges from the smirky to the ponderous. All the same, a rich vein of comedy is tapped. It is, as I say, a funny show, although it may not be everyone's dish. And it is, further, a long remove from the savage assault on public morals that the clamor would have you believe.

Susan Harris, the creator and writer of "Soap," has this to say: "We deal with subjects that are being dealt with in daytime TV all the time. Women are watching during the day. Who's going to be shocked by moving it to prime time? Husbands?"

Probably. But that doesn't keep them from the set.

Debased by Watching TV?

"What if you were the President of the United States," said Nick

Johnson, who is a former FCC commissioner and now head of the National Citizens Committee for Broadcasting, "and they came to you with irrefutable evidence that television was bad for people? What if the doctors had all this evidence that TV was a harmful drug? Now as President you had the right to disconnect all the tubes in the country, disband the networks, shut down all the TV stations, put the whole TV industry away because it was harmful. What would you do?"

"I don't know," I said, boldly.

And I still don't. Nick Johnson is a man of vast persuasive force and a lot of charm and wit, and he had been talking about a new book by Marie Winn called "The Plug-In Drug," which refers to television. Nick Johnson doesn't like television, but then he doesn't watch much of it, either, even though the burden of his complaints lay in the area of public affairs programming.

There isn't enough of it, Nick Johnson insists. And of course he's right. There is much that is amiss with television but Nick had been reading this book and he had been taken with its premise which is, simply, that all of the talk about improving television is irrelevant — television, says Marie Winn, should be shut down altogether, tossed to the winds.

Marie Winn is the author of 10 books for parents and children, a graduate of Radcliffe College and Columbia University, who lives in New York with her husband, Allan Miller, and two young sons. "The Millers" — I quote here from the dust jacket — "own one small black-and-white television set that is used for special occasions."

And there, on a most intriguing note, it stops. What are those special occasions? Are the occasions literally that — is the set flipped on, in its glorious black-and-white, only occasionally? What I am saying is that, as a fellow who views the medium professionally, there are many special occasions that don't come along occasionally, if I make my point.

They come along frequently — every day, in fact. And the Millers, and their kids, are apparently missing most of them, if they are missing "Upstairs, Downstairs," "Barney Miller," "M*A*S*H," the William Buckley interviews, Georg Solti and the Chicago Symphony, Andre Previn and the Pittsburgh Symphony, the "Today Show" and "Washington Week in Review" and Cronkite and Chancellor and the plays on "Visions" and — I wonder if they missed the enchantment of the Olympics on ABC, or was that enough of a special occasion?

In "The Plug-In Drug," Marie Winn dismisses whatever virtues one might claim for the foregoing. It is her thesis that the very act of watching television affects us adversely — children, mainly — and she argues that it makes no difference "whether the program being watched is 'Sesame Street' or 'Superman,' 'The Descent of

Man' or 'Popeye.'" Possibly she means "The Ascent of Man." Small matter.

Television, Marie Winn argues, stunts the child's development in every possible way; television is passive, it is addictive; it is, in her view, a drug that exacts a ruinous price; it causes "television trance" and dominates family life.

Before the invention of television (and once, in the long ago, Edward R. Murrow whimsically wondered if the gadget could be "disinvented"), there were families and I presume they sat around and conversed. That is to say, they spoke to one another instead of to the television set and, of course, they spoke in Latin and discussed the finer points of Shakespeare's sonnets and frequently there was wit exchanged as to make Oscar Wilde and Lord Chesterfield numb with envy.

Isn't it a shame that television had to be invented and end this idyllic family existence?

"The role television has played in the national decline of reading and writing skills has not been precisely assessed — perhaps it never can be," Winn writes. "But the non-verbal nature of television, and the great involvement of children with television from their earliest years to the end of their school careers makes a connection between television watching and inadequate writing skills seem inevitable."

It does? Has there ever been a time when complaints weren't aired about the writing skills of students? Would the burning to ashes of all the TV sets in the Republic suddenly bring to yield a generation of authorship unparalleled in history? Would that really happen?

"In the television experience," Winn writes, basing her views presumably on occasional watching of her black-and-white set, "a viewer is carried along by the exigencies of a mechanical device, unable to bring into play his most highly developed mental abilities or to fulfill his individual emotional needs. He is entertained while watching television, but his passive participation leaves him unchanged in a human sense. For while television viewing provides diversion, reading allows and supports growth."

Contrarily, librarians say that reading has increased markedly with television and that many programs inspire viewers to get on to the library to acquire further information. The people who are the book readers in the nation would read books whether or not television existed. Is it too easy to point to the "Roots" phenomenon? Probably it is. But it is there, nonetheless, the extraordinary instance of an excellent book furthered in its sweeping popularity by a remarkable television series.

And why, I keep wondering, must "television" serve as the nasty pejorative and "reading" as the ennobling pursuit? In contrast to Marie Winn, I ask: what television are you watching? What books are you reading? Would you trade an hour of "Upstairs, Downstairs" for an hour of Harold Robbins?

Some Surefire Lines

I have been working on what I hope will prove an absolutely smashing script although as yet I seem to be a little short on plot and characters. All that I have so far, in fact, are assorted lines of dialogue, the result of a fairly exhaustive study of the late show.

But then, these are all surefire lines and once I get around to sprinkling them into one simple story — well, I just think we'll have a surefire script on our hands. Here are the lines; we'll dream up a plot later:

"Say, you look different tonight, Cynthia. You've taken off your glasses. Why, Cynthia, I never noticed before but — you're beautiful . . ."

"What did you say just then, Mr. Crumley — did you say a 'pearl-handled revolver?' Nobody here at Scotland Yard has said anything about a pearl-handled revolver. We said merely that Amantha Loot, the heiress, had been found with the murder weapon at her side . . . Crumley, you're under arrest — for murder!"

"Hello? Yes, this is Sally Glow — oh, that's awful! She tripped and broke her leg? But how can she go on tonight? It's opening night and . . . sure, I've heard it so often at rehearsal, I think I know the part . . ."

"We don't cotton much to strangers in these parts."

"Kid, you got moxie."

"I've never been more serious in all my life."

"You and me, Marsha, we belong to different worlds . . . It wouldn't work."

"Those drums! Those infernal drums!"

"Duvall, I've gone into the tank for you for the last time."

"Don't say a word. Just let me look at you."

"Farbishaw, I like your spirit. There's not a brighter intern here at Chart General. But, my boy, hospitals have rules . . ."

"All right, I'll tell you he couldn't have murdered Fernwell on the night of June 10. Because (sob) that night he was — with me ..."

"But ... but ... all that the letter said was that a J. K. Crisp was flying in to supervise the mine and we, uh, just naturally assumed it was a man ... Boy, help Miss Crisp with her bags!"

"Slim, I'm not rightly sure where to begin. You're the finest dadgum hand I ever hired here at the Bar B Q. Last week, when you asked for Emmy Lou's hand, I was proud to give you my blessing. But yesterday I was over to Dodge and the marshal gave me this 'wanted' poster ..."

"It's quiet around here. Too quiet ..."

"Objection! Prosecution is badgering the witness!"

"You fool. You crazy — wonderful fool."

"And that man was — your father."

"Ah, you silly, silly girl. We have only just met and yet I feel that I know you so well. You Americans are like children, as my mother, the contessa, often says. You save and scrimp, teaching school in this place you call Iowa. You come to Rome on vacation and here you expect to find romance — as you put it — in one day, one week, one summer. Do you not realize that romance is a way of life? It must be savored as one would savor a new spring wine — slowly. Very slowly. Now then, my little cabbage — first you and me, we will have luncheon then a stroll down the Via Veneta, then cocktails at a little place I know, then dinner at my apartment ..."

A Secret For Popularity

On the "Today Show," beamed over from London where they were celebrating Queen Elizabeth's Silver Jubilee, Tom Brokaw passed along one theory for the queen's enduring popularity in that 25-year span from 1952 to 1977. "It is said," Brokaw confided, "that her secret is simply that she has never once spoken to a journalist."

Now I, myself, have never spoken to royalty for an even longer period than 25 years, although I did have a conversation once with Benny Goodman, the King of Swing. This probably doesn't count.

Why, I wondered, hasn't the Queen deigned to converse with us ink-smeared wretches of the press? Perhaps she has seen us eating. Or drinking. My own private theory is that, years ago, before assuming the throne, she must have seen the Hecht-MacArthur newspaper classic, namely "The Front Page," and observed its hero, the free-wheeling Hildy Johnson, all too closely. And thereafter, perhaps, she made her vow of never speaking to anyone with a press card in his hat.

If I could have but one word with Queen Elizabeth on the subject, I would tell her that we aren't all of us like Hildy Johnson in "The Front Page." Most of us aren't that well-mannered.

The foregoing does not apply to one Charles McCabe, the San Francisco columnist of impeccable button-down civility, who recently wrote about Her Majesty in an essay headlined, irreverently: "Madame Queen."

"Trying to explain the Queen of England is rather like trying to explicate the mysteries of the Holy Ghost," McCabe begins, "or why money is accepted as a symbol of value. She is a mystery rooted deep in the British character."

It is this particular mystery, even as much as the attendant festivities, that seemed to be absorbing those who covered the big event. On "Today," for instance, Jane Pauley found herself moderating a heated debate in a London pub. The combatants were a young man dressed to the nines, wearing insignia that upheld the monarchy, and a young woman vigorously opposed to such notions.

"Why are you dressed like that?" the young woman snappishly asked the young man.

"Because," he said, airily, "I can afford it."

However the issue of the monarchy is eventually resolved (an astrologer on "Today" foresees no real problems until the 1990s because of moons and cusps or something), the Silver Jubilee celebration is a mighty festive and colorful occasion. And grand television.

And like all stars of television, Queen Elizabeth earns a bundle, maybe even more than such American royalty as Farrah Fawcett-Majors, who, after one season of "Charlie's Angels," lacked only 24 years of her own silver Jubilee.

Nobody, in fact, knows just how rich Queen Elizabeth is. A recent pay boost, obtained without a whimper from the constituents, brought her income up to 1,665,000 pounds a year, or $2,830,500. She pays no taxes. She is assuredly one of the richest women in the world. One estimate of her personal fortune puts it at 50 million pounds, or $85 million.

Most of the journalists to whom she has never spoken in her reign don't even have half that much.

The Night of The 1977 Oscars

Just before the 1977 Academy Awards ceremonies were beamed across the land on ABC, Regis Philbin and Sarah Purcell, cohosts of "A.M. Los Angeles," had their own interview show as they tracked down the celebrities entering the theater. Along came Rocky himself — Sylvester Stallone, the Italian Stallion, the man who made Cinderella look like a hard-luck case.

He's a good-natured sort, this Stallone, with a disarming air of self-deprecation. "Last year," Stallone said. "I'd have been parkin' your car."

Regis smiled. Sarah smiled. Sylvester shrugged. "Listen," said the author and star of "Rocky," the picture which would later be hailed with the Oscar, "I may be a flash in the pan. And next year I may be back parkin' your car again."

But don't bet on it. As a chalk player, I usually root for U.S. Steel and John Wayne and the Yankees. This time around, I was all for "Rocky," the long shot. Sylvester Stallone turned out to be a gracious winner on a show that emerged, as always, as a curiously heady tribal rite, an annual showcase of show business glamour. What hair-dos, what ruffles, what frills — and you should have seen the women!

Basically, the Oscar show is a televised news event. Year after year, we tune in to see who won (and if they'll show up) and who thanks who and at what length. It's always a compelling show, a parade of Hollywood glitter in its own peculiarly individual way and always a big smash in the ratings.

There is something indisputably special about movie stars. Certainly they are bigger than life — they are, in fact, enormous on the big screen. And they are less available. To see them, you must depart the comforts of home, including the 21-inch view of the lesser TV people, and shell out coin of the realm to see them in the movie houses.

Speaking here as a guy occupied with television, I have to say that the motion picture Academy Awards program does offer a built-in excitement that TV, for all of its impact, has never captured and which the TV people might well study. Mary Tyler Moore is terrific, but it is something special to see Liv Ullmann plain, if I make my point and I think I do.

One memorable highlight on this night was the comedy routine performed by Red Skelton, absent from television these last few years. Skelton stole the show from all those glamorous people. And he did it with the sly, ingratiating polish of the old pro come to illustrate to the neophytes the difficult art of capturing an audience and then, without strain, holding it in thrall.

Usually, in these affairs, it is a young newcomer who comes out of nowhere and wins the plaudits of the multitudes. Ann-Margret did it one year. Bernadette Peters did it another. But here was Red Skelton, practically retired, an elder statesman of comedy, doing his stuff and making the folks out front — and you and me at home — sit up and take sharp notice of a great clown at work.

Red Skelton, to put this another way, still has his fast ball. And I devoutly hope that the moguls who produce television shows, munching on larks' wings up there on Mt. Olympus, observed what we groundlings found so manifestly obvious — that there should be room for Red Skelton somewhere on the schedule.

Clearly, the evening's high drama came when Paddy Chayefsky, author of "Network," brought on Peter Finch's widow for a tearful acceptance of the late actor's award. "Network" was a nominee, of course, and it seemed ironic that this corrosive study of broadcasting — a picture so roundly despised by the network people themselves — should be heralded on one of the year's highest-rated programs.

It is an irony that Paddy Chayefsky, once a writer for TV, must have appreciated, having the success of his anti-television film proclaimed on the most commercially successful of the networks. But then one recalls the Gene Fowler line: "What is success? It is a toy balloon among children armed with pins."

A Long Day's Impressions

Finally, the day and the night came to an end, "the day," in Chet Huntley's apt phrase, "a nation put aside its anger and measured its grief." As Huntley observed by way of summation: "This was a day crowded with thousands of impressions ... and one of the impressions is the emotion that grief imparts to a face — here the face of Ethel Skakel Kennedy. We can think of no more appropriate way to close our coverage."

A moment later on NBC we saw again that numbingly moving portrait of Robert Kennedy's widow, head bowed, kneeling in prayer at the bier of her husband at St. Patrick's Cathedral.

The one picture on our television screens said it all with such completeness — this study of fortitude, of nobility, of despair and grief, of course, and of faith. It was a picture whose outlines will undoubtedly cling like few others with a searing permanence to the nation's collective memory.

Thousands of impressions from a June day in 1968.

So many impressions we had on this one day, all of them prompted by the television cameras: John Glenn at the graveside with the pallbearers, crisply, meticulously, with a sense of heavy duty, folding the flag that had draped Robert Kennedy's coffin; the solemnity of the Mass at St. Patrick's; Andy Williams singing "The Battle Hymn of the Republic;" all the familiar faces in an unfamiliar context; the young son of the senator helping to carry the casket; those of the Poor People's Campaign singing, their arms upraised; Ted Kennedy giving the eulogy.

The funeral train presented its own impressions, with its crowds at each depot waiting for a final glimpse and the girl, holding a picture of the senator in one hand, a tape recorder in the other. NBC's Ellie Abel, after disembarking, expressed himself in introspective terms about the long train ride from New York: "It was as if eight years of our lives had come together on that train — and it all ended when we arrived in Washington."

"It's an inner world on this train," said Harry Reasoner, "that appreciated the love and affection that poured in from the outside."

On ABC, Frank Reynolds engaged in a revealing dialogue with correspondent Bob Young.

"The world inside the train is much different than it is outside," Young told Reynolds. "It is less deliberate, less grieving, perhaps. There is an Irish wake going on here, relaxing the tension. We've got our own world here and it is ... relatively relaxed."

"An Irish wake, you would say?" Reynolds asked.

"An Irish wake preceding the burial, as sometimes occurs," Young replied. "Mrs. Ethel Kennedy has made a walk through the entire train, preceded by her son, Joseph Kennedy III. She is shaking hands with everyone and she has something to say, a reminiscence, a story, something personal that concerned the senator and the person she talks to, to everyone she sees. It is very hard, though, for most of us to reply ...

"It's an amazing example of composure and inner strength," Young went on. "And Mrs. Rose Kennedy is here, too. She is concerned about three things, which she dismisses immediately — age, weariness and defeat ... There is certainly cognizance and sensitivity to what this train means but the atmosphere is not all gloom."

Young added: "The Kennedys are seizing life where it can be seized. They seem to be saying that they are not afraid, even at a moment like this, to try to smile."

At the conclusion, just before the picture of Ethel Skakel Kennedy flashed on the screen, David Brinkley gazed at the burial plot above the Lincoln Memorial and his voice, always so measured and resonant, assumed a tone of leaden resignation. He spoke of the two Kennedy brothers, set to rest almost together.

"Between them," Brinkley said, "the presidency, a seat in the Senate, a presidential campaign unfinished ... a nation wounded and upset ... grieving parents ... two widows ... between them twelve children — and a child yet unborn."

These are some impressions. There were many more.

Some People I've Met

One of the benefits of interviewing celebrities is the custom, usually dictated by their schedules, of conducting them at lunch at very fine restaurants. If it weren't for an interview lunch I had once with Zsa Zsa Gabor in Beverly Hills, I would still think that escargot was an obscure French playwright.

"You must try the escargot, dolling," Zsa Zsa implored. I did. They were the best snails I ever tasted.

I remember talking once with Merv Griffin, the singer who became a durable talk show host. We were exploring my theory that as interviewers we tend to differ from other professional listeners such as doctors, lawyers, psychiatrists, insurance adjusters and those assigned to the complaint desk at the department store. They hear people at their worst.

Contrarily, it seemed to me, when we do our professional listening, we hear people at their best — or trying, in various degrees, to get there. The reason is apparent: we are not Woodward and Bernstein asking questions to track down involvement in a crime and its coverup. We are not, in short, involved with the cosmic. We want our questions to be met with charm and witty, quotable replies. And sometimes, if we're lucky, they are.

Here are a few of the people I've enjoyed meeting, most of them having appeared on television at one time or another or with some regularity.

King of the One-Liners

Henny Youngman was wearing the uniform of the comic's trade, the tuxedo with the ruffled shirt and the outsize bow tie, and he looked terrific. His jokes get older and Henny gets younger. And now, to his vast surprise and delight, he has become a beloved comedian.

Many comedians win laughs with their antics but our affection eludes them. People care about Henny. They are solicitous about his well-being. He is a part of our lives, a spur to that special lode of laughter in our memories.

"After 40 years, I'm an institution," Henny says. "People see me, they say, 'Henny, how ya feeling? Henny, ya lookin' good.' They say, 'Henny, take care of yourself.' They want me to look good and feel good. They want me to be young forever. I remind 'em of the good times they've had."

And that's about as serious as Henny Youngman gets. He picked up his cup of coffee and lifted it to his mouth but instead he hit the bottom of his nose. "Oops," he cried. "I thought I was taller!"

He lifts his coffee cup again and this time it found his mouth. Henny shakes his head. "I'm so near-sighted I can't even see my contact lenses!"

Henny Youngman is a big man with elfin eyes and a mischievous grin scrawled across his merry features. He is, of course, the King of the One-Liners, a master stylist, a one-of-a-kind performer. With his outlandish jokes and machine-gun delivery, Henny Youngman reflects the essence of the comic spirit, the true comic mind, the man who thinks funny, who says funny things and says things funny.

Once, he was invited to play golf with author Dick Schaap. As they stood at the first tee, Henny admitted that his knowledge of golf was meager. Holding his driver, Henny said, "What do I do now?"

Schaap said: "You address the ball."

Henny flexed his knees and leaned over the ball. "Dear sir," he said.

As he recalls the afternoon on the links, Henny says gleefully: "I broke 70 — and that's a lot of clubs to break!"

Wherever he goes, Henny is recognized. He had breezed into town to tell his jokes to a convention of industrial equipment distributors at the Town and Country, San Diego. As he strolled near the pool, a woman spotted him and a look of incredulity crossed her face.

"Henny Youngman!" she cried. "Are you in town?"

"Yes," Henny said.

Someone else saw him and shouted: "Take my wife — please!" Henny grinned. "I get it all the time, every day," Henny said. "People give me back my own lines. Wife jokes is what people know me for. Like I'm married 47 years to the same woman — where have I failed?" Beaming now, Henny said: "When my career started going good, my wife said she wanted a mink. I got her a mink. Then she wanted a sable. I got her a sable. Then she wanted a chinchilla. I got her a chinchilla." (Pause.) "The house was full of animals!"

Jokes are Henny's business but he admits to an occasional puzzlement at an audience's reaction. "Sometimes people applaud my jokes. Like take my mother-in-law. She's very neat — she even puts paper UNDER the cuckoo clock! With that line, I always get a laugh — and applause. Who knows why?"

I asked Henny how one becomes a comedian. "Are you kidding?" he said. "Listen, first you train your voice. Put a dozen marbles in your mouth and try to talk. Each day you get rid of one marble — by the time you've lost all your marbles, you're a comedian!"

Now there was no stopping him. "I had a sore leg. I went to a doctor. 'I'll have you walking in an hour,' he said. He stole my car!"

"I got a terrific doctor," Henny says. "If you can't afford the operation, he touches up the X-rays!"

And: "I got a friend, a lawyer. I won't mention his name but he's trying to break a girl's will!"

The Purest Kind of Sonnet

To begin on a note of metaphor, the interview is the golf swing of journalism. Or the tennis serve, depending on what form of punishment you choose for exercise. The interview can be likened to any minor art form that strikes the eye as simplicity itself and which is, in reality, so terribly difficult to do well, with rhythm and flow and a seamless precision.

In the perfect interview, there is an unmistakable strain of poetry. A perfect interview, to the journalist's ear, is the purest kind of sonnet — and just as rare.

"The big trick in the interview," Barbara Walters was saying in June, 1977, "is not necessarily to ask the tough questions. You can ask a lot of tough questions and people just won't answer, and then where are you? The idea in the interview is to get people to reveal themselves.

"A lot of people ask much tougher questions than I do. Women's Wear Daily asks tougher questions. Connie Chung, when she was doing interviews on CBS, asked tougher questions. Connie was very tough. But it's not always the tough questions that put people at ease so that they tell us, in their answers, who they are. I am very proud of the interview I did with Fidel Castro, but it wasn't the tough questions necessarily that got him to reveal himself the way he did.

"There are really two different types of interviews. Sometimes they are in conflict. We in television are very impressed if something we do on TV gets picked up in the press. So if you're interviewing someone in the news, do you ask questions that you think might be picked up and make headlines? Most often you do. If it's a personality interview — with Elizabeth Taylor, for instance — you are not looking for headlines but for her to reveal herself, to make the viewer know her better, to know who she is."

Barbara is speaking now with an easy warmth, if it's possible to be warm and moderately crisp at the same time. And I think it is. She has good humor, she is candid and she is honest and she is, seen plain, very likable. And she knows what interviews are all about. And she does a good newscast. And she knows how it is being in the eye of the hurricane of hoopla.

As everyone knows, in the spring of '77 she moved over from NBC to the coanchor berth with Harry Reasoner at ABC. For Barbara, the profound complexities of venturing over to ABC were comparable to getting on the air in the first place.

"This goes back to 1964," she said, "and there had been a big splash of publicity about Maureen O'Sullivan, who'd been hired by the 'Today Show.' It was a disaster. They had to pay her off. And then they began looking around for a replacement."

Al Morgan, who was then the "Today" producer, wanted Barbara Walters, a staff writer. He ran into tremendous opposition from the sales department.

"The people in sales said, 'Who is she? Who knows her? What can she do? She'll never sell.' So they gave me a straight 13-week contract at scale, the union minimum. I was on 'Today' for 10 years before I got any real attention. Dean Rusk made the difference. In those days, nobody thought a woman could even handle an important interview. But when I made my request, Dean Rusk said, 'Fine,' and that was a major breakthrough.

"And that," Barbara said, "was as recently as 1969. All of this happened very quickly."

It happened very quickly indeed: The ascent to celebrity, the big interviews, the furor over her million-dollar contract with ABC.

She turned reflective now. "Just a few years ago, before the big move, I was becoming an elder statesman at NBC. I won some awards — an Emmy for the first time. I thought I'd be on 'Today' until I was 65 and they'd retire me in my gray dress. Then it all happened and I wish it had been handled better."

There was, beyond dispute, a double standard put into motion. "At NBC, David Brinkley had been brought in to work with John Chancellor as a coanchor," Barbara said. "John Chancellor did not cheer because who wants a partner? But Harry Reasoner says a few things when I move over to be his coanchor and it's headlines.

"If I'd have stayed at NBC for the same money ABC offered, it wouldn't have been the same uproar. When Tom Brokaw came, even without doing the commercials as we had to do, he made more money on 'Today' than I ever made. Walter Cronkite makes more money than I do. Harry Reasoner makes exactly the same, dollar for dollar, and I do specials besides the news. But people say about me, 'How dare she?'

"A part of it was, of course, being the first woman to anchor a network newscast. There was always that feeling that network news is a man's domain, with that right kind of look and the pompous writing and the taking for granted that everyone knows what a 'petrodollar' is and what the 'GNP' is.

"I was on a panel with John Chancellor and Walter Cronkite and Bill Moyers and at one point in response to a question, I said, 'Look, bear in mind that we don't know everything. We're not demigods.' John Chancellor laughed and said, 'Speak for yourself, Barbara ...' "

The Reticent Mr. Cooper

Gary Cooper, who came out of Montana to epitomize the strong-silent cowboy on the screen, always had an affectionate interest in the old West. No one else would have been quite so appropriate a narrator for "The Real West," an NBC Project 20 special aired in spring, 1961.

However, the narrator's function is to talk and Mr. Cooper, as everyone knows, had a long established reputation for reticence.

In fact, when I saw Mr. Cooper, I informed him that I came armed with plenty of questions and that, if he had a hankerin', he could answer with a simple yes or not or even a nod and I would understand. He seemed amenable.

To begin with, I asked, is the real West portrayed accurately on television?

"The real West," declared Mr. Cooper, sitting tall on a couch in his Beverly Hills office and looking resplendent in a yellow shirt and a green-gray suit of continental cut. "You hardly ever see anything like the real West on TV. It's all who killed who and who has the fastest draw west of the Pecos. You look at some of these westerns and it's strictly 'Hamlet' at the Bar X corral.

"There's just a few basic western plots and they've been plagiarized from hell to breakfast. They've taken Al Capone stories from Chicago and transplanted them into westerns. But the public likes westerns whether they're good or bad, accurate or not, and that makes it even harder to do a good, accurate one.

"You take the people who went West. They were strong and gutty. Yet there's westerns where a whole yellow-livered town is scared stiff of one blinking gunslinger. In the real West a whole town could never have been swayed by one lawless punk."

Mr. Cooper paused to deposit a butterscotch Life Saver into his mouth and went on: "There's 'High Noon'. It opens with the marshal running out scared and the whole town turns yellow. Frankly, I had my doubts about that aspect even then. But dramatically it was awfully good. So . . ."

He shrugged, meaningfully. "Oh. I've done a little stretching of the facts myself," Mr. Cooper admitted, wryly. "I glorified Wild Bill Hickok — who was no saint in real life — in a picture that had him in love with Calamity Jane. Boy, what fiction! In real life, Calamity Jane was an ugly old bat who drank more'n the men.

"All the same, I've tried for accuracy where I could. Now you take these TV shows. 'Wagon Train' is quite good and so was the early 'Wyatt Earp' and I thought 'The Westerner' was very good.

"But what you see mostly in westerns is a little guy with four guns starting fights in the town saloon. And some fights! They land 15 or 20 haymakers on the jaw and when the brawl's over, nobody's winded and the hero's got one small grease mark on his pretty face.

"The real West," continued Mr. Cooper, "gave America what you could call our King Arthurian period. It followed the Civil War which threw a lot of young fellas off balance. If life bumped you a little, you could always go West.

"Remington did a fine painting of the cowboy and called him 'The Last Cavalier,' which he was. It didn't last long, though, the old West. They discovered gold and that started to change the West. Then, when the railroads made connection, in 1881, a fella said, sadly, 'The West isn't any more, boys.'

"People change too. You see it in their faces. I remember as a kid in Montana I'd see these oldtimers and they had faces with character. I'd see the Indians with their great, savage faces. It's all changed.

"I often think," Mr. Cooper said, "that mebbe I was born 50 years too late. I'd like to have seen the West before it got all trampled under, before the buffalo was slaughtered, when the West was all big sky and land without fences."

As Mr. Cooper rose long-legged from the couch, a smile formed on the familiar face of his that might well have belonged to a cowboy in the old, real West.

"You get enough there for a column, mebbe?" he asked.

"Yup," I said.

Mae West, A Lively Legend

"I was the first sex symbol," said Mae West, the words flowing lightly, insinuatingly out of the corner of her mouth. "And I was the first to use the word alone in a play I wrote called 'Sex.' Before that, it was a word in, y'know, medical books. Or people said, 'the fair sex.' The newspapers wouldn't even print the title in the ads. They said, 'See Mae West in that certain play.' But that was in another day, another time . . .''

Mae West. There she sits primly — well, almost primly — on a sofa in her luxurious sixth-floor apartment in Hollywood. The decor is all chastely white. On one wall hangs a nude portrait and on the white piano rests a nude statue — both are, of course, Miss West — and atop a record player is her "Way Out West" album wherein she sings, in her inimitable fashion, rock 'n' roll songs.

Mae West. Looking at you through very clear eyes with their glint of delicious candor — they are ageless eyes, very blue-green. She wears a floral dressing gown and her platinum curls topple over her shoulders.

"Here, feel the skin on my arm, feel the skin on my neck," she says. In both areas, the skin is soft and as taut as a banjo string. She looks pleased, this new darling of the college crowd, who flock to her old movies and send her presents, such as diamonds.

"Exercise, honey," she explains. "I'm always exercisin'. And I have my diet. One steak a week. One egg a day. Don't smoke, don't drink. Lots of salads with subtle dressin'. No white bread. No canned goods. It's all to keep my measurements and to keep me in my 20s." A throaty giggle. "I used to be 26. Now I'm 28."

Whatever her age, the indestructible Mae was full of fire and plans on this spring day in '67, and she talked about a TV special she had in mind whereupon I mentioned the censors, her old bugaboo.

"Censors?" Miss West smiled. "Are they still around?"

Maybe not in the movies, but in television they are.

"I never had trouble with the censors," Mae said. "They were my friends. They'd come with me to see scenes from my pictures and they'd laugh and scream and then they'd say, 'Oh, Mae, that's gotta go!' But I never did anything in bad taste. I'm a person of good taste. I'm regal and subtle. I never disrobed like some do today. It's my personality. It's not what I say, it's the way I say it."

The way she says it is soft, languid, purring — and wonderfully funny.

"The time on radio, when I played Eve and Don Ameche was Adam," she said, eyes wide in mock astonishment. "They approved the script but I must've put somethin' into the words when I said 'em. And I said to Charlie McCarthy, 'Come on up and I'll let you play in my wood pile.' What's so terrible about that? I'll say something innocent like 'Too much of a good thing is wonderful' and the censors squirm in their shoes."

She paused. "Grayson!" she called out. "Somethin' cool and refreshin'?" she suggested. Grayson, the butler, silently entered with servings of diet cola.

"They wanted me to do an advice to the lovelorn show," Miss West resumed. "It woulda been like educational TV. I'd answer questions that puzzle women, like how do you hold a man? I always say, 'In your arms, honey, in your arms.' I tell 'em the ground rules — 'Love thy neighbor but not thy neighbor's husband.' It's all psychological. But I turned it down. My audience doesn't want me at a desk, with only 50 per cent showin'. They want to see me movin' around."

Somehow the conversation drifted to "sex personalities," a descriptive phrase that struck her fancy.

"I consider Elvis Presley the No. 1 sex personality," Mae said. "Sinatra is a sex personality but only when he sings. Dean Martin is a sex personality and so is that big one from 'Cheyenne' — Clint Walker. But you don't have to be big — James Cagney was always a sex personality."

How about Johnny Carson? "Oh, he's cute and I'd mother him if I was the mother type," Miss West said. "But he's no sex personality. Now this little Sue Lyon in 'Lolita' looks like she has it. But you gotta have it without tryin' — like Bardot, but she goes in for nudity. Liz Taylor has a certain amount. But Garbo was in a class by herself. They all have their techniques and I have mine."

I had heard that of all the words bandied about Miss West (whose measurements were once listed as 42-26-38) preferred being described as "buxom."

"No, no," she drawled. "Not buxom. The word I like best for me is — voluptuous. People are surprised that I'm only 5 feet 4 'cause I look so big on the screen, with my hair piled up and the big hats. But mainly it's my carriage, how I walk. Always straight and tall. I never slump over."

Personality Parade

"Laughter is really love," said Gabe Kaplan, who stars in "Welcome Back, Kotter" and is one of the fastest rising comedians around. "An audience responds with laughter and applause and that's the way a comedian finds his acceptance. It's people saying in a very positive way that they like you.

"You can be well adjusted in other aspects of your life, but, if you're a comedian, you always have this strong desire for acceptance, for love from an audience. You face an audience and you are able to say things about yourself that you might not dare say to people as individuals. In some crazy way, an audience becomes one, they turn into a unit, and they're receptive.

"As a comedian," Gabe said, "I can share experiences with an audience. They don't have to answer me. I can tell them maybe about this girl who I asked how I could reach her and I think I'm doing terrific with her and, later, I call her and it turns out she's given me a wrong number.

"I talk about this to an audience. What am I talking about? My own insecurities, right? But when the audience gives me laughter and applause, what they're saying is, 'It's okay, Gabe. We understand.'

"With individuals, I tend to be shy. But I'm never shy in front of an audience. A lot of comedians are like that, basically shy people, introspective. But what we all have is a definite neurosis. It's not just that we want some laughter and applause. It's not just wanting. It's needing. We need it, like we need air to breathe. That's how much we need the love that we get from an audience that laughs and applauds."

Lou Rawls remembers how it was, on this special night in San Francisco, singing with Duke Ellington's powerhouse band going at full throttle behind him. "It was so mellow," Lou says. "It was like putting on a perfect fitting pair of shoes."

Lou remembers the Duke himself, that nonpareil of musicianship, with admiration and fondness. "The Duke," says Lou, with wonder in his voice, "was such a gentleman, so worldly and debonair, the master of the kindly gesture. I'm thinking of something that happened at intermission during the gig while we were sitting around rapping, the Duke wearing his fine silk robe and sitting majestically on the couch.

"Now some guy comes into Duke's dressing room, an old acquaintance that Duke hadn't seen for 25 years. The Duke gives him a big handshake and, right off, he remembered everything about him from way back, and the guy is beaming that the Duke hasn't forgotten him. He has his wife with him and he introduces her to the Duke. The Duke smiles in that gracious way of his — don't you know? — and he says, 'How do you do?' And she just sort of grunts.

"Well, her jaw is tight," Lou goes on, "and the Duke realizes that the man and his wife had obviously had some kind of flap and things weren't cool. The Duke is a very perceptive cat. He's still smiling and he says to her, 'My dear, may I show you something beautiful in the mirror?'

"And then he takes this little hand-mirror and he puts it up to her face. And she looks at herself in the mirror and a big, big smile crosses her face and I swear she looks like melted butter."

"Life is a parade," Erma Bombeck said, "and I'm standing behind Bill Russell! I'm the kind of woman who always has to stuff toilet paper into her shoes. What I am is the original loser. A woman said to me the other day, 'Erma, you're not fat any more but you keep writing as though you were.'

"And she was right. So I've lost 20 pounds — I did it the easy way, by starving — but I still feel fat and dumpy and slovenly inside. It's the feeling inside that matters. It's all those feelings of frustration that build and pop out, and that's where so much of humor comes from. But I'm still an incurable optimist. My husband calls me 'Peter Pan in a Pantygirdle.' "

It is typical, vintage Bombeck, tapping a rich vein of self-deprecation, alive with bright picture images, and deliciously funny — and her expression, as she shares the familiar from a comedic tilt, is attuned exactly to the words she utters.

In this coupling of funny words and funny demeanor, Erma Bombeck is a lineal descendant of Robert Benchley, a wry and self-effacing humorist of the '30s and '40s who once entered somebody's home after walking through a rainstorm and cried: "Let's get out of these wet clothes and into a dry martini!" It is appropriate that this similarity of the two writer-performers should exist because Erma says that Robert Benchley was her alltime favorite.

"I remember when I was a kid in high school, back in Dayton," Erma says. "I'd read Benchley and laugh and laugh. I used to read H. Allen Smith and Max Shulman and James Thurber and Corey Ford, but I'd always return to Benchley. His humor was always so gentle."

Now her favorite is another cherubic funnyman, Art Buchwald. "I did a review of Art's new book," she said, gleefully, "and my lead went: 'Art Buchwald has often been compared to Pope and Swift — and you know how funny Pope Paul and Tom Swift were.' I finished with: 'I loved the book — I don't care what anyone says.' Actually, I did love the book and I think Art Buchwald is a genius."

Erma Bombeck belongs in the same company.

☆　☆　☆

Once, as Ray Bradbury remembers with vast pleasure, he was struck with the notion of working with Walt Disney on an animation film project. He approached Disney with his proposal. But Disney shook his head. "You're a genius and I'm a genius," said Disney to Bradbury, "and that's why it would never work. We'd end up tearing each other apart."

Thus was mayhem avoided but also, to our loss, a uniting of creative energies by two of the most imaginative and prolific innovators of our time. Bradbury is a wizard at his craft, the master of fantasy fiction, the author of close to 400 short stories, novels, poems, plays and essays, and a man, further, who is exuberantly aware of his own considerable worth.

"I knew exactly what Walt Disney was telling me," Bradbury said, his eyes alight behind his horn-rim spectacles.

"Walt was undoubtedly right. The sight of egos in conflict is never a pretty one to contemplate. The ego is essential. You need the ego to do your work — and to survive, to continually believe that you're immortal."

Hans Conried, who has a richly theatrical manner, was in a reflective mood as he dwelled ruefully on the injustices that time, the cruelest of casting directors, can inflict on one who treads the boards. "How sad," said Mr. Conried, the tones pure Smithfield, as ripe as pears in autumn. "How very sad to be a boulevardier in an age that lacks a boulevard."

How sad, indeed. "Ah, but it is a blessing," Mr. Conried went on, "to be born in a time when one can be useful. Put your mind on the plight of, say, a George C. Scott if he were to have emerged as an actor in another time, when drawing room farce was all the vogue. 'You an actor, sir?' he would have been told. 'Go, sir, and do your proper work on the drayman's wagon!'

"As for me," he continued, "it is small matter what role I play. I haven't changed my performance since I was a lad of 18, tall for my age, when I would go on stage and convince an audience that I was older. Since I undoubtedly did convince them, I must have been a better actor then.

"It is nice to report that I have been working steadily at my wandering gypsy's trade for 42 years. This is rather satisfying to an old trouper, never to have set foot in an unemployment line and to have a home, my retreat from all the slings and arrows, that is all paid for."

He sighed. "As an old radio actor," he said, mournfully, "I feel at one with the maker of buggy whips."

At once he brightened. "Ah, radio," he cried. "The theater of the mind, where the rubies were always flawless and as big as the mind would will them. Once — this goes back some years now — I was trying to explain the greatness of oldtime radio drama, its glories and its grandeur, to my daughter, who was 8 at the time.

"She said, 'Radio? Oh, I know daddy, you mean the thing in the car.' I promptly sent her to her room!"

Singing Is Her Security

Dinah Shore! A flash-flood of warm memories — the old Sunday night variety show and the hostess wafting a big smack of a goodnight kiss to the cameras, the soft, southern voice melting out "Skylark" and "Blues in the Night," those swinging duets with Ella Fitzgerald, the pinpoint perfectionism that blended into the all-American girl exuberance. If she were a man, you thought once, her picture would be on a box of Wheaties.

For seven years, Dinah had put her considerable talents to hosting her own daytime talk show and she had come to town in October of 1977 to tape segments at such places in San Diego as the Zoo and Wild Animal Park and Sea World, where she was now, taking her ease in an air-conditioned trailer dressing room.

She wore white denim slacks and a knitted white sweater and she looked like several million dollars, before taxes. She uses almost no makeup, even while facing the cameras in the harsh light of the Southern California sun.

We were talking about the television talk show, that peculiar beast of show business, and her own approach to its demands.

"You can't pretend to be something you're not," Dinah was saying, the voice still retaining vestigial pinfeathers of her native Tennessee. "You can't pretend to listen. You can't pretend to feel. Maybe you can do these things, but you can't get away with it for long.

"You can't ever doze off mentally. You have to keep your guests on the show comfortable. But you can't be too cautious and yet you can't be offensive. You can't intrude but you can't be a sponge and never exude anything in return. You can't be nebulous. You've got to be a giver and a taker, a little bit of both. And the guests — and the audience — have got to trust you."

It was suggested to Dinah that singers dominate the ranks of the talk-show hosts that endure. Besides Dinah, the successful people in that line of work include Merv Griffin and Mike Douglas, both of whom often lift their voices in song, and Johnny Carson, who is a comedian.

Success is its own mystery and a pleasant voice — all singers have pleasant speaking voices — would seem to be an incontestable asset to a talk-show host. Beyond that, however, the theory evaporates.

"If it were based on a great voice," Dinah said, "then the greatest of all talk-show hosts would be Beverly Sills or Robert Merrill. I was lucky that I became one of those singers who talk. I think of Tony Bennett and Peggy Lee, both great singers but not so great at talking to an audience."

Dinah paused. "I still find myself dropping an occasional 'er' or 'uh,' a fumfer while I gather my thoughts. But I know I can sing. Singing is my security, my anchor, my blue blanket. I still think of myself as a singer who asks questions."

The cameras were in position now, outside, and Dinah, having changed into some terrific outfit, was about to return to work. "What you need in this business isn't talent but stamina," Dinah said with that warming smile. "Health and vitality are two of the most attractive qualities we can offer. You can't simulate it. Either you are healthy and vital or you aren't. I can't let myself get even three pounds over-weight — well, make that five."

Dinah said: "I know I've been kidded about my rosy optimism. But I have a philosophy that each of us has something to offer that no-body else has. I have never really envied anyone, ever.

"Oh, momentarily, I might envy a girl who's prettier or younger — but the envious people of the world are always looking over their shoulder. They never give the most of what they have to give. They never really taste much of life."

The Sweet Smell of Success

Bemusedly, with a bow toward the grinning gods of adversity, Merv Griffin was saying that he found himself, in the first years of his ca-reer, merrily buffeted by every sudden sea-change of popular tastes. But he plodded onward, undismayed, with the airy confidence of the passenger who assumed that the Titanic was merely stopping for ice.

"I got into radio just when television was coming in and radio was going out," Merv said. "I was hired to sing with a dance band just when people stopped dancing. I made a record and it went out in the same shipment with a record by another new singer. His name was Elvis Presley. The name of his record was 'Hound Dog.'

"I got into the movies and in my first picture I costarred with Kath-ryn Grayson. Just as the movie was released, the studio announced something called Cinemascope with the great big screen. Our little movie looked like a postage stamp.

"I went into television game shows," Merv went on, with mock solemnity, "just when the game show scandals broke and everybody was going to jail. I became Jack Paar's substitute host but when he quit, Johnny Carson got his job.

"And yet I made it. How I made it, I don't know. The first night I substituted for Jack Paar, I did a monologue and walked off the stage and I was about to keep going out the door. The producer stopped me. 'Merv,' he yelled, 'you can't leave. We've got 80 more minutes to fill.' And I said 'But I bombed out there. I can't do it.' He pushed me back onstage and I've been there, facing those cameras, ever since."

Today, Mervyn Edward Griffin roosts among the aristocracy of the talk show hosts, his syndicated entry an unqualified success, a model for the tyros to follow. Dr. Martin Grotjahn, an elder statesman among psychiatrists, issued the ultimate compliment to Griffin's skills.

To his fellow analysts, Dr. Grotjahn advised: "If you want to learn the best technique of psychiatric interviews watch Merv Griffin."

Now in April, 1976, after playing a match at the La Costa pro-celebrity tennis tournament, Merv sipped his Tab and munched cashew nuts and talked about the problems in his line of work.

"The big problem for any performer is fear," Griffin said. "Fear takes odd forms on TV — the nervous tick, the throbbing neck, the quivering lip. The fear can be — frightening."

"Have you known fear?" I asked Merv.

He nodded. "But not lately. Most of the time fear is a case of not being prepared. I go in totally prepared and so I'm just not intimidated by anything. Even Bob Hope, who intimidates all the other hosts, doesn't intimidate me.

"The show may look simple but many hours go into the preparation. I remember Jack Paar saying to me, 'Pal, always be prepared. Make it look like adlibbing but know what you're doing every minute.'

"I owe everything to Jack Paar," Merv said. "One day, I was doing my game show — this is years ago — and Paar accidentally wandered into the studio. He was stunned. I talked with him as though it were all planned. Later, he asked around, 'Who's that kid? He's funny.' That's how I became his substitute."

As a rule, Griffin steers his first guest to stage-center and they talk casually. It is, he notes, a carefully plotted maneuver.

"Once," said Merv, "Dustin Hoffman said to me after a show, 'That's it. Now I get it. The only problem is fear of an audience. So you bring 'em down to the audience immediately.' Exactly. I keep the guest there, close to the audience, until he's conquered fear. Some nights, I've had to hold on to a guest, literally, until I see his fear is gone. Then we sit down and go on with the interview."

The television talk show is a strange hybrid of show business, Merv contends, an uncharted form that has become, in a curious way, an extension of himself. "Basically, I'm shy," Merv says, "but what I do is, I put up a good front. I'm happier on the show than I am off. Off camera, people say to me, 'You're so easy to meet.' What they don't know is, I'm uncomfortable with groups until I get on-camera and then I'm relaxed.

"In fact, that's my whole interviewing technique — I'm so relaxed myself and I try to make my guests so totally relaxed they'll reveal more than they ever thought they would. I sit close and look them right in the eye and they start blurting things out.

"As an interviewer, I'm a performer," Merv says, "but, strictly speaking, I don't 'perform.' That's why people never say, 'Merv wasn't funny tonight.' More likely, they'd say, 'Merv's guests weren't so good.' I get credit for the good shows and I don't get blamed for the bombs."

A Trust Symbol Named Carson

"Johnny Carson," wrote Tom Shales, the Washington columnist, "is just thin enough, just funny enough and just vaguely defined enough to have become one of the most enduring and broadly popular figures in the history of television. He is the Walter Cronkite of comedy, a trust symbol."

The Walter Cronkite of comedy? Not a bad phrase, for in the best sense of that comparison, Johnny Carson has achieved a stature of dependability and of durability; he has an identity and a style and a distinctive pace and he has earned his niche in our late-night viewing.

"We're called a talk show but to me a real talk show is Bill Buckley discussing the big issues," Carson reflected. "We've done the Margaret Mead interviews and I'll do interviews with Carl Sagan, the astronomer. But we keep things in balance. I think it would be easy to do a straight talk show. Just say to a guest, 'Now tell me, what do you think of busing or recidivism in crime or the death penalty?' But that's not what I want. I'm a comedian. I'm not there to lead everybody out of Armageddon. I go for laughs.

"It used to bother me when people said we weren't 'serious' enough. Basically we've got an entertainment show with the accent on comedy. Why do I always have to defend myself? Ed Sullivan didn't have to defend his show.

"There's a myth that there are so many exciting people just waiting to go on TV as a guest," Carson said. "Well, where are they? I'd be delighted to get them. Try to make a list of great conversationalists, stimulating and witty people, and it has to be a very short list.

"Actors, especially, find it just a little bit uncomfortable being on this type of show. I've had actors on the show, monumental stars, and they'd turn to me during the commercials and their eyes are blank — they're lost because they aren't playing a role and they can't handle it."

In common with other performers going back to the ancient Greeks, Carson finds audiences a mystery. "I don't think there's ever been an entertainer who's ever understood an audience. We see 500 people in our studio audience and we do a show that gets a great reaction. If we could do the exact same show for another 500 people, we might get a different reaction.

"There's no pattern to audiences. Some audiences are wild and the atmosphere gets wild and things pop out. Sometimes I'll do a joke that's too easy and maybe the taste's not too good. But you react automatically to a situation. One time I said that Mike Douglas was as indigenous to Philadelphia as cream cheese — and just as funny. Mike hasn't spoken to me since."

Sinatra: A Way of Singing

If Henry Fonda's acting could be transformed into singing, it would come out, I suspect, sounding like Sinatra. Both share singular artistic nuances — the lean, spare, graceful economy of expression with no wasted motion, verbal or physical. It is performance cut to the bone, with an arrestingly individual sound and distinctive — and matchless! — phrasing and, above all, an inner fire.

The foregoing theory, when I mentioned it to Sinatra himself, is one that he found entirely acceptable. Sinatra was taking his ease now in his dressing room suite at Caesars Palace in Las Vegas, where he would assume stage-center in the evening's first performance. Only then would he wear the saloon singer's uniform, the tuxedo, saloon singer being his own description of his line of work.

Now he was dressed casually in sports shirt and slacks and he puffed on his pipe and, for the moment, the subject was Fonda, and Sinatra, in buoyant good spirits, observed: "Henry has a way of inserting his pauses and taking a breath so that his sentences flow longer than an audience expects. He breathes well."

Breathing well is of the essence to a singer. It is the heart of Sinatra's phrasing, the floating, easy vocal line he achieves. Even before he joined the Tommy Dorsey band, Sinatra was saying, he was aware of Dorsey's long, mellifluous melodic lines on the trombone.

"I listened to Tommy," Sinatra said, "and I said to myself, 'That's as close to the vocal range as an instrument can get.' But how did he breathe and sustain the notes? His trick was never to let the public know he'd taken a breath. I'd sit there on the bandstand, leaning way over staring at Dorsey as he played the trombone for 10, 15 bars and seemingly without breathing. And Jo Stafford sitting with me the way the girl singer always did, would say, 'What are you doing, Frank?'

"I told her I was trying to figure out how the hell Tommy breathed. Where did he get the air to play his instrument? I couldn't spot any breathing movement in the back of his jacket. It was a mystery.

"Finally, one night, Dorsey takes me aside. A great bandleader, by the way, a strict disciplinarian. 'Haven't you seen it yet?' he says. 'It's in the corner of my mouth.' Then he explained how he'd keep his mouth open ever so slightly in the corner and then let the air pop in, like a pinhole, and you couldn't see it because his mouthpiece was there. 'Now,' Tommy said to me, 'you have to find a way of doing that when you sing.' "

Sinatra smiled in recollection of the moment. "That's what I worked to do, and I worked hard. And I'd swim and run laps around the track to expand my lungs to be able to take in as much air as possible — and sing longer and longer musical phrases."

I asked Sinatra: "What if you had joined Glenn Miller's band instead of Tommy Dorsey's?"

"Then," Sinatra said, "I might never have learned the finer points of breathing and singing."

After learning breath control from Tommy Dorsey, Sinatra acquired an unexpected lesson. "One day, by accident, I was listening to Jascha Heifetz on the radio. It dazzled me, the way his constant bowing carried the musical line straight on through without a break. I bought every Heifetz record I could, and so from a violin virtuoso I learned more about singing."

I asked Sinatra how he acquired his clarity of enunciation with a lyric, how he softens the hard consonant sounds. "Rudy Vallee," he said. "I'd listen to Vallee's crisp, precise enunciation, the way he said his D's and T's. He overdid it. But he made me conscious of clarity and this wasn't easy for me because you've got to remember I was a dese-dem-and-dose guy from Jersey.

"In my old neighborhood in Hoboken," Frank Sinatra said, "all of us would-be singers were Crosby-stricken. We loved Bing. I had Bing's picture hung in my room. But I was influenced as much by Billie Holiday and Louis Armstrong and Mabel Mercer, a very liquid singer.

"Even as a kid," Sinatra said, thoughtfully drawing on his pipe, "I knew that singing was acting. The ballads were a story with a musical backdrop. The orchestra was like a curtain on a stage. The lyrics were like dialogue. But there are things I do as a singer I can't explain. It was always a part of me, a certain way of singing."

Once, in the long ago, Sinatra conducted a full-size orchestra on a Columbia recording of Alec Wilder's compositions. It is a collector's item now, this record with Sinatra and the orchestra (with symphony musicians here and there) and the wonderfully lyrical music of Alec Wilder, and a treasure to possess.

Who is Alec Wilder, you ask? He's a composer and a songwriter and, as they say about him, a musician's musician. His book, an authoritative tome called "The American Popular Song," served as the wellspring for a PBS radio series that won him a Peabody Award in 1977. His musical works are strikingly individual, with a whimsical charm, and they are a delight to the musical cognoscenti.

"It's 10 o'clock in the morning," said Sinatra, still casually puffing on his pipe, "and I walk into the studio and the musicians look up and they're wondering what the hell the skinny singer is doing here? I told them: 'I'm going to conduct the Wilder.' A lot of funny glances. Him conduct? Him who can't even read music?

"Then I said: 'Look, I've never done this before, I need some help. Wherever you can help me with this, I'll appreciate.' And then, a minute or two later, I give the downbeat. I can't read music, the way a player does, but as a singer I know solfeggio — what do, re, mi would be on the scale. And I know something about what a tempo is. And we're dealing here with marvelous music, Wilder's music, and we have some of the top musicians to play it."

Sinatra conducted one side of the record — on the other an octet played Wilder pieces — and the session went on for hours. "The guys helped me," Sinatra said, "and we cut a record."

Sinatra the conductor, an interesting concept. Although Frank Sinatra is undoubtedly one of the most musicianlike of our singers, it is still an unexpected role for him, standing in front of an orchestra, his voice not raised in song.

"After doing the Wilder album, I conducted on a few more," Sinatra was saying. "I did one with Peggy Lee and Dean Martin and the remarkable thing about it was, I made them sing. I love her, Peggy, but she has a tendency to try to sing without opening her mouth and you just can't do that. 'No, no,' I said to Peggy, 'let those notes come out.'

"And Dean was clowning around. I said, 'Listen, Dino, this is serious. I want you to sing.' And he sang and Peggy sang, and I conducted the orchestra, and we cut a record."

Sinatra remembered another occasion wherein he conducted an orchestra of topflight studio musicians. The music was based on interpretations of various colors, a novel idea.

"What color did you choose?" I asked.

"None," Sinatra said. "I was strictly the conductor."

"But what color would you have chosen?"

"Orange," Sinatra said, without hesitation. "A lovely color, the happiest color, a nice musical color."

If the notion of Frank Sinatra as a conductor seems unusual, there is yet another unexpected offshoot of the man's self-expression along artistic lines — photography. A few months earlier in New York, I had dropped into Jimmy Weston's restaurant, which is a place where sportswriters and other low types congregate.

Along one wall at Weston's, as you enter, are huge blown-up photographs from the first Ali-Frazier fight. The photographer: Frank Sinatra. And they are damned good pictures.

"They used seven of my pictures in Life Magazine," Sinatra said, proudly. "They told me beforehand, 'Having been an amateur boxer, you'll be able to anticipate what can happen in the ring,' which fascinated me. That's how it turned out. By remembering how it was, I could anticipate. I could see their moves when Ali or Frazier were about to throw a left hook, for instance.

"I had three cameras, Nikons, and I had three loaders working, and I got some marvelous pictures of the fight. But I got pictures of a more human nature that they didn't use."

We talked about the Sinatra voice, a sterling instrument that Sinatra likens to the reed of an alto sax. "I still vocalize to keep the reed in shape," Sinatra said, "and every so often, I get together with Robert Merrill — we're both baritones, you know — and we have a clinic on breathing and singing. Good for the reed."

This is an era when so many of the singers write their own songs but Sinatra demurs. He did write the music for one of his songs — "This Love of Mine," and that goes back to 1941. "If I started writing songs, it'd look like I was getting into their act," Sinatra said. "I'll just sing. It's what I know. Singing is what I know."

A Writer and His 'Roots'

One year later, in January, 1978, a tumultuous year after the explosive success of his "Roots," first as a novel and then as an epic television venture, Alex Haley wondered if he will ever truly get back to where his writer's heart remains — back to the typewriter.

"I haven't been able to write a coherent paragraph," Alex Haley said. Then he added, firmly, on a note of resolve: "I've got to write again."

Haley, a successful man in whom serenity clearly resides, was relaxing over coffee and a fellow asked him, as one asks those in the profession, how the writing was going.

It was not going well. It was not, in fact, going at all and Alex Haley is saying that he must get back to the typewriter to write a work which he proposes to call "Search," a chronicle of the 12-year inquiry that preceded the authorship of "Roots." Haley put in 20 years with the Coast Guard and it is at sea that he learned to write and it is where he prefers to write still, on board a ship.

There is a pleasant legend that Haley, as a Coast Guardsman skilled with the pen, wrote love letters for his less-verbal shipmates, a seagoing John Alden. Haley, with a grin, confirms the legend as fact.

"Over the years, I had a couple hundred shipmates," he says, "and about 50 of them would ask me to write their love letters home to their girlfriends. In 20 years, I must have written a thousand love letters. With that kind of practice, I must say I got fairly good at this rather specialized art form."

Later, he would write about half of "Roots" aboard ship, usually on a freighter as a passenger. The rhythm of the sea bestirs the creative juices and the isolation helps.

"The thing is, I'm a sailor," Alex Haley says. "I can write on dry land but I think I write better at sea. I like writing at sea."

Nearly 20 years have passed since he left the Coast Guard with its security for the precarious gamble that is free-lance writing. He tasted a moderate success from the outset, selling to Harper's, the

Atlantic Monthly and the New York Times Magazine. Then he originated the journalistic form of the intensive interview for Playboy. After his interview with Malcolm X, he devoted two years to writing "The Autobiography of Malcolm X."

"I am now really, legitimately, a millionaire," Alex Haley said, "but it means not a damn to me. Since "Roots," I haven't spent more than $10,000 on myself. No new fancy cars, no new homes. I'm driving the same car I had back in 1970. I can now afford to give financial help to the widow and family of Malcolm X. Before 'Roots' I had one corduroy jacket. Now I have six suits. I don't live all that differently than I did before."

It pleases Alex Haley that "Roots" has assumed an enduring niche in our culture. "All of this happened, I think, because 'Roots' touched something universal. The show has been seen in 33 countries, dubbed into 14 languages. The book has been published in 28 languages. It is astonishing — it is so rewarding — to be in Norway, say, and you hear people talking in a language foreign to you and suddenly, in the middle of a sentence, you hear someone say 'Chicken George.' "

An Irish Tenor Named Mike

Mike Douglas can remember, as a kid of 8 or 9, when he'd wander into the Irish bars in his old neighborhood in Chicago, toss back his head and, in a voice as sweet and pure as the morning bells, sing "The Rose of Tralee."

"Another kid was my shill," Mike was saying. "When I hit that high note at the end, he'd toss a quarter at my feet and the men at the bar would dab at their eyes and toss coins. 'What's your name, lad?' some guy at the bar would say. I'd say: 'I'm Michael Delaney Dowd, sir.' And the guy'd nod and smile and say: 'Sure, and 'tis a foine lad from the Ould Sod you must be.' And I'd sing 'Did Your Mother Come From Ireland?' and the tears would flow and the coins would fly. It was grand."

And Mike can remember the moment when he was first beckoned by the siren song of show business. It happened at the Chicago Theater in his hometown and a fellow named Bob Eberly, deep-voiced and slick-haired, was singing with Jimmy Dorsey's orchestra. Mike sat in the audience, his eyes twin beacons of awe.

"Bob Eberly," Mike said. "He was up there on the stage in his cream-colored jacket and the lemon slacks and the brown and white shoes. The girls in the audience were all screaming with excitement. He looked so — so regal, on top of the world. I saw him up there singing and I said to myself, 'Boy, that's it! That's what I want to be, just like Bob Eberly!' "

Some years later, Michael Delaney Dowd would become Mike Douglas, singer, TV host and proprietor of his hugely successful daytime show. Mike still has the same easy-going charm and the same way with a song — he still goes for the high notes — that go back to those Irish bars in Chicago when the walls rang with the sound, clear as crystal, of young Mike Dowd singing "Galway Bay." And tears filled every eye.

The Delicate Art of Comedy

Jackie Gleason, that most exuberant and gifted of players, was once summed up in a twinkling of sentences, as follows: "A comedian who works solely to support a stomach that seems to exist independently of the body in which it is housed, or insulated. Do not see Gleason when he really is eating. So much food is consumed, the ordinary human can be put off his own feed for a week."

These words were set down by the late Richard Gehman in his book of recipes called "The Haphazard Gourmet" (the funniest volume on comestibles I know of) and his assessment of Herbert John Gleason remains basically accurate. Already assured of a niche in the eater's hall of fame, Jackie may have tapered off some but with a knife and fork in his hands, he is still awesome.

On this night in March, 1978, at George Pernicano's Casa di Baffi, in San Diego, Jackie first cleared his palate with a Scotch and water — one or three or five, but who was counting? — and then laid waste to six huge Icelandic lobster tails Italian style, some Italian greens, a sampling of someone else's pork chops, and a bulging plateful of linguini with red clam sauce, topped off with a dessert of creamy cannoli.

Wherever Jackie Gleason sits is the head of the table. The table also was occupied by, among others, director Arthur Penn and playwright Larry Gelbart, whose Broadway hit comedy, "Sly Fox," was about to begin a national tour on a San Diego theater stage with Gleason in the title role.

The talk now was of show business and acting and the delicate art of comedy, and Jackie was saying: "Laughter is the only emotion that can't be faked. You can look sad, amazed, querulous and fake it. But honest laughter demands a set of muscles you have no conscious control over. The good comedians can make an audience cry. And except for Groucho, who was special, the real great ones can make an audience cry when they are doing something funny."

Someone at the table mentioned Chaplin and Gleason nodded. "One of the greatest, Chaplin," Jackie said. "One time, I'm workin' at Slapsie Maxie's in Hollywood and this goes back a few years, I'm outside taking a smoke. Chaplin had just seen my act. He comes up to me and says, 'You're funny.' Then he walked away in that odd way he had. It was like giving me a check for $20,000!"

Jackie puffed on a Carleton and arched an eyebrow. "But could Chaplin have done a new television show once a week, every week?"

Jackie Gleason did just that, with a considerable boost from Art Carney, and the Gleason shows are now rated as classic television. There is a school of thought (including me) which says that Gleason, in his Poor Soul characterization and in his brilliant movie "Gigot," even surpassed Chaplin.

One of the great raconteurs of our time, Gleason was talking now about Jack Oakie, whose passing left a large void in the ranks of the funnymen.

"He was beautiful, that Oakie," Gleason said, warmly. "In some old movie when he's found out that Alice Faye loved John Payne instead of him, he'd do maybe nine fast, funny takes."

And here he demonstrated and, doing Oakie he was wondrously funny, and you knew at once that Jack Oakie was one of the influences that shaped Jackie Gleason.

"Jack Oakie," he went on, "was not only a great funnyman, he could do a soft roll into drama. And the way he did it" — and here he demonstrated again — "you'd never see the seams.

"This is the difference between a dramatic actor and a comedian," Jackie Gleason said. "An actor can take two hours to claim an audience, but a comedian has to do it right now. Being a comedian is a struggle for affection — people won't laugh at you unless they like you. Some comics tell a lotta jokes and afterward people may remember some of the jokes but nothin' about the guy who told 'em.

"It's a tough business, being funny. There's never been one great dramatic actor who became a comedian, but comedians have become dramatic actors, which says something."

"When are you going to play Hamlet, Jack?" someone asked.

"I did it once," Jackie said. "I did the Hamlet Soliloquy as Reggie Van Gleason III and afterward I got a wire from Richard Burton. It said: 'Dear Jackie, that's the first time I ever understood it!'"

Here Gleason released a great guffaw. When Jackie started out, a kid getting laughs around the candy store on Chauncey Street, in Brooklyn, his idol was not a comic but the prince of Hamlets, John Barrymore.

Jackie cherishes the praise from Richard Burton almost as much as the warming words that would come from Oliver Hardy. "They used to watch our old show, Babe Hardy and Stan Laurel. One time, Carney and I actually did a Laurel and Hardy bit and Babe Hardy was on the phone and he said, 'Jack, you did us beautifully.' A lovely man."

Jackie figures that over the years he has lost about 44,000 pounds in dieting and he was saying that he once had a terrific idea to get into shape. He went up to Brockton, Mass., to work out with Rocky Marciano. "We put on the gloves in Rocky's backyard," Jackie remembers, "and there's a bunch of neighborhood kids there hollerin' away: 'Kill him, Rocky!' Finally, I said, 'Rock, pal, this isn't for me.' There are other ways to lose weight."

One of them, Jackie concedes, is spurning a friendly glass, which he rarely does. "I've said it before, I'll say it again," Jackie thunders. "I never take a booze to stimulate my appetite. Or to quiet my nerves. Or to get to sleep. I take a booze only for the ancient and honorable purpose of getting bagged!"

Portrait of a Genius

Once, when my son Tom was about 9 or 10, I asked him if he would like to meet Dr. Seuss. The boy's response was by turns puzzled and gleeful. "You mean, really see Dr. Seuss?" he said. "You mean, the real Dr. Seuss?" I assured him that I had no intention of passing off an imposter. "Let's go!" he cried and so we drove to La Jolla, which is really a northernmost neighborhood of San Diego that cherishes its own post office and posh identity.

Dr. Seuss is, in reality, a writer-artist named Ted Geisel and, with his wife, he occupies a beautifully spacious home atop one of the hills of La Jolla. He met us at the door, a tall and gangling man with a shock of stubborn, free-form hair and a warmly benign expression. There is this fact to remember about Dr. Seuss — he has never fathered any children of his own and he is wary of them encountered in the flesh.

I said, "Hi, Ted. This is my son, Tom. Tommy, this is Dr. Seuss."

Seuss was obviously surprised to see the kid, and the kid was stunned to see Dr. Seuss. They shook hands. We entered the house. "Uh, Tommy, would you like some milk and, uh, cookies?" Ted said. Tom nodded and was escorted to the kitchen where he remained throughout the interview. It was easier for Dr. Seuss, the world's foremost writer of stories for children, to talk with the kid out of the way.

With his crinkly-soft eyes, his grandly equine nose and the loping mooselike walk, he looks for all the world as though he had sprung full-blown from his own drawing board. When you see Theodor S. Geisel plain, all that seems to be missing is his signature below, two words warmly familiar to millions of children the world over and their grateful parents. The two words are — Dr. Seuss.

They are, of course, one and the same — Ted Geisel of La Jolla, Calif., and Dr. Seuss, the pseudonym he has employed for over 40 years while writing and illustrating, very slowly and with the deepest pains of creation, his 40-odd children's books that have sold over 70 million copies. A number of the Seuss stories have been adapted by Geisel himself into animated television musicals, one having brought him the prestigious Peabody Award.

"Counting Lewis Carroll and allowing for A. A. Milne," an observer once noted, "Dr. Seuss has become the most important name ever pressed on a children's book jacket." The late Bennett Cerf, Seuss's publisher at Random House, once declared: "I've published any number of great writers, from William Faulkner to John O'Hara, but there's only one genius on my authors' list. His name is Ted Geisel."

Geisel shrugs off the compliment, whipping a hand through his unkempt silver-gray hair. "If I were a genius," he demands, logically, "why do I have to sweat so hard at my work? I know my stuff all looks like it was rattled off in twenty-three seconds but every word is a struggle and every sentence is like the pangs of birth." Geisel, in the jargon of the writers' trade, is a bleeder. Each of his illustrated books, none over 50 pages, requires a year or more of intense Seussian gestation.

Unconcerned about his genius standing, Dr. Seuss's juvenile readers have responded through the years with their own brightly turned words of praise. "Dr. Seuss," wrote one admiring child, "you have an imagination with a long tail!" ("Now there," says Geisel, "is a kid who's going places!") "This is the funniest book I ever read in nine years," a nine-year-old wrote to Seuss. Another wrote about a Seuss book: "All would like it from age six to forty-four — that's how old my mother is."

An eight-year-old wrote the letter that Geisel finds most perplexing: "Dear Dr. Seuss, you sure thunk up a lot of funny books. You sure thunk up a million funny animals ... Who thunk you up, Dr. Seuss?"

Geisel admits that he thunk up Dr. Seuss with relative ease — Seuss is both his mother's maiden name and his own middle name. The "Dr." he lightly assumed in view of his postgraduate pursuit of a doctorate in literature, which he never obtained. The "Dr." preceding Seuss still bestirs some confusion among those who are uncertain of his profession. Invited to a state dinner at the White House in 1970, Geisel was nonplussed to see himself on the guest list as Dr. Theodor Seuss Geisel.

The world of Seussiana, however, he thunk up only by that inexplicably mysterious process from which, over four decades, have flowed such classics as *And To Think I Saw It on Mulberry Street* and *How the Grinch Stole Christmas* and *The Cat in the Hat* and *Horton Hears a Who* and *I Had Trouble in Getting to Solla Sollew* and on and on and on to his latest, and one of his funniest, *There's a Wocket in My Pocket.*

The years have also brought from Seuss such wildly fanciful creatures as the Drum-Tummied Snumm who can "drum any tune you care to hum" and Yertle the Turtle and Thidwick the Big-Hearted Moose and the sneetches and nerkles and nutches "who live in small caves; known as nitches for hutches," and the Hippo-no-Bungus from Hippo-no-Hungus, not to mention Mrs. McCave and her 23 sons named Dave and the Tufted Mazurka from the Isle of Yerka and the Scrooge of a beast known as Grinch who very nearly stole Christmas. And, with the Seussian juices turned to fierce invective, in his musical version of *The Cat in the Hat,* on TV, a goldfish named Karlos K. Krinklebein sings out with soaring, yeasty chunks of language: "I'm a groffulous, griffulous groo. I'm a schoosler! A schminkler! And a poop-poodler, too! I'm a horrendous hobject which nobody loves ... I'm untouchable unless you wear antiseptic gloves ... I'm a punk! A kartungulous schnunck. Nobody loves me — not one tiny hunk!"

For another slice of Seuss invective, in the award-winning TV production of his *How the Grinch Stole Christmas,* he has a chorus lash out with: "You're a bad banana with a greasy black peel. Your brain is full of spiders; you've got garlic in your soul. Your heart is full of unwashed socks; your soul is full of gunk." And then the gleefully malevolent topper: "You're a three-decker sauerkraut and toadstool sandwich with arsenic sauce!"

The style of his words, as with most writers, reflects the man himself, for inside Ted Geisel there resides a full complement of wry, restlessly impish demons that help him view the world from a special, charmingly eccentric tilt.

With his wife, Audrey, who has a smile that would surely bedazzle a snerkle or a grinch, Geisel lives and works in a pink stucco showplace of a home, once a World War II watchtower atop the highest hill in La Jolla, overlooking the Pacific.

The Geisels have no children of their own and kids, says Geisel, are invariably disappointed when they encounter him in the flesh. A shy man, although not as shy as the legend he has nurtured, Geisel tends to be at his shyest and most uneasy in the presence of children.

"Kids expect Dr. Seuss to be a baggy pants character," says Geisel. "They expect big whiskers and a nose that lights up. Instead, I come to the door, a normal old poop. Some of the kids say, 'Go on, you aren't Dr. Seuss.' It can be embarrassing. Frankly, I'm terrified of kids in a mass. Individually, some kids are nice, some are little stinkers. But I don't hold with that nonsense that children are all little angels."

In 1978, he was 74 and still coltish and youthful. Ted Geisel says that he has heightened his pace with age. A late riser, he usually puts in an eight-hour day at the desk and drawing board in his expansive studio, with illustrations for his current project lining the walls. If the work is going well, he may press on for 10 or 12 hours, slowly, meticulously, painfully and usually into the night. "At night," he explains, "nobody calls you on the phone and tries to sell you insurance."

Geisel views himself essentially as a writer who draws. "I'm a writer who throws in the drawings for free," he says. "The drawing is fun, the writing is murder." When the words won't come, Geisel will stare morosely out at the Pacific. And if the creative well turns temporarily to dust, he may topple his lean, six-foot frame on a nearby couch, groaning and thrashing the air.

For every 60 pages of manuscript he deems usable, he hurls at least 500 pages into the wastebasket. Ninety-five percent of his drawings he tosses angrily on the floor. The efforts he would formerly throw away he now dispatches, at the university's request, to the UCLA library, which also contains the original drawings and manuscripts of most of Seuss's works.

He bristles at talk of retirement. "People of my age are all retiring," he says, "which is something I would never want for myself. I'm afraid the average guy enjoys his retirement because he never enjoyed his work. I've got more things I want to do now than ever."

Juggling several careers at once, Geisel laboriously churns out his children's books — on the wall now were preliminary sketches for three new stories — and he's an editor of the Beginner's Books division of Random House. He administers charitable works through his Dr. Seuss Foundation, which provides money for various zoos and scholarships for worthy students and has underwritten the salary of a professor of humanities at his alma mater, Dartmouth. As a relief from the delicate drudgery of authorship, he paints with serious intent.

Geisel says: "Television is the biggest, the most exciting medium there is. I just want to live long enough to do something terrific on TV." With his television commitments Geisel must commute frequently by shuttle flight from San Diego to Hollywood. Recently, at the Los Angeles Airport, he was returning home after a working day at the TV studio and a Los Angeles Library Association luncheon at which he was presented a bronzed Flit gun, a vintage device for spraying insects.

Years ago, in the 1930's, Geisel worked in advertising in New

York and he conceived of one of the big promotional slogans of the day, with an accompanying Seussian drawing: "Quick, Henry, the Flit."

"So I'm at the airport," Geisel relates, "and the guard says, 'What's that you've got there?' I said it was a bronzed Flit gun. 'A gun?' he said, 'You can't pass through here with a gun in your possession.' He was about 20 years old and had never heard of Flit. I told him to call the next man in charge, who turned out to be about 25 and he hadn't heard of Flit, either. 'Please,' I said, 'there must be some old poop in charge here.' They brought out the supervisor, who *was* an old poop. 'Why, that's a Flit gun,' he said. 'Haven't seen one of them in years.' Then he laughed and sent me on my way."

☆ ☆ ☆

Lately, to his bemused astonishment, Geisel has been the target of several women's lib groups. At once, he says, he began receiving almost identically phrased letters ("with the same words misspelled") from fifteen cities scattered across the country. All complained about a line in his book *And To Think That I Saw It on Mulberry Street*, published in 1937.

The story, a testimony to the power of a child's imagination, dwells on a young boy who walks along Mulberry Street and sees a car and a horse. He continues to imagine other improbable occurrences, but one flight of fantasy he dismisses as too pedestrian. Referring to his little sister, the boy says: "Even Jane could think of it."

"Suddenly, after all these years, I'm deluged with protests over that one line," says Geisel. "They say that line will cause boys to grow up feeling superior to their sisters. They demanded that I change the line. I wrote back saying that I agree with some of their goals and I know their request may be well-intentioned. But the boy in my story did feel that way about his sister and I wasn't about to change a word."

Another letter brought a similar feminist complaint. It seems that the works of Dr. Seuss had been put through a computer and it was concluded that 99 percent of the animal creatures he drew in them were male.

"The woman who wrote to me said this was demeaning and why didn't I draw females?" says Geisel. "I wrote back that I was ashamed of my oversight but I've got this problem — I asked her, did you ever try to draw a female hippo-griff?"

Geisel concedes that he has never had the knack of drawing females of any kind. In 1939, he wrote a humor book for adults called *The Seven Lady Godivas*. As he recalls, thumbing through the pages, "I tried to draw my Godivas as very sexy babes. But look at them here — they're neuter and sexless and they have no shape at all."

On the door to the Geisels' home is a small printed sign that warns, with typical Seussian waggishness: *Beware of the Cat*. There are no cats in the Geisel household unless one counts the 400 or so feline specimens in his various paintings. One painting contains 200 faces of cats in a cluster. Geisel calls it appropriately "A Plethora of Cats."

In contrast to another cherished writer-illustrator, the late James Thurber, whose specialty was wistful dogs, Geisel leans to cats although he admits he has no particular affection for them. "The truth," he says, "is that I like dogs better than cats but I don't know how to draw a dog."

It was a cat drawing, in fact, that led Geisel into a hitherto uncharted area of children's books. In the mid-1950s, when parents were concerned that Johnny was unable to read, Geisel's publisher urged him to fill the void with a book for six-year-olds. The story would be limited to a prescribed list of words, all of one syllable.

After months of helpless thrashing, Geisel was rummaging through his discarded sketches one day when he saw a drawing of a roguish-looking cat. It was a true Seussian cat, wearing a stovepipe hat. Since both "cat" and "hat" were on the word list, and rhymed, Geisel parlayed them into *The Cat in the Hat*, a comic masterpiece now a supplementary text for first-graders.

Geisel's feeling for animals can be traced to his boyhood in Springfield, Mass., where he was born of German stock on March 4, 1904. His father's duties as supervisor of public parks included the overseeing of the city's zoo. Young Ted and his sister often romped with the animals and they would listen to animal stories related by their mother.

One incident in his boyhood left Geisel with a permanent dread of audiences. He rejects all invitations to give speeches and he refuses to appear on television talk shows. There is still a haunted look in his eyes as he recalls the day when he was thirteen and Theodore Roosevelt came to Springfield to address a World War I bond rally and to present medals to Boy Scouts with the best bond-selling records.

With the other boys, Geisel sat nervously as the names were called out and the medals given. Finally, young Ted was sitting alone with Roosevelt on the platform. Sadly, Ted Geisel's name had been inadvertently omitted from the list.

"I can still hear it now," Geisel says. "Teddy Roosevelt looking around and asking, 'What is this little boy doing here?' And all those eyes from the audience staring right through me, people whispering, 'Ted Geisel tried to get a medal and he didn't deserve it.' I can still hear them saying, 'What's he doing there?' Even today, I sometimes find myself asking, 'What am I doing here?'"

At Dartmouth, Geisel majored in literature and went on to Oxford for graduate work. His plan was to return to his beloved Dartmouth as a professor. At Oxford, he was chagrined to learn that he knew much less than his fellow British students and he casually devoted his time to drawing. Subsequently, he spent a year at the University of Vienna and at the Sorbonne. In 1927, he returned to the United States and his cartoons, with funny two-line captions, began to appear regularly in the top magazines, including *The Saturday Evening Post*. He chose to sign them "Dr. Seuss."

"I used to tell myself I used 'Dr. Seuss' to save my own name for when I write The Great American Novel," Geisel says. "What isn't generally known is that I already wrote my Great American Novel. I wrote it over 40 years ago. It went unpublished and deservedly so. First, I wrote it in two volumes. Then I cut it to one volume, then to a long short story, then a paragraph. In the end, I sold it as a two-line caption for a cartoon."

While he was involved in the advertising campaign to promote the Flit spray-gun, he learned that his contract specifically forbade outside writing. There was one exception — he could write for children. "It was not through my love of children that I began to write for them," Geisel says. "It all happened through a loophole in my contract."

Then he wrote and illustrated *And To Think That I Saw It on Mulberry Street*, which was turned down by 27 publishers. The 28th was much more perceptive and the book, by now accepted as a classic, has since appeared in over 20 editions. All of Geisel's books are printed in a number of foreign languages and enjoy a vast international popularity, from Germany to Brazil to Japan.

In contrast to the heavy-handed sermonizing found in so many children's stories, the Dr. Seuss tales reveal Geisel as a master of the subtle moral. "It's impossible to write anything without making some kind of statement," he insists. His tale of the Star-Belly Sneetches who are snooty to the Plain-Belly Sneetches is clearly a blow at snobbery. In *How the Grinch Stole Christmas*, the nasty Grinch makes off with all the presents in Who-ville, but the resourceful Who's celebrate without presents, saying for Seuss: "Maybe Christmas doesn't come from a store. Maybe Christmas ... means a little more."

Aside from his *Yertle the Turtle*, a parable on Hitler, Geisel rarely aims for a moral. Shortly after producing a film documentary on Japan — it brought him one of his three Academy Awards — Geisel wrote *Horton Hears a Who*, wherein the tiny Who's symbolized the Japanese people, humiliated in World War II and searching now for their own kind of democracy. One line from the story: "A person is a person no matter how small." Another exception was *The Lorax*, in which he lambasted the spoilers of the land.

Several years ago, Geisel campaigned against what he termed "linguistic untidiness" with a book called *Fox in Socks*, which included the following tongue-twister: "Clocks on fox tick. Clocks on Knox tock. Six sick bricks tick. Six sick chicks tock." An eminent English professor wrote in admiration: "Peter Piper has picked his last peck of pickled peppers."

As a craftsman, Geisel has never set out consciously to write for children. He treats his young readers as equals. "Too many writers have only contempt and condescension for children, which is why they give them such degrading corn about bunnies," Geisel says. "When you write for kids, you can't lose them for one second. If you don't take the child forward with each turn of the page you're cooked. I write for myself at my own level first; then I go back and shorten and simplify the sentences. A kid can understand anything."

As he looks back on a lifetime of creativity, Ted (Dr. Seuss) Geisel, a perfectionist with every stroke of the pen, sums up the body of his work with characteristic humility. "I just wish it were better," he says. "But it's all as good as I could do."

Is there anyone who could have done better, this side of Who-ville, not far from the River Wah-hoo, near the wilds of Hippo-no-Hungus, on the way to Solla Sollew?

Some Places I've Been

A fine writer named Leo Rosten once put together a collection of travel pieces which he chose to call "The 3:10 to Anywhere," a provocative title that he went on to explain: "My wife described me in despair; 'He'll take the 3:10 to anywhere.'"

Rosten went on further to quote Hazlitt, as follows: "The soul of a journey is freedom — to think, feel, do just as one pleases." That is a poetic definition, but I think that Rosten himself scored points on Hazlitt with his own, more prosaic description. "Whenever I yearn to see Venice again," Rosten said, "or Taos or Hong Kong or Ottery Saint Mary, I take a token trip — in that wrinkled, grayish vehicle that weighs around three pounds, and is called the brain."

Unlike Leo Rosten, I have no ingrained passion for travel. I don't like to pack. I'm not fond of airports. I can never remember anything I ever read in an airplane. Or ever said or heard. Half of the fun, for me, is not in getting there but in being there. I am not, in short, a good traveler. But the nature of a writer's job is to get about and, in retrospect, I think that is a good thing — when I'm back home. I suspect there is more than rueful rumor in Frank Gifford's line about jet travel: "Breakfast in New York, dinner in Los Angeles, and your luggage in Honolulu."

Nonetheless, it is always a pleasure to write about the places.

Georgia on My Mind

In this restaurant in Athens, which is a lovely college town in north

Georgia, the waitress smiled as she listened and then she said in a voice of rich magnolia: "Do I detect a Yankee accent?" A Yankee accent? Me? You mean to say that WE sound strange to THEM?

Many years ago, not long after what's known in the South as the War Between the States, a Union officer named John William De-Forest reported on postbellum South Carolina for Harper's Weekly as follows: "We shall do well to study this peculiar people, which will soon lose its peculiarities."

Such dire fears have been expressed for the last century, with each study of each new generation of southerners. But the "peculiarities" remain, these distinctive and intriguing differences. The South is different. Southerners are different. Who has ever heard of "northern charm"? Or "northern hospitality"?

And is it possible that the myth of southern romanticism is more truth than legend? Northern boys stationed in Army bases down south are always falling in love with those southern girls. But who's ever heard of a southern boy stationed up north falling in love with a northern girl?

I had come to the University of Georgia and its distinguished Henry Grady School of Journalism to sit in solemn conclave with the other judges of the Peabody Awards, which is television's version of the Pulitzer Prizes. And then, later, it was time to look around at other parts of the South and to learn about grits and red-eye gravy.

Grits, to begin with, is singular. I learned this from a professor who, by way of illustration of perfectly good English, stated: "These grits is great." You can say, "These grits are great," but folks would know you're an illiterate Yankee.

I'll tell you about red-eye gravy. It comes from the pan on which the ham has been fried. With a serving of grits on your plate, you mark a small hole in the middle with your fork and then ladle in the gravy, which really does look like a red eye staring out from all that whiteness of the grits.

They tell about an incident during the big Army maneuvers in Louisiana in 1941. A farmer approached a visiting northern news-paperman. "What's all the excitement about?" the farmer asked.

"We're training," the newspaperman said.

"For what?"

"Well," the newspaperman explained, "we may be getting into the war over in Europe."

"I thought so," the farmer said. "But one thing bothers us down here. You reckon that when we do get in the war, you Yankees are goin' to help us any?"

History records that the Yankees did offer some help and now, a generation later, the South is booming through the roof. As a symbolic example, consider the Omni in Atlanta. Now I have been to a number of county fairs and three goat ropings, but I've never seen anything like the mammoth new Omni International Megastructure, which is practically an enclosed city stretching 14 stories into the Altanta sky — a posh hotel (Jimmy Carter spent election night at the Omni in a suite now designated the Presidential), six theaters, discotheques, gourmet restaurants, fancy shops, a playpen for the basketball Hawks and the hockey Flames, and, just off the hotel lobby, a public ice skating rink.

They have gone daft over ice skating in Atlanta. And in Atlanta they have one of the nation's largest ski clubs. Where, do you ask, do Atlantans ski? Why, naturally, up to the snowy mountains of North Carolina.

At Savannah, on the Georgia coast, there is a pronounced boom in such verities as charm and historic grace. In any rating of beautiful cities, Savannah must rate as a contender. "Savannah," wrote Chandler Brossard a few years ago, "is a secluded spot of exquisite humanness." It is all of that, with a legend attached to each of the many Colonial homes restored to original stateliness along the city's 24 leafy squares. And there is languid beauty in the riverfront section with its cobblestone streets, its galleries and museums.

And one can't overlook the Savannah Saw Works which proclaims as its slogan: "Business Is Good When Things Are Dull."

And there is proper obeisance to a hometown boy, the late Johnny Mercer, who wrote great lyrics for great songs and still had a home in Savannah he called "Moon River." Another native Savannahian, Herb Traub, runs a splendid restaurant called the Pirates' House in a building dating back to 1733, and in it there is a Hall of Fame room with such Mercer memorabilia as the sheet music for "Something's Gotta Give" and other Mercer tunes. A nice, warming touch.

I can tell you about the fabled Okefenokee Swamp near Waycross, Ga., where a place called the Green Frog offers terrific frog legs and the slogan: "Service With a Hop." And I can tell you that "cracker" is derived from the whip sound made by the old muledrivers of the South. And 200 years ago, the settlers would boil the bark of a tree in water and the stuff would cure the dogs of mange. Hence: Dogwood.

The great editor Jonathan Daniels once wrote: "We southerners are of course a mythological people." Ingenious, too. I think of the waitress in Mobile, Ala., who poured salt on the napkin so the beer-filled frosted mug wouldn't slip. And down the road, a gas-station attendant came out wearing roller skates. "Saves my feet," he explained.

Aboard the Urban Titanic

NEW YORK — Years ago, the old gunfighter known as Bat Masterson came to the big town and wondered aloud: "Is New York an unfinished mining camp?" A more recent visitor, sportscaster Keith Jackson, suggested along similar lines that New York is "a town that works overtime trying to defeat you."

And Bob Hope insists that a friend of his in New York was mugged by a 3-year-old wearing high heels. New York, as everyone knows, is an urban Titanic beset by troubles on every side. Even Joe Namath moved out to the suburbs. Broadway Joe was no more. But who could ever refer to this symbol of the good swinging, Upper East Side life as Scarsdale Joe?

To survive in New York clearly requires ingenuity. One thinking cabdriver, for instance, shelled out $5 for the cheapest cigars possible. Then he put the cigars in a box next to a sign reading: "Congratulations! I Have Just Become a Father! Please Have a Cigar!"

"This is a terrific gimmick," I said to the cabbie. "Does it work?"

The cabbie shrugged modestly. "It makes me up to $200 a month in tips," he said. "I'd say it works. A passenger looks to leave a two-bit tip. But he takes a cigar and the tip's got to go up 50 cents."

Another cabdriver gives lollipops to his passengers to promote tips. This might also be interpreted as a tribute to Telly Savalas, TV's Kojak, the town's most visible show business figure, a lollipop fancier who is seen everywhere in his velvet suit telling people: "It's chic to be Greek."

Ingenuity is everywhere in this town. At a store with the marvelous name of Hammacher Schlemmer's, they're advertising a gadget known as a "Sound Sleep." The thing makes a humming noise to promote sleep in this noisy city and it costs about $25.

Occasionally, the pressure of big-city living mounts to a breaking point. They tell about a woman who took her husband to a Park Avenue psychiatrist.

"My poor husband!" she cried. "He's convinced that he is a parking meter."

Regarding the woe-begone fellow, the analyst inquired: "Why don't you let him speak for himself?"

To which she replied: "How can he — with all those dimes in his mouth?"

Small wonder, with the present so overwhelming, that nostalgia for the recent past is so much a part of the New York of the mid-1970s. At the Drake Hotel, for example, the newest supperclub known as "After Ten" breathes an atmosphere out of a 1940s movie on the late show. You hear "As Time Goes By" on the piano in the background and, in the dim light, could that be Bogie himself sitting at the bar?

The double-deck buses of old are again trudging down Fifth Avenue and Madison and Riverside Drive. The city shelled out $800,000 for eight buses from London and they are enormously popular — and evocative of another day.

Once, the rhythms of the city were reflected by its columnists — the "cafe Prousts," in Ben Hecht's apt phrase. They are all gone now, the Ed Sullivans, the Danton Walkers, the Louis Sobols, the Leonard Lyons and, of course, the Walter Winchells. And something of the city's special tone and flavor went with them.

A City of Country Music

NASHVILLE — They call it Music City, USA. Or, with an eye on the money that keeps rolling in, just plain Cashville. Or, with a respectful nod to Marshall McLuhan's learned notions on the worldwide effects of the electronic media, it's the "musical marketplace of the global village."

Nashville is where "Grand Old Opry" was spawned over Station WSM in 1925 by a newspaperman-emcee named George D. Hay, who had a column called "Howdy, Judge" and referred to himself as "The Solemn Old Judge," and, of course, the "Opry" thrived in the 3,481 seat Ryman Auditorium, a storied mecca of country sounds, with its ancient wooden pews forming a huge semi-circle around the stage.

The Ryman was born when hoofbeats and buggy wheels clattered along Summer Street and Sam Jones, a Georgia preacher, was doing battle with the devil for local souls. Tom Ryman, a riverboat captain on the Cumberland, used to barrel in with his roustabouts and tear up tent revival meetings. But one day, just as the captain was about to signal his men into action, he paused and listened to the words of Rev. Jones, speaking now with unexpected softness.

The subject of the sermon was "Mother." Large, sentimental tears fell from Capt. Ryman's eyes. Penitently, he rose and vowed to start a campaign to build a tabernacle, which went up 15 years later. He never again broke up a tent meeting, either.

In time, the Union Gospel Tabernacle became the Ryman Auditorium and the altar to which sinners once shuffled hesitantly gave way to a theater in the round. And, over the years, legend began to attach itself to Ryman the way a sheep dog collects cockleburrs.

Around the first of the century, the Metropolitan Opera was there putting on "Carmen." The great symphonies from New York, Chicago and Boston played at the Ryman. John Philip Sousa led his brass band within its walls. In 1917, already past 70, Sarah (The Divine) Bernhardt performed on the stage.

On two successively glorious nights in April, 1919, audiences heard Caruso and then Galli-Curci. Enthralled, the local boosters called it "the greatest week in Nashville music history."

Music still flows in Nashville but with themes that Caruso and

Galli-Curci never sang about — diesel trucks, Wichita linemen, Harper Valley PTAs and Nashville skylines. They sing songs by the original Jimmy Rodgers, The Singing Brakeman, who wrote tunes with names like "My Carolina Sunshine Gal" and "I'm in the Jail-house Now."

You can drop into Tootsie's Orchid Lounge, a beer parlor where the country music people hang out. The walls are full of pictures, the tables are shaky and it's said that Tootsie, a motherly, good-natured woman, has four or five cigar boxes full of IOU's.

"See that booth back there," says Tootsie. "Roger Miller wrote 'Dang Me' right there in that booth."

Better yet, visit a spectacularly attractive and splendidly assembled place called the Country Music Hall of Fame. They have tours, a literal "hall of fame" with portraits, films, animated displays and loads of memorabilia — Eddy Arnold's guitar, Roy Acuff's fiddle, a gold record from Tennessee Ernie Ford, even a horseblanket that Will Rogers owned and many others including a guitar once played by Arkie the Arkansas Woodchopper and Vernon Dalhart's 1917 recording of "Can't You Hear Me Callin', Caroline?"

At the Hall of Fame you can listen to Cecil Whaley, the publicist, who knows every country tune ever written, tell about the late Red Foley going to Chicago for the first time to play on the "Barn Dance." Says Whaley: "Red's parents warned him about city slickers and gave him $75, which he changed into fives and ones and stuffed into his shoes. He limped around Chicago for a week!"

Whaley also can bowl you over with statistics. Nashville puts out nearly 52 per cent of all the music recorded in the land and half of that is country music. There are 42 recording companies here and over 900 songwriters. The local chapter of the musicians union has over 1,500 members, but it's doubtful if half that number could pass a written musical test.

"Oh, they read music all right," says guitarist-executive Chet Atkins. "But they read it with their ears instead of their eyes."

The City That Care Forgot

NEW ORLEANS — Outside of Antoine's, a landmark restaurant of some antiquity, a woman was startled to see an imposingly familiar face. "Bob Hope!" she cried. "My goodness, is it really you?"

"No," Hope grinned. "I'm on tape."

It's Mardi Gras time, in this City That Care Forgot, a city that is also a state of mind, where crayfish is called "crawfish" and they accent the word Burgundy on the second syllable, the city where jazz (and Louis Armstrong) was born and where now they have a bus named Desire.

And for a lagniappe, which is what New Orleanians call an added attraction, they had Bob Hope himself to reign as king of the Krewe of Bacchus parade, a magnificent spectacle where the monarch waves to the roaring crowds and, in true mock regal fashion, tosses out doubloons and shiny beads.

It seemed a splendid notion, in this atmosphere of frolic and gaiety, for Hope to tape his monthly NBC special here in such storied French Quarter boites as Pete Fountain's and Al Hirt's and at the new Theater for the Performing Arts.

Phil Harris is here, too, as a guest on the show and he had introduced Hope to a potent local concoction known as a Hurricane. "It's 90 per cent tiger's milk and 10 per cent panther's breath," Hope explains. "One guy had two of them and they removed his appendix while he was singing "Honeysuckle Rose'!"

The spirit of Mardi Gras is everywhere and the infectious mood of carnival knows no boundaries of age. Says Hope: "I saw an 80-year-old couple doing the Funky Chicken while drinking Geritol out of a slipper!"

They are at Al Hirt's place now, with the cameras and the sound booms and the bright lights and the tangle of wires. How is a Hope show put together? With great care and painstaking effort. It is axiomatic that hard work makes for easy viewing.

Bob also functions as the executive producer, which means that he oversees every minute detail. His mood is light and the banter flows but he is working with precision and a strong sense of discipline. He nods at instructions from the director.

And, of course, he jokes with the people at the tables. "You know, we're trying to get the Rams interested in sports," he confides. "They said a prayer before every game and four times last year that was intercepted."

He grins at Barney McNulty, for years his lieutenant in charge of the cue cards. "Would you mind holding up my adlibs, sir?" Hope requests. It looks deceptively easy, holding up cue cards but McNulty does his job well because he is tuned into Hope's speech rhythms and he knows how to listen.

Now Al Hirt strolls onto the bandstand, horn in hand. He's shed some weight but he's still massive. "Al's done a wonderful job of dieting," says Hope. "Oh, he slipped a little and ate a catering truck."

"You were in the Army," Hope says to Al at one point in their exchange.

"Yes, that's right," says Al.

"What were you?"

"I was a battalion."

A Woman Named Mary

KETCHUM, Idaho — "The earth abideth," it says in Ecclesiastes, the biblical epigraphs from which Hemingway chose the title of his first and, some say, his best novel: "The Sun Also Rises." Here in the abiding Idaho earth, where Ernest Hemingway was buried in the summer of '61, the Hemingway presence endures and it grows — strange, haunting and singularly memorable.

He was big enough in life, God knows, a man as vivid as a flash of lightning, full of swagger and charm and courage and, above all, for this was the core of his essence, artistry. Now his towering presence seems a part of the mountain air, itself as clean and pure as the carefully crafted Hemingway sentence.

At the Alpine, one of the town bars that Hemingway frequented, they reminisce about him still. Everybody calls him "Papa." The ones who knew him least call him "Papa" the most. At the Ex Libris, a book shop in nearby Sun Valley, five shelves are devoted to his works.

And in the quiet, homey elegance of the Sun Valley Lodge, where he lived periodically in the late '30s, No. 206 is still known as the "Hemingway Room." It is a sunlit corner suite, actually, with a fireplace in each of the two rooms.

A visitor enters 206 with a sense of awe, which is heightened by sitting at the desk where Ernest Hemingway, just back from Spain, his creative juices in full flow, wrote "For Whom the Bell Tolls."

For a number of years, the lodge decorated the suite with a portrait of Hemingway and a notice saying the picture could be purchased. But at least a dozen of these pictures were permanently borrowed, each in turn replaced, and now the walls stand bare of any Hemingway memorabilia.

Out on the road to Trail Creek Cabin, a memorial was erected to Hemingway. Carved in granite are words taken from a eulogy Hemingway wrote and delivered at the funeral of a friend who died of gunshot wounds on a hunting trip in 1939. But they could apply to Hemingway himself:

Best of All he Loved the Fall
The Leaves Yellow on the Cottonwoods
Leaves Floating in the Trout Streams
And Above the Hills
The High Blue Wordless Skies
... Now he Will Be a Part of Them Forever

His grave is a flat stone under a cross and between two fir trees, with only his full name inscribed: Ernest Miller Hemingway. Someone had placed three short-stem roses on the grave. Not far from the simple cemetery, atop a bluff overlooking the Wood River, where Hemingway fished for trout, is the home where he spent his final years with the last of his wives, Mary Hemingway.

She is a marvelous looking woman, rich with warmth and good humor and she sat on the porch at dusk, a gin and tonic in her hand, and she talked about Ernest.

"Ernest liked only one of all the adaptations they made of his stories for the movies or TV," Mary Hemingway is saying. "That was 'The Killers,' the movie version. He objected to all of the rest. I remember watching Gary Cooper in 'For Whom the Bell Tolls' on TV one night. Ernest scoffed and said, 'Look at old Coops, the Spanish guerrilla fighter in his damned Abercrombie and Fitch outfit!' "

I asked Mary Hemingway how she liked the latest Hemingway film, "Islands in the Stream."

She issued a faint smile. "The last part, about the refugees and the German sub, was all phony, all screwed up from the book," she said. And how did she like George C. Scott as Hemingway? Again the smile and a deliberative pause. "Let's just say that Mr. Scott is a very good actor."

We talked about a book called "Papa," by Hemingway's son, Gregory. "A lot of lies and nonsense," she judged. "I called him up and pointed out errors of fact and Gig just said, 'I'm not a reporter. It's how I remember it.' "

She shrugged. "Everybody else has written so many lies about Ernest, why not his own kid?" A splendid writer herself and once a war correspondent for Time, Mary recently wrote her own autobiography, "How It Was," which MGM is turning into a movie.

With only a trace of irony, she says: "MGM bought the book to make a biographical movie about Ernest."

There are a few unpublished Hemingway works. "I found one enormous manuscript called 'Garden of Eden,' " she said. "Parts of it are good. Other parts are, I'm afraid, worthless. Ernest made me the executor of all his works and I made two guiding principles. First, anything published, such as 'Islands in the Stream,' would be Ernest's work and Ernest's only. No fiddling around by someone else's pen. Second, we will not publish anything that Ernest would not have wanted published. We have a few more short stories, one piece on Africa and another on World War II — all okay, not great, but publishable."

Mary Hemingway had been in Cuba and she had just returned to Ketchum for the annual birthday party she gives in Hemingway's memory. "It's nothing formal or solemn," she says. "Ernest's friends sing and dance and drink wine, and there is laughter and good talk and somebody makes a brief toast to Ernest."

Ernest. Not once did she call him "Papa."

Local Customs in Montreal

MONTREAL — As the man was saying on the television, French is an extraordinary language with some terrific nuances. The man on TV was giving a French lesson, which seemed strange because even the smallest of children here in Montreal are so smart they speak French like a professor.

"Give regard to the matter of the insult," the man said. "If one should call you 'a pig' in French, he would say that you are 'espece de cochon' — literally a kind of a pig but loosely translated, the 'espece' means 'alleged.' Thus, in French, the insult doesn't libel anyone."

Working in French would obviously put a damper on Don Rickles. Actually, the French spoken in Montreal is full of local mannerisms and idioms and is given short shrift by the purists of Paris. But then, the Parisians really don't care for much of anything outside of Paris.

"The Parisians are secure in their knowledge of one essential belief," Heywood Hale Broun once said. "They are certain that God speaks French."

The province of Quebec — La Belle Province — spends millions each year on its Office of the French Language, which is in the vanguard of the struggle to save the tongue of Zola and Voltaire and Robert Clary from subversion at the hands of "les Anglais."

Dread signs of ominous decay are everywhere — Coca Cola is edging out the famed Quebec cider, the "chansons" are yielding to Elton John. And there is the growing intrusion of "franglais," which is English words given French pronunciations such as "le parking" and "le hot dog" and "en blue jean" and "les bestsellers" and "le hamburger" and so on.

At a restaurant, I learned of another local custom. Seeking a restorative after a long flight, I asked the waiter if, "s'il vous plait," I could have a beer.

The waiter rose to his full height of indignation. "Monsieur!" he snapped. "This is a restaurant — we serve WINE!"

Inflation has struck this enchanting city with the force of a slap shot by Maurice (Le Rocket) Richard. A good Havana cigar costs up to $4. Taxis start at 60 cents to get in and 60 cents for each mile traversed. Dinner for two, including an amusing Bordeaux with pretentions of laconic charm, runs up to $100 in the best of the 6,000 restaurants in Montreal.

To the Montrealer, money is "foin," which is French for hay. This goes back to when the French-Canadians, traditionally distrustful of banks, hid their money in a sock under the mattress. Others, still more wary, would spend all of it in one joyous weekend. Their money would therefore be considered burned — just like hay.

On the subject of money, when a woman accompanies a man to a restaurant in Montreal it is assumed that her menu will not be sullied by a listing of prices. Innocent of the ways of vulgar commerce, madame or mademoiselle simply gives her order to monsieur. In Montreal, Women's Liberation is as vaguely arcane as the Wars of the Roses and Gloria Steinem is a myth.

Nearly half of the six million inhabitants of Quebec Province live in Montreal, which is the world's second largest French-speaking city. They enjoy a surprisingly mild climate, warmer than Minneapolis. But the winter brings severe snowstorms. To ward off the chill, Montrealers turn to a devastating mixture of sweet red wine and whisky known as Cariboo.

This Cariboo of which I speak is served only at special parties or on hunting and fishing expeditions. I can attest that this Cariboo could have been conceived by Alfred Nobel before he decided to invent dynamite.

Along such lines, they tell the story of Henry Fonda in a Montreal boite, resisting the waiter's urging that he drink a glass of absinthe.

"Why are you so insistent?" Fonda said.

"Because I want you to stay healthy," the waiter said. "I happen to know that absinthe makes the heart grow, Fonda."

The story is not guaranteed for accuracy.

A Monument to Beer

MUNICH, Germany — After the second act of "The Bartered Bride," an opera by one Bedrich Smetana that ranks among the lower draft choices, a sports columnist from Texas summed up the feelings of his fellow journalists. "I think," said this squint-eyed Texan whose name is Blackie Sherrod, "this sumbitch'n opera is goin' into overtime."

It seemed prudent, thereafter, to repair from the stately Munich Bayerische Staatsopher — National Opera House — over to the near-by Hofbrauhaus, which H. L. Mencken once called the "Parthenon of beer drinking."

As everyone knows — it is common knowledge to every child in Bavaria — beer was invented long ago by a Flemish king named Gambrinus. No better or noisier monument to good King Gambrinus exists than the Hofbrauhaus, which was founded in 1569 to sell the beer of the court (hof) brewery.

A three-level beer hall, massive enough to serve 4,000, the Hof-brauhaus is aglow with Bavarian music and a warming gemutlichkeit, a happy German word that means joy, comfort, good fellowship. With a few drams of enzian, a schnapps made from herbs found atop the ridges of the Bavarian Alps, followed by a liter or two of that incom-parable, velvety Bavarian brew, you can reach a heady gemutlichkeit as fast as you can say "Red Baron."

They also serve a mouth-watering pigs knuckles, potatoes and sauer-kraut. "Would it be possible," I asked, "to have something instead of the sauerkraut?"

Our waitress frowned. "You vill eat the sauerkraut," she said. (She really did. I'm not making this up, folks.)

And, of course, I did eat the sauerkraut. It was fantastic.

In the Heart of the Tyrol

INNSBRUCK, Austria — Among the ABC people here, who were preparing to televise the Winter Olympics of 1976 from this picturesque city in the heart of the Tyrolean Alps, the memories return of another time, another Olympics. They were here before, in the winter of 1964, the first time that the network had ever fastened its cameras on the world's premiere athletes in a setting of snow.

Roone Arledge, president of ABC Sports, remembers the difficulty then of cutting through the barrier of language. "One day, I was explaining some details of the telecast to one of the top Austrians on the Olympics committee," says Arledge. "He had let it be known that he understood English completely. As I talked on, he would nod at appropriate times. Then I finished and he looked at his watch, put on his hat and coat and said to me, 'Well, I see that the time is getting late and now it is time to say hello.'

"I had," says Arledge, reliving the moment, "what might be described as a sudden sinking feeling."

Presumably, in the years that have since passed, the Innsbruckers have been too busy schussing and sledding and enjoying the good mountain life to have added appreciably to their storehouse of English. The German they speak is, after all, remarkably flexible. One thinks of "bitte," for instance, a dandy utility infielder of a word that means both "please" and "you're welcome." And there's "*loewenzahne*," which means "lion's teeth," literally, but refers colloquially to dandelion wine.

And there is "fensterbolster," which is the plump pillow that the hausfraus of Innsbruck place on their window ledges to rest their elbows if the outdoor conversations, also known as gossip, go into overtime.

Status is important and duly acknowledged. The University of Innsbruck is 400 years old — the city itself has graced the map for over 700 years — and a highly respected institution. Some of the faculty members have earned two doctorate degrees. Therefore, their mailboxes have this inscription before their names — "Dr. Dr."

On the highways, known as autobahns, there is no speed limit and most drivers go at a steady 85 or 90 miles an hour. When informed that the national speed limit in the United States is 55, an Innsbrucker expresses amazement.

"But surely," he says, "if you drive only at 55, you will fall asleep at the wheel."

Otherwise, speed is not a vital part of the Innsbruckers' existence. An old joke, in fact, may well have had its roots here in the story of the Innsbrucker who left his shoes to be repaired. "They'll be ready next Wednesday," the shoemaker said.

Soon thereafter, the customer was called off on international business which kept him away for six months. On his return, he remembered his shoes and went to the shop.

"Oh yes," the shoemaker told him. "Your shoes will be ready next Wednesday."

On such occasions, and sometimes on no occasion at all, the Innsbrucker can turn to his schnapps, which is a spirituous liquor favored to ward off the chill and, possibly, snakebite in the Alps.

Here at Innsbruck, there had been speculation on the effect of the foehn, should it strike around these parts during the Olympic competition. The foehn — pronounced "fern" as Goethe is called "gert-uh" — is, like the oboe, an ill wind that blows nobody well. Clockers of winds make it the most troublesome of them all. It is the wind that wears a black hat.

Suddenly, carrying its own electric charges, the foehn will swoop up malevolently from Italy in the South. The warm, alpine current lasts for several days, a benumbing period known in retrospect as a time when things were rotten. Headaches abound, traffic accidents increase, divorces multiply.

Usually, the foehn hits in late autumn and is known therefore, as the "turken roster," or corn ripener. But the foehn, as erratic as the behavior it causes, has been known to visit in February as well.

How would the foehn affect Howard Cosell? The question is put to Roone Arledge, who smokes missile-size cigars and is innovative and wise and good-humored. "Fortunately," says Roone, "if the foehn should come at Olympics time, it wouldn't bother Cosell since he won't be here."

Why won't Cosell be here? "Quite simply," Arledge muses, "because it is too mind-boggling to imagine Howard Cosell in stretch pants."

Surely if the mind must be boggled, let it be done by Innsbruck itself, a lovely, historic, mountain-ringed city whose name stems from the bridge ("bruck") over the River Inn, which is a Celtic word meaning "flowing one." If you ask an Innsbrucker why any Austrian river has a Celtic name, you get a Gallic shrug.

If the Olympics are, in Jim McKay's phrase, a "mirror of the times," it is hoped fervently that they will become only a reflection of magical Innsbruck.

"Heaven," an Innsbrucker tells you, "is by definition an English apartment, a Japanese wife, Chinese food and an American salary. What we have instead is English food, an American wife, a Japanese apartment and a Chinese salary."

These are the jokes, of course. I am talking with Dr. Karl Heinz Klee, a practicing attorney in Innsbruck and secretary-general of the

Olympic committee, and he adds a line to the old definition of hell as a place where the English cook the food, the French direct the traffic and the Germans tell the jokes — "and the Austrians," says Dr. Klee, "do the organizing."

This is, in short, not Germany where earlier, in 1972, the Olympics head there had said: "We Germans can't improvise, so we organize." The Austrians and Germans share the same language but the difference in mentality is sharp and historic. In bad times, says Dr. Klee by way of illustration, it was said in Berlin that "the situation is very serious, but not hopeless; whereas, in Vienna, they said the situation is hopeless but not very serious."

This is Mozart country and Wagner gets short shrift. Every Innsbrucker knows that a Wagnerian opera is where you go in at 8 o'clock and four hours later it's 8:30.

Most Innsbruckers own a smattering of English. Still, there are language barriers beyond hurdling. An ABC fellow was ordering breakfast one morning at his hotel. On the first day, he asked for "scrambled eggs mit bacon." The waiter nodded and returned instead with eggs and ham. The second day, he again requested "scrambled eggs mit bacon." And again, despite nodding in agreement, the waiter returned with eggs and ham.

On the third day, admitting defeat, the ABC fellow said, resignedly: "May I have scrambled eggs mit ham?"

"What," the waiter cried, "no bacon?"

Although the foregoing isn't guaranteed for accuracy, it is true that Geoff Mason, ABC's director of planning for the Olympics, left a wakeup call with the hotel operator one night. "I'd like a wakeup call for 6:30," he said, "and in case I oversleep, I'd like another wakeup call at 7."

"All right," he was told, "which one do you want first?"

In Innsbruck, as in all of Austria, the most invaluable of phrases to know is "gruess'Gott," an all-purpose greeting which means, vaguely, "God's greetings." There are no waiters in the restaurants — all are head waiters and must be addressed therefore as "Herr Ober." The check in German is "die rechnung," which translates loosely into "the reckoning." Nearly all of the cabbies drive a Mercedes Benz. It is difficult to know how much you tip a man who owns a Mercedes. Gin is cheap, vodka expensive, the coffee is steamed, bitter and almost undrinkable.

Instead of the formal "auf Wiedersehen," one says, simply, "Wiederseh'n" in leaving Innsbruck, which isn't easy.

Time for Cockney Rhyme

LONDON — "Have you grown accustomed to our ways?" the Englishman wanted to know. I had been in London four days. "Why, yes,"

I lied. "I can truthfully say I no longer believe it odd for cars to keep to the left of the road. It seems perfectly natural for me to refer to the elevator as the 'lift' and the subway as the 'tube.' I always remember to ask for a glass of 'bitters,' which I used to call beer, at a public house, which I used to call a bar. And I now thoroughly understand the difference between guineas, pounds, quid, half-crowns, shillings, six-pence, three-pence and ha' pennies. I learned it all zip zip, just like that."

"Sure you did," the Englishman agreed. "And now, since Cockney talk is always popping up on our late, late movies you chaps must see on your television, it is time you learned something about the Cockneys and their rhyming slang."

And so I did. To begin with, the true Cockney, by a definition fairly accepted throughout England, is a Londoner who was born within earshot of the bells of the St. Mary's Bow Bells church in the East End of the city. What the term itself means no one seems to know. Chaucer used it — spelling it Cokney — to mean a rural simpleton. But the Cockney is anything but simple and he is far from rural.

Today the Cockney is a shrewd, chirpy, often undersized Londoner who has an irreverent attitude toward the respectable side of life (although he is generally very respectable himself) and he expresses himself in a racy form of speech, laced with a characteristic rhyme. There are roughly two million Cockneys in London, all of them easy to identify once they utter a sound. The first tip is their substitution of the "f" sound for "th" — as in "fing" for "thing." The other, most conclusive giveaway is their happy dedication to the rhyming slang.

Originally, rhyming slang was a jargon of thieves and cutpurses, who found it a valuable tool in deceiving their marks, or victims. In time, rhyming slang elbowed into ordinary usage among Cockneys and now it's as honest as a grasshopper (which, as we all know, means policeman, the transition flowing from copper to hopper to grasshopper.)

Most of the rhymes are a bit more complicated than that one and there's a sound reason for it. Above all else, the Cockneys are a talkative people, speech representing one of their most potent weapons against adversity and the haughtiness — either supposed or real — of other Londoners. The Cockney will always take the longest verbal route.

"Stairs," in Cockney, become "apples and pears." But not always, for the Cockney is a most ingenious fellow. He may omit the word that rhymes with the original — so that stairs will frequently be, simply, "apples." Now you may be astonished to hear this, but there are stuffy people who contend these omissions render Cockney talk difficult for the outsider to understand.

If a man wants to understand Cockney rhyming slang — well, he'd best have a smattering of British history in his head. Anyone here know what a "Darby Kelly" is? "Darby Kelly" was a melodrama popular in London in the 1830s; it has nothing in common with cooking but Kelly does rhyme with belly, doesn't it?

For another throwback to the past, the British suffered a moderately grave defeat at Khyber Pass in Afghanistan, a fact which may emerge in ordinary daily conversation and possibly may not. More than a century later, the Cockney refers to his drinking glass as a "Khyber" (taking scrupulous care to omit the rhyming word, pass).

Drinking and eating, in fact, furnish a sizable share of the rhyming slang. To a Cockney an egg is a "clothes peg." If you ask the barkeep for a "stand at ease" on a slice of "Uncle Fred," naturally you'll receive some cheese on a piece of bread.

It's also best to have only a "down the sink" (a single drink) so you don't become "elephant's trunk" (drunk, of course) else you may spend the night in the "flowery dell" (a cell). But then, a true Cockney always uses his "loaf of bread," (meaning his head).

The Women

"It is only a question of time," James Thurber wrote more than two decades ago, "before the male factor in the perpetuation of the species becomes a matter of biological deep freeze, an everlasting laboratory culture, labeled, controlled and supervised by women technicians."

Thurber, who referred to us men as "the insecure sex," also mentioned that the Encyclopedia Britannica had for years listed nothing under "Woman." Instead, the notation went: "See Man."

Such notions come to mind in putting together the following chapter on certain areas of television that have focused on women. Actually, television started as a woman's medium. The first truly big national star was Faye Emerson who practically owned the industry in its Pleistocene Age, in the late '40s and very early '50s.

Since then, women have done very well in the medium, up to and including a long-running syndicated show moderated by Virginia Graham called "Girl Talk," where mostly women graced the panel. Then they summoned a man on board, which was probably a mistake since the man was the acerbic Broadway producer, David Merrick, who immediately proclaimed: "When a ship is sinking, why is it always women and children first? I think men should go first!"

Merrick was rewarded for his candor by a request to leave forthwith.

The Judging At the Miss USA

"Good evening, y'all," said Miss Louisiana, each word a soft, soothing driblet of warm honey, as the contestants strutted to open the "Miss USA Pageant" telecast on CBS. It's all over now, I shouted. The rest is mere formality, I predicted. A shoo-in, folks. Southern girls always win these beauty contests in a walk — a very nice southern walk.

But she didn't. Instead, the judges, in their state of collective myopia, gave their nod to a northern entry, Miss Pennsylvania. Some judges, anyway, who don't know the rules governing southern womanhood and beauty contests.

You can't win 'em all, as I keep telling Eddie Fisher. But how they overlooked Miss Georgia is an even greater puzzlement. Listen, Miss Georgia — never you mind those judges. To me, you'll always be the true Miss USA. As for you, Miss Louisiana, you're my runnerup, y'all.

How gloriously mindless they are, these televised beauty contests, but somehow they are also irresistible and I am as captivated by them as the next fellow. I suppose, moreover, that we should offer a respectful if cherished tolerance toward such tribal rites while we still have them. It is well known that when the Women's Liberation folks rule the roost, they'll be switching things around and they'll have the guys competing for the beauty crowns and the girls sitting in judgment.

"And then see how you like it," snapped this Women's Liberation lady on the phone, "parading around half-dressed, being ogled and regarded solely as a sex object."

I said: "Hey, that sounds swell. Where do I sign up?"

As I have long maintained, it is the sun spots that hover around Miami Beach which are responsible not only for the curious assessments by the judges but for the oddments of behavior as well. The conversations between emcee Bob Barker and the contestants should, I firmly believe, be engraved in marble for generations unborn to ponder.

Said Mr. Barker to Miss California: "You're a beautiful girl but you have a twin brother. Is he an identical twin?"

"No, he's not identical. He's fraternal," she said. "He's very good looking."

"I'm sure he is," said Barker.

"Thank you," said Miss California.

And there was Miss Florida who confided that she met some fellow who told her that he was a son of one of the pageant judges.

"You didn't fall for that, did you?" Mr. Barker inquired apprehensively.

"Just for a little while," said Miss Florida.

It's those sun spots, I tell you. Even sensible June Lockhart, formerly on the "Lassie" show, a beaming den mother at the microphone at these activities, was heard to say: "Miss Arizona sings and plays the flute — but, of course, not at the same time."

For this particular event, they followed tradition with the staging of, in Barker's words, "the parade of states." In this segment, the contestants venture forth garbed to represent their states in a novel way, if that's the phrase I'm groping for here.

Novel? Well, Miss Alaska was dressed like a totem pole. I call that novel. Miss Kansas was a sunflower, Miss Maryland a jockey, Miss Michigan an oldtime car driver with goggles and Miss Idaho was — a potato? No, of course not. She was a cowgirl.

Miss Texas was also a cowgirl. She said, "Howdy!" Miss Oklahoma wore Indian garb. She said, "How!"

Law of Feminine Infallibility

If you will cup your ear, I should like to pass along Freeman's Law of Feminine Infallibility as it is reflected in TV and in the movies but not, save us all, in real life.

Remember this scene? The young composer is at the piano, playing his new concerto for his girl. At the finish, he turns to her.

"Is it — any good," he asks, hopefully. "Is it — really good?"

She nods. "Yes, it's good," she says. They embrace.

Who is this girl all of a sudden — Leonard Bernstein? Here he is, a fellow who's studied at Juilliard, who's devoted 10 years of his life to writing a concerto and this girl, who wouldn't know a C scale if it fell into her hairdo, has the effrontery to pass judgment.

What really throws me is that he seriously accepts her opinions and, what's more, as it turns out, she's right. Next scene: Our hero is playing his concerto in Carnegie Hall. Camera pans to the critics. They smile. Camera pans to the girl. She smiles. Oh, brother!

Two more familiar scenes. The young poet doubtfully reads several lines of his epic work. His girl nods. "Yes, it's good," she says. He wins the Nobel Prize for literature.

The young attorney hesitantly outlines his courtroom strategy. "No," his girl says, lowering her eyes. "It's unethical." He bites his lip but follows her advice. He wins the case and is elected governor of the state.

Gentlemen, I give you — The Infallible Female.

These women in fiction — they know more about music than composers, more about poetry than poets, more about legal ethics than lawyers. And don't get me started on the nurses who know more about medicine, for heaven's sakes, than Marcus Welby.

I ask you, did Beethoven turn for advice to his girl?

"Ludwig, it's good," she says, as he first rattles off the "Moonlight Sonata."

"Back into the kitchen and prepare it the weinerschnitzel," Ludwig van Beethoven snaps. "If I need YOUR advice about MY music, I'll ask, but don't hold your breath."

You don't think that's closer to the truth? Anyway, this particular siege of irascibility on my part can be traced to an "Alcoa Premiere" in which Bethel Leslie (an excellent actress) knew more about the law than her employer, a judge, and more about journalism than a newspaper editor, played with iron-jawed severity by Hugh O'Brian.

The details of the plot I'll forego except to say that it explored the nuances of collective guilt and wasn't at all bad — if you overlook this flowering of Feminine Infallibility.

There she was again, friends, that favorite stereotype of our popular culture we all know as (fanfare from the trumpets!) the Unfallible Female. Of course you know Little Miss Infallible. Certainly we've seen enough of her — the secretary who knows more about law than her boss, the attorney; the nurse who can tell the surgeon a thing or two about performing an appendectomy.

And now, on that last bastion of masculine assertiveness, there she was again — the Infallible Female out West in "Death Valley Days."

This time she was Nancy Cooper, blonde and pretty and it was she, we learn in this particular episode, who pointed Charles Russell, the cowboy artist, on the right path. Russell (played by Robert Taylor) likes to paint and draw well enough but when these sodbusters come around, he slaps on his nickel-plated six-shooters and joins his old trail pals for a good, old-fashioned shootout.

Does Nancy let him enjoy a nice companionable shootout? Ha!

Will Nancy implore him to put away his trusty six-shooter and go back to his easel? Yep.

Will Nancy succeed in this noble aim? Listen, you've seen the Infallible Female operate in fiction as much as I have. Historically speaking, the odds go all in her favor. Don't bet against it.

In the big scene, Nancy confronts Charlie Russell and reminds him that his art is vital, important and probably full of vitamins. It is he, Charlie Russell, she tells him, who has set down the Old West as no one before him had done on canvas. Will he risk all of this just to shoot at some sodbusters?

Poor Charlie Russell! A great artist, full of sensitivity and soul, but he can't resolve one of life's simple problems. Without the Infallible Female, what on earth would he do?

"Last evening," says Nancy, as taut as a lariat, "I stood in the presence of something wonderful, I saw the greatness of a wiry, whipcord-tough giant who could keep alive a dying era! That man still exists — but only in a few scattered canvases!"

Significant pause, then: "After today, maybe that's *all* there'll ever be of him!"

Brother, that's dialogue.

"I'm sorry, Nancy," says Russell, as taut as a 10-gallon hat. "I'll see you at supper."

But he knows that she's right. And he doesn't for various reasons, engage in gunplay with the sodbusters. And he does marry fair Nancy. For details, please consult your nearest art historian.

On the "Mike Douglas Show" the genial host introduced a team of acrobats and added that this particular couple was, indeed, out of the ordinary in one regard — the lady, he explained, holds up the man. The lady, in short, provides the strength.

"I don't think I've ever seen anything like this before," said Mr. Douglas. Well, who has?

And on they trotted, the acrobatic act known as Duvall and Trina. She's a little wisp of a blonde, Trina, and Duvall is a short, husky guy with the bulging forearms of a Tennessee plowboy. But she lifts him on HER shoulders. Is this progress? Or, as the Thinking Man's Disc Jockey, Jean Shepard, suggests in an essay entitled "Captain Ahab Is Dead, Long Live Bob Dylan," is this The Great Role Reversal?

'The Most Scandalous Woman'

"Notorious Woman" was the title affixed to PBS' seven-part "Masterpiece Theater" series about George Sand (actually Amandine Aurore Lucille Dupin), who smoked cigars, wore trousers and wrote books and became, in the early part of the 19th Century, "the most scandalous woman in Paris."

But "notorious?" I can hear Gloria Steinem now, plaintively inquiring: "If the program were about a male, would they have called it 'Notorious Man?'" Of course not. As everyone knows, a man becomes notorious in a number of ways, usually involved with power or money or recognition, which just about taps all the bases. A woman, contrarily, becomes notorious in the public image almost solely in regard to sex.

To phrase this particular thesis another way, a "bad" boy is not quite the same as a "bad" girl, if I make my point and I think I do. Within those rigid confines of conventional morality, I guess Ms. Sand was "notorious," all right.

If the expression had been in vogue, Ms. Sand might well have been called a groupie with artistic leanings. To her great good friend, Chopin, she was "my eternal soul." Victor Hugo called her "my breathless ideal." To Flaubert, she was "my elusive goddess." She knew, in a manner of speaking, everyone.

But George Sand, a pseudonym she borrowed from one of her early lovers, a chap named Sandeau, was also described by Elizabeth Barrett Browning as "the finest female mind of our country or age." And the best of the day's composers, writers, actors, politicians and musicians flocked to her salon, where the conversation often as not dwelled on questions of women's rights.

At the conclusion of the opening episode Alistair Cooke, in his lofty tones, issued this patronizing view: "We can say she was a lady of high birth and low breeding." In other words, "notorious."

Dramatically, this production would hardly qualify as a model of clarity, the pace being recklessly swift and the dialogue, for all its emotion (not to mention its truths), occasionally too pat, too contrived, with too many intrusive echoes of the 1970s. Any minute in that first episode, I expected to hear talk of "consciousness-raising" and other contemporary — and therefore anachronistic — jargon.

Nonetheless, Rosemary Harris, an English actress of tremendous gifts, was just about perfect as George Sand — steely and rebellious and churning with intellect. At the outset, however, she is in her teens, convent-educated and ready to accept the advice tendered by her well-born grandmother (splendidly played by Cathleen Nesbitt).

Grandmama, in these scenes, could have been Mama Gabor passing on the secrets of womahood to Zsa Zsa and Eva. "You've been educated as a great lady," says Grandmama in her worldly fashion. "It's time you looked like one."

Whereupon she dwells on the use of lemon as a hair bleach and, in her phrase, "the arts of makeup."

"Is all this really necessary?" Aurore inquires. "Why must I present a false face to the world?"

"Because," Grandmama informs her with a sigh, "your true face is unspectacular."

Now she is introduced to the clothes of high fashion. "You have so few attributes, we must magnify the good ones," Grandmama suggests with her whim of iron.

"But, Grandmother," says Aurore, "there are other things in life — books, music, being good and kind."

To which Grandmama airily replies: "Goodness and kindness are to be found in nuns and spinsters."

Could Mama Gabor have expressed it better?

A Great Free-Style Talker

Virginia Graham is saying that she won't be competing in the Olympics only because free-style talking has unaccountably been omitted from the competition. A world-class entrant in the volubility sweepstakes, Miss Graham held sway for about 14 years as hostess-conferencier of "Girl Talk."

Miss Graham did not, as some suspect, invent talking. But she did provide a new dimension to the art, giving a high gloss to rusty nouns, adverbs and a stray conjunction or two. As a talker, she is terrific in the sprints and she can also go the distance.

I should add, however, that Miss Graham is by no means gabby. She is, instead, a woman of vast charm and good humor who articulates well.

"Tell me, Virginia, about women," I ventured.

"Women," she said, "are much franker, more honest than men. Ask a man a question and he hedges, he looks around the room, fills his pipe, adjusts his tie and then — even then, mind you — he comes up with a rationalization that may not really be what he's thinking.

"Women are impulsive, amenable to change. But I must say I liked them better before they wanted more applause than their husbands. Women's Lib — I call it Women's Glib — is right on economic conditions but as for Betty Friedan, who wrote 'Feminine Mystique' and started it all, she's a condition. Her husband — former husband now — was strictly Pablum with legs."

Miss Graham went on: "I do want to salute the women of America for one thing — I don't see as many haircurlers as I once did. I much prefer a bald woman to one wearing haircurlers. A bald woman? A Tillie Savalas? And speaking of hair, the worst hairdos in the country are to be found in Los Angeles. I could make a citizen's arrest of half the beauty parlors in L.A."

"Well, it seems to me that —" I began.

"Time was, women would meet to discuss recipes," Miss Graham said. "Now it's hair colors they talk about — this rinse, that rinse. It adds up to one thing — women are more basically honest than men. Of course I dye my hair. Why, I don't know now if I'm gray or not — only my embalmer will know for sure.

"Now men are dyeing their hair but I love a doctor with gray hair or a lawyer or a newscaster. I like to see an accountant with gray hair. It means they're worrying over my money. And I hope everyone at the IRS turns bald!

"And those old goats who marry young girls! I've never seen a young girl marry a poor older man. Marry 'em and they're loaded — with arterial sclerosis. Change of life equals change of wife!"

"What do you think about — ?" I began.

"Listen, life is better in a patriarchal society," Miss Graham said. "Why do we have all these 'Moon children' and this thing they call 'est' and 'TM'? It's because people have nobody to look up to, no heroes, no idols.

"And everybody looks alike. I remember when people in the public eye, in the movies, looked different. You knew who was Carole Lombard and who was Bette Davis. Now I can't tell the Bionic Woman from Laverne and Shirley, or Donny from Marie!"

"But don't you think that — ?" I began.

"Time really does make people look more contemporary," Miss Graham said. "Today I look 20 years younger than I did 20 years ago. The styles help and the makeup helps. And I've learned about eyeshadow. I used to have eyes that when I'd laugh they'd disappear and only the FBI could find them!

"Actually, there's one thing wonderful about today's styles — there's no way it could get any worse. Those T-shirts! Those unisex clothes! We're living in a drip-dry world — too many drips, not enough drys!"

"On the other hand — " I began.

"I like to see women improve and better themselves," Miss Graham said. "When I first interviewed that exercise girl, Debbie Drake, on 'Girl Talk,' I swear I thought she'd graduated cum laude from the third grade. She said to Cornelia Otis Skinner: 'What a wonderful stage name you have!' But Debbie grew and now she's a terrific guest.

"To me, the funniest women in the whole world are the Gabors, including Zsa Zsa, who tickles me. They're outlandish, utterly and devastatingly beautiful creatures. The Gabors make men feel 10 feet tall and I admire any woman who can do that . . ."

Social Note on Joanna

At last count, there was only one actress in Hollywood who could truthfully lay claim to being a native of Boston and a Smith College graduate with a Phi Beta Kappa key. (Of course, there may be dozens around in Hollywood, but this was a quick survey.)

The actress with that rare distinction was Joanna Barnes, an enticing ash blonde whom I met at MGM, where she was guest-starring on some series or other.

On the desk of Miss Barnes' trailer dressing room rested a copy of Cleveland Amory's "Who Killed Society?" It seemed pertinent to ask why she was reading that particular book, a mystery thriller, I believe.

"Oh, I was just kicked out of the Social Register," Miss Barnes announced.

"I'm sorry," I said, sympathetically.

"Well, I'm not," Miss Barnes said, airily. "I'm delighted beyond words. It can mean only one thing, that I've been recognized by the Register as an actress."

"They wrote it up in the Social Register that you're an actress?"

"No, no, no," said Miss Barnes. "The Register has a big thing against the acting profession and such showy nonsense. Once they find out you're in show business — it's out, out, out. So, they must have learned about me, which is wonderful."

I told Miss Barnes that since absolutely no one in my set had ever been kicked out of the Social Register, I wondered as to the procedure. Do they send the malefactor a testy note?

"You'd think they would, wouldn't you?" Miss Barnes said. "But they don't. You're not even informed. One day you look in the Social Register and your name is gone, perhaps forever."

"Then you do feel a slight twinge of regret," I suggested.

Miss Barnes gave momentary thought to the notion. "No," she said. "No. When one's name is in the Register one is always getting throwaway letters from odd outfits requesting money. I won't miss that."

She paused. "On the other hand," she added, "the Social Register is a convenience in size, I mean, in looking up one's friends it's much easier to use the Social Register than the phone book.

"What else shall we talk about?" Miss Barnes said with a warm smile. "I really am a Phi Beta Kappa. I know — your expression is doubtful. For a while there, every other blonde in Hollywood was claiming to be a Phi Beta. But I'm not kidding. You could check with the Phi Beta Kappa people.

"What else? Well, I read a book a day. My reading speed is from 80 to 100 pages an hour. And I write. That's why I use this flashy cigarette holder. I'd be smoking and concentrating on my writing and the cigarette would burn my lips.

"At Smith I was a real campus outcast," she breezed on. "I wouldn't ride a bicycle like everyone else. I wouldn't wear Bermuda shorts like everyone else. So everyone else thought I was a kook. And maybe I am.

"But then, I think actresses should be different from other people, don't you?"

How To Be 'Outrageous'

Once, in writing about Helen Gurley Brown, a biographer saw fit to mention her "capped teeth, padded bra, straightened nose, pancake makeup and wig." Somehow, in beginning an interview with Mrs. Brown, I heard those very same words come rushing haltingly out of my mouth.

"True," she said, nodding, with a beaming smile. "All true. Most girls wear all or part of those things. Being natural is not necessarily the most desirable, the ideal. You know, when I wrote 'Sex and the Single Girl,' and then 'Sex and the Office' and 'Sex and the New Single Girl,' I wasn't writing for the Wellesley graduates. I was writing for girls who may have looked like hummingbirds but inside they felt like birds of paradise."

As she uttered the above, in pleasantly modulated tones, Helen Gurley Brown sat almost motionless on the edge of a couch in her

New York office at Cosmopolitan Magazine, where she holds the editorial reins. I remembered a line from one of her books. In "Outrageous Opinions," she had written, as follows: "Sitting still is sexy." I stopped wiggling in my chair and asked her if that thesis was still valid.

"Sitting still IS sexy," she said. "Being quiet is sexy. It's difficult for a man to get excited over a jittery girl. And a girl can't be expected to go wild for a man who's a nervous scurrier. Long hair on a woman is sexy. Looking straight at a man while you talk is sexy."

Whereupon she turned slightly and looked straight at me. I averted my eyes.

"Are you still outrageous?" I blurted.

"The only way to be outrageous today," Mrs. Brown said, "is to be very old-fashioned — and stick to it."

There is about Helen Gurley Brown an air of quiet candor, an unpretentious calm that seems as guileless as it is disarming. These characteristics she brought to television each Friday on ABC's "Good Morning, America" where, she had replied to a letter-writer's complaint about her usage of "girls" instead of "women."

"It's absurd," Mrs. Brown was saying, "to get into a big flap over 'girls' versus 'women.' In the office here, I might tell my assistant, 'Get the girls together at 4:30 and we'll have a meeting.' It would be ridiculous to say 'women.' But I would use the following sentence, 'Women have different degrees of emotional reaction.' It depends on the context.

"Look, if I have a big talent it lies in a knack of sensibleness. I really have the greatest common sense of anybody I know, aside from other successful women who see through the nonsense and follow their instincts."

"Is it outrageous," I asked, "to follow your instincts?"

Mrs. Brown nodded. "To give your age is outrageous," she said. "I was on the 'Tonight Show' and I asked a young actor how old he was. I thought he was 14. Later, I heard the actor's agent hollering at him, 'Why did you let that bitchy woman ask you such a personal question?'

"It's outrageous, nowadays, to think that living together before marriage is rotten, which I happen to believe. I don't base my feelings on morality. I just think it's grubby, although I think many experiences are desirable before marriage. Sex seems to me far less sexy since it got so permissible and it's not much more than a soapy bath.

"But I still think the sex revolution is fabulous," she said, "and the gains far outweigh any loss in human relationships. Certainly men and women are more alike emotionally than they are different.

"The time is coming," she said, "when it's not at all outrageous for an older woman to be as free to have younger men as an older man is to have younger women. It's all a matter of money. You don't see a penniless, 75-year-old man with young girls. Now women are freer economically and if they are rich, they can-use their money as rich men do, and women, I should add, are just as driving and ambitious as men."

☆　☆　☆

Can one say, with propriety, that a woman edging into her early 40s is as cute as a little red wagon? The phrase belongs to the late John McNulty, a much neglected author, and the description was applied to someone else, but it could have been inspired by a glance at Shirley MacLaine.

She is a great looking woman with the dancer's sleekness of form, reddish hair, very alert and bemused blue eyes, and a smile with enough candlepower to light up an average-sized city for months.

There are those who see her as a dilettante trouble maker, an actress who shouldn't be out stirring up the status quo. Others embrace Shirley MacLaine as an engaging rebel with, perhaps, a touch of naivete. But her talent and the charm are beyond dispute.

As everyone knows, Shirley MacLaine is outspoken (but not by many, as the line goes), but she was saying that her articulated views have never dampened her career. "If my ratings were low or if my pictures didn't make money, then maybe my comments would hurt. As for the press, I suspect they are much more resentful of those stars with the yellow Jaguars who sit by their pools and say nothing quotable."

And that's the truth.

☆　☆　☆

One Star and Two Satellites

I was sitting around one day in the spring of 1977 whistling the theme from "Charlie's Angels" and wondering what it was the shrinks used to do before there was such a fuss over the show and its three stars. One star and two satellites, actually, Farrah Fawcett-Majors being the star, or self-illuminating body, and Kate Jackson and Jaclyn Smith filling out the marquee, not to mention the bikinis it seems necessary for them to wear to solve all those mysteries.

As a newspaperman, I must say that I have a certain indebtedness to psychologists and psychiatrists for their quotability. You want a quote, you go to a shrink and you are repaid with marvelous glibness, solid, well-rounded quotes with a slick patina of scientific phraseology. They can make words dance, those shrinks, and, as I say, they are invaluable in fleshing out a story.

I see in TV Guide, for instance, that one psychiatrist in Los Angeles says about the Fawcett-Majors phenomenon: "The key to the whole thing is that men think of her as a sexpot and women invariably describe her as 'adorable.' When women call another woman 'adorable,' that means she poses no threat to them in terms of seducing their husbands . . ."

And another psychiatrist says: "She's a throwback to Lana Turner' and Brigitte Bardot. She seems to have skipped the whole unpleasant decade of the 1960s, which people want to forget."

☆   ☆   ☆

Terrific. All deeply analytical. All based on years of study of the human condition, the vexing problems of our existence. All students of the mind with staggering insight.

And all evasive of a simple truth which was articulated by Farrah herself, to wit: "When the show was No. 3, I thought it was our acting. When we got to be No. 1, I decided it could only be because none of us wears a bra."

I guess the shrinks didn't notice. Turn now to a recent edition of The Star, subtitled "The American Women's Weekly," which has a special panel of psychiatrists employed to come to grips with the issue of "Charlie's Angels." One of them, a Dr. Anthony Pietropinto, of New York, had this to say:

"Farrah is emerging as a sex symbol of almost a Marilyn Monroe magnitude. Yet she is very different from previous sex symbols such as Monroe, Betty Grable, Rita Hayworth and Ava Gardner who all had a remote type of glamor.

"A man could fantasize about seeing them in the Casbah or in some plush far-out nightclub, but he wouldn't dream of running into them in some ordinary way. But Farrah is the kind of girl you could fantasize about running into in Central Park."

Anyone who would harbor such a fantasy has obviously never set foot on the bleak greensward of Central Park. But press on, doctor:

"She's a very down-to-earth, active type of girl. Farrah doesn't seem to be haughty or unapproachable, but has a friendly attitude, a very chummy, down-to-earth attitude rather than a remote sex goddess aura. Men are finding this very appealing.

"In her role in 'Charlie's Angels,' Farrah is a very competent girl and today's man is relating to this kind of woman ... someone he feels is very competent and self-assured. Men are beginning to feel they have enough responsibility as it is and they are looking for women who can share life's responsibilities with them.

"Another aspect of Farrah's tremendous sex appeal is her long, wild hair. Long hair emphasizes the sex difference, especially now that men are getting away from the long hair they were wearing during the hippie era."

Now he turns to the other two angels, as follows: "Jaclyn Smith in some ways has a more classical beauty than Farrah ... Farrah has an almost hardness about her that Jaclyn just doesn't. In fact, she is the softest of the three. Jaclyn is the more demure type ... Even in her role on the show, although she is active, she seems to be the least physical of the three. Jaclyn is the kind of girl you would most want to protect.

"Kate seems as if she could be a home girl and perhaps the one most like 'the girl next door.' She seems to be the most quick-witted, the one most given to making jokes, the one with the most leadership qualities. Kate is the kind of girl a man could fantasize being married to. You can see Kate going to pick up your kids at school. But you couldn't fantasize Farrah or Jaclyn sitting in on a PTA meeting ..."

And if you believe any of this, I've got some swampland in Florida that you might be interested in buying.

A Mirror of The Times

On the subject of Women's Liberation, television is, as one might expect, a mirror of the times, demonstrably stylish, even chic in its pronouncements. Suddenly, in the mid-'70s, news sources on TV were referred to as "spokespersons," a language-jarring phrase uttered by women, usually young and pretty, known as "anchorpersons."

When television did tackle the women's movement, conceivably a social eruption as far-reaching in altering the structure of our lives as television itself, it did so in terms of trite, superficial, cliche-ridden pop-sociology — three hours worth, for example, on a special entitled "Of Women and Men," a sequence of billing that could hardly go unnoticed. The co-hosts were Barbara Walters and Tom Snyder, also announced in that order.

At one point, a commentator interviewed by Miss Walters told the viewers that pinup pictures in the men's magazines, from the old and innocent petty drawings in the Esquire of the '40s to the more specific and pinkly enticing photographs in Playboy and Penthouse, are "like trophies." They are, further, she insisted angrily, reflective of "male hostility" to women. Then there were glimpses offered of the new phenomenon of nude male centerfolds but not a word was uttered about any likelihood of "female hostility" toward men.

After the show, in New York alone 260 phone calls were received the following day. Of that number, 200 expressed approval, 30 complained of being deprived of regular programming, others saw the show as "demeaning" to housewives, still others, a minority, decried the low-cut gowns that adorned Miss Walters, usually most circumspect in her dress. Why Miss Walters chose a program on Women's

Liberation to go glamorous and low-cut remains a puzzlement for students of human behavior to ponder. Tom Snyder, the purists noted, retained the same dark blue suit throughout.

It was also inevitable and, possibly, a sign of the times that television would cloak its most cherished and enduring product, the western, in terms that Feminist Gloria Steinem would find praiseworthy. A brace of such films came along, in one recent season, both of them easily catalogued as a new form — a new Maiden-form, one might say — namely, the Women's Lib western.

In a distant time, the westerns were pure and simple, like the western hero who might say, to lasso a line out of memory: "Saddle yourself a horse and I'll swear you in with the others and then we'll track down that no-good, hoss-thievin' side-winder." Then came the psychological western, in which a posse is rounded up by having a mass group therapy session and the town shrink picks out the most qualified riders. And by that time the no-good, hoss-thievin' side-winder has galloped clear out of the country, beyond the Pecos.

Television went from the psychological western to the adult western to the eastern-western — there is no other word to describe the pretentious drivel called "Kung Fu" — and then, by the ghost of William S. Hart, there arrived the Women's Lib western. It came, unheralded, in an episode of an ABC series called "The Cowboys." It is necessary here to document the full rich progression of the story line which began with Pippa Scott, an actress with a firm chin and crisp voice, passing through town.

In contrast to the Annie Oakleys of another TV era, always portrayed as dead-eyed sharpshooters who smiled sweetly, Pippa is a professional faro dealer and she gets into a friendly game of poker with the town's leading citizens. She cleans them out. Soon thereafter, the men sign a complaint, charging her with the ignoble practice of dealing seconds, or the card second from the top. She is aghast at the accusation. Confronted by the marshal, she admits that she is, indeed, a professional at dealing. "I also play poker," she says. "I never dealt seconds in my life. I never had to."

"You won that money honestly?" the marshal asks.

"I did," she says. "Not that it will make any difference."

Then she uncorks the zinger. "A man," she says, "gets a reputation for being a card player and people line up, just beggin' to lose. But let 'em sit down with a woman and get up with empty pockets — will they give her credit for card sense or know-how? No sir! A woman only wins by cheatin'. Code of the West."

As the marshal learns, she was right. It turns out that the leading citizens had actually been trying to cheat *her*, and then, that failing, they accused her of cheating them. This is known as Male Chauvinist Hog Gall, western-style. Later, the marshal, hand on his gun, faces these loathsome fellows and his eyes turn narrow and he says: "I suppose it didn't occur to any of you that she might simply be better at the game than you are? No, I guess not, bein' a woman ..."

☆ ☆ ☆

The second example of the Women's Lib western unfolded in a TV yarn called "Sidekicks." In this one, Larry Hagman and Lou Gossett found themselves facing a girl, played by Blythe Danner, with a rifle in her hands. It is pointed at them.

"Give me one good reason," says Hagman, "why I shouldn't walk over and take that rifle away from you."

"Because," she snaps, "I'd shoot off both your eyes before you could take a step."

"That's a good reason," he says.

Later in the film, he says to her: "Whatever happened to those sweet, nice, gentle girls?"

By way of reply, she promptly decks him with the straightest left hook this side of Muhammad Ali.

As a counter-ploy to these shows, another one of recent vintage called "Planet Earth" was a futuristic TV epic set in the year 2133 in a female-dominated society known as the Confederacy of Ruth. There the males are bought and sold like captive animals. "It's Women's Lib gone mad," cries actor John Saxon, playing an American astronaut from the 1980s who is somehow thrust into this strange and perilous new world.

Gene Roddenberry, a producer known as the creator of "Star Trek," conceived this show, an outgrowth of his theory that if the women did take over, they would be fiercer in their dominance than any man ever dreamed of being. These women in the Confederacy of Ruth are also pretty fierce toward each other.

"He is my property," says one woman, referring to her male captive. Another woman comes up and belts her one in the kisser.

"He *was* your property," she says, taking the guy and dragging him off to — to what? To a fate worse than death, probably.

Out of This World

Many here said it before and I will repeat that television reaches its great fulfillment in recording events live, as they are happening. This immediacy was best reflected in the coverage of the big story of the '60s — the advent of man into space.

Over a span of years, the television cameras were at hand as the heretofore unknown names popped into our consciousness — John Glenn, Neil Armstrong, Wally Schirra, the latter an astronaut who went on to become a most lucid and welcome commentator on such events on TV.

There was something extraordinarily dramatic about television's space coverage and then, suddenly, space flights became commonplace. I miss those flights and the excitement they afforded. In a decade that saw the nation torn apart by a war in Indochina and riots on the campuses and in the ghettoes, by the awful trauma of assassinations and revelations of Watergate, space was a positive achievement that exalted rather than demeaned us.

Space gave us a collective pride and unity — space, moreover, was mighty terrific television and the memories are good to cherish.

Man's First Small Step

"We've seen some kind of a birth here," said Eric Sevareid in the wake of man's first small step up there on the moon in July, 1969. "This new world, this new reality ... They've peered into another life." A new world and a new reality and there it was, unfolding hour

135

after hour on the television screen, a series of events at once humbling and ennobling. It was beautiful.

And we all knew, as the ghostly figures walked at first hesitantly and then so coltishly on that alien planet, that man and the moon would never again be the same. We had climbed our extra-terrestrial Everest.

And, with proper irony, the landing by Neil Armstrong and Buzz Aldrin occurred only hours before the dawn of the day that the ancients, with due sense of awe, named for the moon — Monday.

There was so much to be said and the commentators, wherever you spun the dial, said most of it. Walter Cronkite, the iron man at CBS' mike, observed: "An era, an age has come to an end — the thousands of years in which man stood down here on this small planet and thought, wrote and dreamed of the moon. He gave it names, and gods and goddesses ... composed sonnets about its reflected light and its loneliness ... planted, harvested, navigated, worshiped and romanced beneath its lull and under its spell ...

"Starting today," Cronkite went on, "with this proof that man can leave the earth and land safely on another celestial body, he is now unlikely to be slowed in his stride to go elsewhere in the solar system ... but as we touch this first milestone the nostalgia still remains, at least for most of us ...

"In a generation or two, the nostalgia will be gone ... when those who are too young to remember this day will be grown up ... and unable to remember what it might have been like before and it's kind of sad, isn't it?"

Nostalgia? Well, there was Steve Allen, on ABC, plunking away on the piano and singing all the old moon songs — "Carolina Moon" and "Moon Over Miami" and "Harvest Moon" and on and on. No matter what leaps mankind may take in the future, one thing remains ever constant — moon will always rhyme with June.

And between commentators, there was banter. On NBC, Frank McGee turned at one point to David Brinkley and asked: "Would you like to be the first newsman on the moon?"

"Certainly," Brinkley said.

"You answered too quickly. Why do you want to go?"

"Why not?"

"Not good enough," McGee persisted. "Why?"

Brinkley drew a breath. "For one thing," he began, thoughtfully now, "I'd go as journalist, as you would ... presumably we'd go to do a job of reporting instead of science. They're preoccupied with their work, which is great — very great. But I do know a little bit about news." He paused. "When a poet does land on the moon," he added, "he'll have been put there by the engineers."

And always, there was a persistent reaffirmation of man. In Rome, an Italian space scientist was telling CBS' Winston Burdett: "Why send a man to the moon? A man has initiative, imagination, intelligence. A machine can only obey orders."

Wally Schirra, the astronaut (and an invaluable commentator working with Cronkite), saw the American flag implanted in the moon's bleak terrain. Then he said, softly, "There's no way an automated system could put up a flag such as that ..."

How Much Is the Fare?

One of the most fascinating items to emerge from the epochal 30-hour telecast of the Armstrong-Aldrin moonshot, the biggest TV spectacular of them all, was the brief interview with the president of Pan Am Airlines, who talked about future commercial flights to the moon. He seemed altogether serious about this.

Being a fellow who likes to plan ahead, I placed a call to Pan Am and inquired about the availability of seats on their first moon trip. A girl replied that I should write to Pan Am's Boston office and then I'd be placed on the waiting list. I said I'd be happy to do that.

Later, I phoned American Airlines and the man who answered said they were indeed accepting reservations for the moon right now. "Give me your name and address," he suggested, "and when we have our first flight scheduled we'll let you know immediately."

"When do we take off?"

"Oh, sometime in the early 1980s," he said. "Maybe around 1985 or, at the most, 1990. One, two, five years either way. But don't hold me to it."

"Of course," I agreed. "How many seats will you have and, listen, how much is the fare?"

"We'll seat about 40 people," he said. "So far the CAB hasn't approved a fare for the moon, but I figure it'll be over $1,000. Closer to $3.000"

I whistled. "Hey, that's a lot of money," I told the man from American. "Is it possible you may have something less, uh, stratospheric?"

"You think we're asking for the moon, do you?" the man said, chuckling. "But, look, it's a long way up there. It'll be comfortable, though, I assure you, in our Astrojet — that's what our rockets will be called."

"Is that $3,000 for first class?"

"We'll only have one class," he said. "That's on account of the way the rockets will be constructed."

"How long will it take?"

"Beats me," the man at American said. "We'll probably stop and refuel at a space station about 200 miles out, which should take a few hours. Probably change rockets, too. We'll save a lot of fuel departing from a space station. Well, check back in a year, won't you?"

When I phoned Continental Airlines, a man there said they had a waiting list for their inaugural moon flight but he wasn't sure of the exact date. He told me not to be in too much of a hurry.

"By the way," he said, "are you calling from San Diego?"

"Yes," I said.

"Well," he said, doubtfully, "I don't know whether we'll have nonstop flights to the moon from San Diego. We'll probably blast off from L. A."

"Naturally," I said. "How much will the trip cost?"

"That depends on whether it's first class, coach, economy or excursion," he said. "Our price isn't set yet but we hear the other airlines are thinking in terms of $2,800 for a round trip, based on mileage."

"Will you serve drinks?"

"By all means," said the man from Continental. "It's such a long trip I think we'll have to relax the two-drink rule. We want our passengers to be happy."

I phoned PSA and inquired about their moon service. "Well, we're not an interstate airline, you know," a girl said. "But if California decides to annex the moon . . ."

Finally, I called United Airlines. "On the telecast the other night," I said, "they had the head man at Pan Am talking about commercial flights to the moon. Do you people have any such plans for taking reservations to go to the moon?"

"The moon?" cried the girl at United. "They won't let us go nonstop to Honolulu!"

Song Titles Into Orbit

On the lighter side of the moon, you should know that Johnny Tillotson, who writes songs and sings them, quickly cranked out a tune with the tender title, "The Dust on the Moon Ain't as Pretty as the Powder on Your Nose." And now, of course, it's out on record.

Speaking of records, another songwriter recorded an item called "There's an American Flag on the Moon," sung by Jon and Robin, and rushed it out to radio stations across the land with a warning to disc jockeys: "Under no condition are you to play this record unless the moon flight is successful."

Jimmy Webb, who had already made a bundle with "Up, Up and Away," also joined the lists with a song he calls "Everybody Gets to the Moon." And all the singers you can name suddenly added "Fly Me to the Moon" to their repertoires.

And Al Zimbalist, a producer who specializes in science-fiction, registered a movie title with the Motion Picture Association's Title Bureau — "Sea of Tranquility."

What else? Well, they're hoisting a friendly glass to the big event, with innovations. A club in Texas introduced a new drink called a Moonshot, served with a tiny American flag — you salute before you swallow. In Cocoa Beach, Fla., near the launch site, a barkeep put together something he calls a Moon Glow to sell at $1.25, with plenty of takers.

And columnist Hank Grant, in Hollywood, referred to a just-divorced movie couple as being "as split as the Eagle module and Columbia."

Along more serious lines, perhaps the most gifted and certainly the most eloquent of today's science-fiction writers, Ray Bradbury, turned up on NBC to discuss the implications of the moonshot with Roy Neal.

"It has everything to do with immortality," Bradbury pointed out. "We've been asking the questions for thousands of years. We've gone to our theologians. We've said, 'What is life? What is it all about? What are we doing here?' The great mystery stands at the center of everything.

"The theologians have tried to help us ... But the mystery remains. And we've gone to our scientists and we've said, 'Tell us about the atom and the molecule and the stars.' And they've done their very best ... But the mystery remains."

Bradbury continued: "So now we come to this time when we've asked ourselves, 'Why bother being alive? Why be born upon this earth if we must die? What are our chances for survival?' And suddenly the space age gives us our huge chance to survive forever.

"Once we make it to the moon, once we touch down on Mars, once we move on to the stars and go to planets revolving around stars so far away we can't even imagine it ... Once we do this we become the thing that we've always wanted to become, and that is immortal ...

"The race doesn't have to die. It doesn't have to be destroyed by the dying of the sun ... And in future generations, other races of people, other generations ... will look back to this summer and say, 'Oh, how wonderful it must have been to have been alive then when this huge step which insures the victory over time and space and eternity for all of us, how wonderful to have been alive when that happened.'"

Astronauts Face the Press

Neil, Buzz and Mike. They have, somehow, achieved the warm familiarity of faces in a family album. We went with them to the moon, Neil and Buzz, and we felt their cool elation as they descended cautiously and then, briefly, frolicked on the moon's alien surface before getting down to scientific business, such as picking up rocks.

Somewhere I remember reading that Dr. Harold Urey, watching intently as Armstrong and Aldrin hopped around joyously on the moon, suddenly rose and blurted at the TV screen: "Oh, hurry up and get the samples!"

And now they're on the tube again — Neil Armstrong, Buzz Aldrin and Mike Collins. (There's a campaign afoot by a Madison Avenue agency to have people, when they want a Tom Collins, to ask the barkeep for a Mike Collins.)

At one point, in answer to a query, they discussed the philosophic implications of their jaunt to the moon. "What this means," said Buzz Aldrin, "is that many other problems can be solved." Mike Collins mentioned the "near" and "far" term results, citing "a nation's will, economy and attention to detail."

Neil Armstrong summed it up well. "I just see it as a beginning," said the commander of Apollo 11. "Not this flight but the whole program is the beginning of a new age."

And it was Armstrong who summoned up the best answer when a reporter asked: "How will you restore some normalcy to your lives?" Neil glanced at the vast assemblage of reporters and grinned. "It kind of depends on you," he said.

The Sporting Life

My first dream, after disposing of such childhood fantasies as riding the range and getting rid of anyone wearing a black hat, was to be a major league shortstop. It lasted, that dream, until the pitchers started throwing curves. There are physicists who have proclaimed that a baseball does not curve, that it is an illusion of the eye. To those doubters I say get out of the laboratory and onto the diamond and grip a bat in your hands and see what happens when the catcher uses two fingers outstretched for a signal to the pitcher. The ball, believe me, will curve. And possibly drop.

Given embarrassing first-hand demonstrations of this phenomenon, I elected to write about the athletes instead of becoming one. Although I was diverted into television (which fortunately includes sports and just about everything else imaginable), my interest has never waned. It seems to me not a bad thing that sports on television has shaped our viewing habits. The fights, the Monday night football, the baseball, the Olympics, all of these televised events have done no appreciable damage to the national psyche. Nor to mine, either.

In fact, of all the activities offered on TV, I find writing about sports the most enjoyable. So long as nobody throws a curve.

Wide World of Words

The thing about the fight guys is the great way they talk. Their language has its own style and rhythm and its own way, sometimes, of cutting right into the truth. For anyone handicapping the field, one of the best talkers around has to be Angelo Dundee, who handles Muhammad Ali and who was on hand at ringside with Howard Cosell, the announcer, for the Sonny Liston-Henry Clark bout in San Francisco. This was televised in 1968 on ABC's "Wide World of Sports."

Never mind the fight. Even for television, which has fewer and fewer great ones (when was the last great TV fight — Archie Moore and Yvon Durelle? And when was that, back in '59?), the Liston-Clark match wasn't much to see. Even on a dull, gray afternoon, it wasn't much even for the buffs.

Still, it was beautiful listening to Angelo Dundee, a wise old fight guy introduced by Cosell as "the renowned, diminutive fight manager." Bespectacled, too, which Cosell left out and I fault him for it. A guy wears glasses around the fights — he's "bespectacled" and Cosell loses points for not having the word up high in his description.

First, on "Wide World," they had a six-round preliminary event, with a pair of tigers named Jimmy Gilmore, who is obese but surprisingly strong and agile, and someone named Harold Dutra. I liked what Angelo had to say about Dutra. Angelo said the words and I wrote them down immediately out of sheer admiration. My business is supposed to be words but right here I bow to Angelo Dundee of the fights.

"Dutra," he summed up, "is a good banger but his chin is suspect."

You could set it to music, that one line of Angelo's. How many different ways is it possible to say that a prize fighter may be able to throw out a punch but most likely can't take a hard one himself? You can say it a lot of ways, even poetically. But if you want the thought expressed with verve and color, you have got to find yourself an Angelo Dundee.

The prelim bout ended, finally, and Howard and Angelo turned their attention to the main event. A few days earlier, Clark tossed out a little publicity gimmick. He sent a wire to TV editors across the land, urging all of us to watch him go after Liston. The wire said how he may not be famous now but we should watch him on "Wide World of Sports" and, wait and see, one day he'd be champion.

"That's not brag," the wire from Clark said, "that's fact."

Just before the fight, Cosell was afflicted with a disarming burst of honesty. It was no championship bout, Cosell said about this thing between Liston and Clark, but it would be interesting. Cosell gave it a terrific soft-sell here — to see if Sonny Liston could make a comeback at 36, the age he claims and which he might be.

"Liston," said Cosell, "has been going around town, waving a birth certificate that says he's 36, showing it to everybody who wants to look."

This prompted another great line from Angelo. Watching these films of Liston in training, Angelo said, almost wistfully: "I wanna see what Father Time has taken outa the guy."

Angelo said about Sonny's opponent: "If he can live with Liston, it might end up a late-round fight."

And Cosell, not to be outdone in terms of language, said about Liston: "He is desperately dreaming of regaining the championship . . . even with the odds seemingly overwhelmingly against him."

There were some very good films of the two fighters, Liston at work and play in his new hometown of Las Vegas, and Clark in the gym and around the neighborhood. Referring to Clark, Cosell said: "The streets of San Francisco are his haven." I was ready to give that line to Angelo but it was Cosell's unmistakable voice that said it.

About the fight itself, what can I tell you? It went seven and all Liston. Clark is no stiff but he's no challenger, either. He never seemed to have a real chance going for him. All he did was absorb punishment and here, I think, my man Angelo wrapped it all up.

"You don't win fights by taking punches," Angelo said. "You gotta throw leather."

Talk about turning phrases, Liston was right in there, too. "He came out fresh, didn't he?" Cosell said to Liston in the post-fight interview.

Liston nodded and almost smiled. "I don't mess with 'em when they're fresh," Sonny said.

A State of Mind — Or Two

Ever since the baseball teams launched their run for the gonfalon, as they say over on sports side, players on both the Los Angeles (formerly Brooklyn) Dodgers and the San Francisco (formerly New York) Giants have been interviewed innumerable times on radio and TV.

My rough estimate is that there have been 1,789 such interviews, all of them starting out with the same question: "Well, Peewee (or Gil or Hank or Willie), how do you like California?"

It's a hospitable question, all right, but it isn't very precise, geographically, and it can lead to pitfalls. Freshly sprung from the East, these ball players believe that California is — well, California.

They can't be expected to know what every schoolboy out here learns at his mother's knee — that California is one state but it embraces several sharply divergent states of mind.

These ballplayers want to endear themselves at the outset as they fit, Dodger and Giant, into their respective communities. And I say they deserve every possible assistance.

Therefore, as a service to promote togetherness and good will, I should like to offer a ready-made set of answers the players can use to the same questions in radio and TV interviews.

First, the answers the Dodgers may use in Los Angeles:

"Well, (name of player), how do you like California?"

"Like it? I love it, especially your grand freeways. I won me a drag race my first day here."

"How about our wonderful California climate?"

"Love it, especially your wonderful smog. Best thing in the world for my sinus. I had a real bad condition in Brooklyn."

"Have you learned some of our wonderful California traditions?"

"You bet. I went to Grauman's Chinese Theater and set my shoes in Clark Gable's footprints. Really gives a fellow a sense of history."

"What do you plan to do in your off-hours away from the ballpark?"

"Naturally, I'll go to the movies — what else would anyone do in California?"

"May I, incidentally, compliment you on your California attire?"

"Thanks. My tailor specializes in these rainbow checked jackets and purple-on-beige striped trousers. The chartreuse bowtie is my own idea."

"How about hats?"

"Never wear a hat — not with all this glorious fresh air and sunshine."

"What kind of a season do you think you'll have?"

"A wonderful season, on account of I'll drink all that vitamin-packed, tasty California orange juice. You want the inside story on why I didn't play so good in spring training? Our camp was in Florida."

"Thank you, (name of player) — you're a true citizen of California!"

Here are the answers the Giants may use in San Francisco:

"Well, (name of player), how do you like California?"

"Like it? I love it, especially your wonderful hills and cable cars. My first day I rode on the cable cars 86 times. Also, I signed 67 petitions not to replace them with buses."

"How about our wonderful California climate?"

"Love it, especially your wonderful fog. It's the best thing in the world for my tired blood."

"Have you learned some of our wonderful California traditions?"

"You bet. I can't wait to get up to the Top o' the Mark and dress up for the opera and ride the ferry boat to the city across the bay, whose name, of course, I forget. Ah yes, Paris reminds me of San Francisco, if you get my distinction. Once I met a man who called it Frisco. I thrashed him."

"What do you plan to do in your off-hours away from the ballpark?"

"Naturally, I'll listen to bearded poets recite their works by candlelight, accompanied by modern jazz — what else would anyone do in California?"

"May I, incidentally, compliment you on your California attire?"

"Thanks. My tailor mistakenly left an ounce of padding in the right shoulder. The matter now rests in the hands of my lawyers."

"How about hats?"

"Like any cosmopolitan man of the world. I'm never without one. But, say, I hear there's a settlement south of here where the men don't wear hats. Must be barbarians."

"What kind of a season do you think you'll have?"

"A wonderful season. Let's drink to it. Mix mine very dry, please. And, if you don't mind, leave out the olive, as I am in training."

"Thank you, (name of player) — you're a true citizen of California!"

The Run For the Roses

Once, while riding a bus, I noticed that virtually all of my fellow passengers were reading newspapers. Then we went into a tunnel and the bus lights dimmed and the reading halted — except for one fellow sitting in front of me. He had a pencil in his hand. He was, in that tunnel, in the shadows, still reading the Racing Form.

A little darkness never stopped a horseplayer and it is 8 to 5 that this anonymous busrider, if his luck and his vision are holding up, joined the rest of us in watching ABC's telecast of the 1977 Kentucky Derby. "If you haven't seen a Kentucky Derby," Irvin S. Cobb used to say, "you ain't seen nothing and you ain't been no place!"

Now we get the Kentucky Derby on the TV in our homes and it's still a grand show. "It is a hot and humid afternoon," said ABC's Jim McKay, "a kind of day that usually depresses the human spirit, but not here. The mint julep is selling like soda pop."

Jim as always captured the mood, the essence, of the event and also its social implications, the elite having assembled along with the $2 bettors. "Lord Derby is here from England," McKay informed us, "and Baron Rothschild is also here." That last name Jim pronounced as though it were spelled "Roth-sheeld." But I don't argue with McKay about the nuances of the language. I remember when we were touring Montreal just before the '76 Olympics, that only Jim McKay knew the derivation of the word, Velodrome. The Velodrome is the name of a large sporting arena where many of the events were held.

A scholar of Latin and Greek, McKay coolly explained: " 'Velo,' from which we get velocity, refers to speed. 'Drone' is from dromedary. A Velodrome, therefore, is a place for fast camels. Common knowledge."

Then, on our screens, there came the magnificently sentimental moment when the band strikes up the theme song of this storied test of horseflesh — "My Old Kentucky Home," of course. Said McKay: "There is a tremor in the fingers, a queasiness in the stomach ... That song does something to you."

It really does, especially when the band hits the part that goes,

"Weep no more, my lady." It's a terrific moment and I was really sore at myself because all through the rendition I was thinking of the twice-told tale about the soprano in a concert singing "My Old Kentucky Home."

A man in the front row started to cry and soon his sobbing filled the hall.

Afterward, the soprano said to him: "I couldn't help but notice that you were crying all the time I was singing 'My Old Kentucky Home.' Tell me, sir, are you a Kentuckian?"

"No," the man said, "I'm a musician."

Anyway, it was a splendid race for the TV cameras and Chick Anderson gave it a crisp and knowing call. Beforehand, however, there were aspersions cast on the character of the eventual winner, Seattle Slew. "The alleged superhorse," Howard Cosell had said, loftily.

Now you know that Howard Cosell is more at home in the more rough-and-tumble events, at the fights or in pro football. Certain phrases from the sport of kings do not exactly tumble trippingly from the Cosell tongue, to wit: "While there is a certain similarity in their conformation, Secretariat was certainly the leggier horse."

All the same, Howard Cosell at any sporting event is a presence to conjure with. "YES," said Howard in his soothing tones, "FIVE TIMES THIS MAN'S WON THE KENTUCKY DERBY!"

Now the voice softens dramatically: "So we are proud to be with him — Eddie Arcaro! Tell me about Seattle Slew, Eddie Arcaro. Can he be beaten? How would you ride him?"

To which Eddie (Banana Nose) Arcaro replied: "I'd like to steal five, six lengths ahead right away, run him, keep him moving. Then in the stretch have him run a breather, we call it."

Now it was post time and Cosell and Arcaro observed the horses as they assembled untidily in the starting gate. Suddenly, Cosell blurts: "Eddie Arcaro has a statement to make! Make it, Eddie!"

"He's broke out," Arcaro said about Seattle Slew, who was jumpy. "He's lathering all over."

"What about his post position?"

"That has nothing to do with his disposition," Eddie Arcaro said.

"What does this betoken to you?" Cosell asked.

"It's not going to help," Arcaro said.

And then it was over and Arcaro was explaining Seattle Slew's recovery from an uncertain start: "He seemed dissatisfied to just set there."

Later, the winners took their bows and Jim McKay, a master linguist, said to the French jockey, Jean Cruguet: "Formidab'!" Jim, you know, stands something under 5 feet 7, or less, and is president of a group he chooses to call the World Association of Men of

Average Height. No doubt he was recruiting the jock for membership.

Dizzy Dean At the Mike

"This boy," said Dizzy Dean during a broadcast, referring to a pitcher with a particularly deceptive motion, "can pick you off between pats."

Between pats? Between pitches did he mean? Between the base baths? Between pats, as when a base runner is patting the dust from his uniform? Frankly, I still have no idea what Jay Hanna (Dizzy) Dean had in mind except that the words had a marvelous ring and flow to them and they were characteristically Dean.

Dizzy Dean was the most amusing, the most effortlessly entertaining and distinctively colorful broadcaster ever to face a microphone and now that he is gone there is, surely, less laughter in the world.

It was H. Allen Smith, the humorist, who reported once on Dean's problems in enunciating the commercials he had to read on his baseball telecasts. One afternoon, according to Smith, Dizzy stumbled his way through a lengthy commercial and then he concluded with: "I admit I cain't read good. But they's one thing I know. When that pitcher thows that ball, he thows it. When that ketcher ketches it, he ketches it. An' when that hitter hits it, he hits it. That's all you gotta know, folks."

It was typically Dean to minimize his special gifts in broadcasting the games. His pitching he could brag on. But announcing, to Diz, was a piece of cake. In the 1974 season, Dizzy was invited to sit in as the first of the celebrity guests on NBC's Monday Night Baseball.

For years, beginning in New York in 1950, Dizzy had announced baseball and until 1965, he shared the booth with Pee Wee Reese on CBS' Game of the Week. But he had been away and someone asked Diz if he were nervous about his return.

"Naw," said Diz. "All I gotta watch is fellas slidin', walkin', thowin' and hittin'."

Listening to ol' Diz that Monday night, his classic delivery unchanged, it was good to reflect on the impact he had over the years as an early day Don Meredith, a free spirit who brought frivolity and irreverence to a game increasingly grown more soberly gray flannel.

One couldn't help but notice, that night, the inroad of subtle refinements, how Dizzy had become, if possible, even more graphic, more linguistically alive.

When the Houston infielders spread out in the McCovey shift, for instance, with all the gloves to the right of second base, the pitcher looked lonely to ol' Diz.

"He looks," said Dean, "like he's by hisself out there."

Dizzy was always turning phrases that struck the ear from a bizarre tilt. Once, as the cameras were fixed on a slow athlete, Dizzy commented: "He runs too long in one place. He's got a lotta up 'n' down, but not much forward."

And there was the time that Diz startled grammarians across the land with his description of a player he had just spotted on the field. Said Diz: "He resembles Crosetti like he used to look."

I don't think I was alone in listening to Dizzy with vast delight at the sheer vitality of his speech, his eloquence in making words work for him, creating phrases that skittered and danced. There were no wallflowers in Dizzy Dean's vocabulary.

"Wal, folks," said Dean as he called a game in San Francisco, "them Gi'nts has got a lotta long ways to go." (Only Dizzy would have inserted that deliciously redundant "lotta" — ah, but what a difference one word makes.)

"Wal, fans, you seen it on yore screen," Dizzy would say. "The right fielder went in there runnin' and made a real good strang catch." (A shoestring catch — what else?)

It was Dizzy who turned the past participle of "slide" into the more lilting "slud." He would talk about an out that "retarrs" the side. To Diz, hard-hit balls — he called them "blue-darters" — would "karm" off a fielder's glove. An infielder would commit an "air" and then walk "disgustilly" back to his position.

And when telegrams flowed in from places like Anoka, Minn., or Bedford, Tex., or Enid, Okla., well, he'd just take time out, with no "pliminaries," to "knowledge all these warrs."

Dizzy always tried to be helpful. "You might as well try to argy with a stump," he said once on the futility of disputing an umpire's decision.

Then, after a momentary reflection, he explained: "Some of you big city folks mightn't not know what a stump is. Wal, I'll tellya, a stump is a wood thing . . . Wal, it's somethin' a tree has been cut down off of."

Dizzy Dean attacked the language as he once threw a baseball — naturally, with the great zest and flavor of a man who enjoyed fully the inhale and exhale of life. It was a joy that he shared with all of us.

Memories of Bill Stern

There was Roger Mudd on the CBS Evening News and he was reminiscing about the late Bill Stern, a sportscaster from out of the 1930s and '40s and a master in infusing an event with his own personal sense of drama.

Stern belonged to the era of old radio, a medium which lent itself to the natural excitement of his voice, his skill at painting word pictures for the listener and his vivid and free-wheeling imagination.

Television presented other, more exacting demands and the late

Bill Stern fell into a gradual decline. All the same, many of today's sports announcers express their debt to Stern's professionalism at the mike and say they found inspiration in his broadcasting style, as intimately colorful as it was dramatic.

So there was Roger Mudd talking about Bill Stern and recalling, wistfully, how Stern once told his radio audience of the circumstances that led to Thomas Alva Edison's deafness. It happened, Stern related, during a baseball game — Stern believed implicitly that every great man had once played baseball — and the pitcher whose beanball struck Edison on the ear was a rather well-known outlaw named Jesse James.

Let the historians tell us that Edison's deafness was attributed to a conductor who boxed his ears when he was a candy butcher working the trains as a boy. It seems unlikely that Thomas Edison and Jesse James, two disparate figures, ever crossed paths. But Stern, given a choice, inevitably spurned dull truth for charming, if concocted, myth.

For nearly 15 years, Stern related his fanciful yarns on NBC's "Sports Newsreel," creating his own world where Frank Merriwell heroes roamed diamond and gridiron and coincidences could be stretched to infinite convenience. Carefree in the face of facts, a teller of tall tales, Stern was never one to feel hindered by the irksome confines of journalism.

In time, the purists complained, and the network began to preface Stern's program with the airy disclaimer that his stories were "partly fact, partly hearsay."

Even "hearsay" was a generous term, with its implication that Stern's entertaining whoppers were culled from the realm of legend. Actually, they were the products of a collective imagination — Stern's and his writers'. It was a Stern trademark, moreover, to withhold the name of his hero until the final triumphant line: "And that man was —." Then the name and usually a famous one.

Connoisseurs of vintage Stern like to recall a typical tall tale which began, as Stern told it, with Grantland Rice, the sportswriter, watching a skinny young boxer sparring in a gym. Later, the sportswriter heard the skinny youngster singing in the shower. Rice took the boy aside and advised him to quit boxing. "What you should do," the young man was told, "is become a singer."

Dramatic pause. "And that young man was — Frank Sinatra!"

It was a good story — all of Stern's stories were good — but wholly untrue and Grantland Rice, normally the most affable of men, was furious. Sinatra's reaction, so far as I know, was never documented.

Pat O'Brien, the actor, remembers listening with astonishment to a Stern broadcast about the Harry Greb-Mickey Walker bout in 1925, in the Polo Grounds, won by Greb. Later that night, Greb and Walker met in a bar and after a few drinks they renewed hostilities. As Stern tells it, a handsome young Irish policeman broke up the fight, whereupon the two boxers urged him to go out to Hollywood and seek his fortune.

"And that young man was — Pat O'Brien." The story's only flaw is that Pat O'Brien was never a policeman in New York or anywhere else.

Perhaps the most fantastic of Stern's stories — and the one most fondly remembered by collectors — dwelled on Abraham Lincoln's dying words. As Lincoln lay on his deathbed, according to Stern, he sent for Gen. Abner Doubleday, who supposedly invented baseball. "Keep baseball alive," the President whispered to Doubleday. "In the trying days ahead, the country will need it."

And that was Bill Stern's view of history, events not as they were but, perhaps, as they should have been.

At the Fights With Phyllis

I can think of no reason why a woman can't report a prizefight on television. Still, it might seem odd, as a guy reporting the Pillsbury Bakeoff could strike one as passing strange. But then, who among us is to say that one day there won't be a female reporter at ringside — and two female heavyweights therein throwing leather, slugging it out for the championship of the world and other planets?

And that woman reporter may well be Phyllis George, who was in fact almost at ringside for CBS' coverage — or, more accurately, over-coverage — of Muhammad Ali's modest exercise with Jean-Pierre Coopman.

This Coopman, a Belgian pacifist known (possibly for his growl) as "The Lion of Flanders," was the subject of prefight chatter by Miss George and her partner in the verbal softshoe, Brent Mussberger. It was, in substance, the classic confrontation of the romanticist and the pragmatist.

"Jean-Pierre is a fine person," said Phyllis, who still smiles as though she were contending for another Miss America title or, per-haps, serving coffee, tea or milk. "He's a painter and a sculptor and a cyclist and a soccer star and ..."

"But," Mussberger interrupted, "can he win this fight?"

Later, Mussberger declared: "And now we will present what journalists like to call the tale of the tape. Phyllis, as a former Miss America, you're better equipped to handle the vital statistics."

"You may get a letter from Gloria Steinem," Phyllis replied, "but I'll let you handle THAT." Then she read aloud the various statistics of both tigers — their respective height, weight, reach and so on. Then she stopped and shook her head incredulously.

"After seeing the two fighters work out," she cried, "I can say that those aren't the correct measurements. Take it from a woman!"

Take it from a woman, eh? There are fight fans around who, in the wake of hearing Phyllis George, are muttering that women should be disbarred permanently from being anywhere near ringside and, just possibly, be deprived of the vote. They aren't suggesting that we repeal the 19th Amendment, exactly, just that maybe we think about it a little bit.

At another point in the prefight nattering (to borrow an apt word from the British), Phyllis mentioned that another European had once ventured to our shores and returned with the heavyweight crown in his luggage — namely, Ingemar Johansson of Sweden, who in 1959 dispatched Floyd Patterson with something called the "toonderbolt" punch.

Mussberger said: "Phyllis, you'd have loved Ingemar Johansson — he's so handsome."

"Oh, the name is handsome!" Phyllis trilled.

Super Bowl — And No Scully

I wouldn't ever dream of telling a network how to run its business — who, me? — but when they are holding the Super Bowl in New Orleans, it strikes me as passing strange for CBS to assign Vin Scully to some golfing match in Phoenix.

Vincent Edward Scully, it says here, is the nonpareil of the sporting announcers, and there he was, on this Super Bowl weekend of '78, his velvet tones dwelling on birdies and chip shots instead of the zesty pompano at Brennan's in New Orleans — "This city," in Jack Whitaker's phrase, "that was not settled by the Puritans."

All the same, CBS did serve up a good telecast with its low-key duo, Pat Summerall and Tom Brookshier, who might have become excited if the Superdome had been rocked by an earthquake but nothing short of that.

But then, it is no easy matter to call a mere Super Bowl contest with the distraction furnished by the Dallas Cowgirls. (Not to say that the Denver cheerleaders weren't keepers, as the fishermen say, but like their Broncos, there they must rank as runner-ups.)

On occasion, Pat and Tom would be deep in conversation about such technical football terms as the overshift (a heavy garment worn by Yugoslavian peasants), whereupon the cameras would suddenly be fixed — closely — on various Dallas Cowgirls.

"My heavens," said Tom Brookshier at one such moment, presumably averting his eyes.

Actually, it is reassuring to note that staid CBS, the button-down network that is usually prim in such matters, found the Dallas Cowgirls irresistible as they pranced about leading the cheers for the Cowboys and, no doubt, accepting a few for themselves. All are top draft choices. None are over-dressed. And for all I know, they are all majoring in nuclear physics at Southern Methodist.

It was in the third quarter, I think, that a CBS photographer abandoned all sense of discretion, his last link to civilized deportment torn to shreds (man is not made of steel) and zoomed in on one willowy Cowgirl with devastatingly superb conformation. She was, so to speak, swaying. It was hypnotic.

A moment later, a CBS camera was dutifully aimed at the field where a penalty had just been imposed. "Illegal motion," the referee proclaimed.

"I'm glad HE said that," Brookshier commented.

Illegal motion, eh? One more motion by that particular Cowgirl and I tell you the place would have been raided.

Politics and Conventions

"*The Fourth of July of politics*" *is how Will Rogers once summed up our national presidential conventions. This is a particularly apt description since the cowboy wit from Oklahoma never lived to see this peculiarly American institution on television.*

It was Walter Cronkite who offered this assessment: "Despite the fact that they're too long, too noisy, too often very dull, they are part of a political process unique in this world and the process seems to work."

The unique process seems to work as well for TV, providing a spotlight on the continuance of the American democratic system, and it is a grand show. Going back to 1952, I have witnessed all of the conventions on television, and some I have attended — Los Angeles in '60, San Francisco in '64, Kansas City in '76.

In Kansas City, where the Republicans convened to nominate Gerald Ford, I interviewed the perennial candidate, Harold Stassen. I had phoned him at his hotel and he said, "I can give you 15 minutes. Be here tomorrow morning at 10."

The night before, I was talking to a good friend, Dick Schaap of NBC, who also was writing a column for the Washington Star. I told him about my appointment with Stassen.

"Can I come along?" Schaap said. "I won't ask any questions."

Now that would have been ridiculous! One of America's finest reporters not ask any questions? "Oh no," I said. "We'll go together and ask anything you want."

The next morning, Dick and I went to see Stassen. He is a man of great charm and the experience was illuminating. Mindful of the 15-

minute limit, neither of us asked very many questions. But we didn't have to — an hour later, Harold Stassen, politician, was still talking ...

Following are some irreverent glimpses of those covering and those being covered at our nation's political conventions.

The "Catch 22" of Politics

As David Brinkley has observed, even at their conventions there is a marked difference between the Republicans and the Democrats, in how they operate.

"The Republicans are more sober in every sense, more punctual, better organized," says Brinkley. "They're not sloppy. They don't throw as much paper on the floor. The Democrats are always late, noisy, milling. At a Democratic convention you're always hearing, 'Will the sergeant at arms please clear the aisles!' And they're never cleared."

There was, at that, a certain air of contentious perplexity as the Democrats convened in the summer of '72 in Miami Beach in what Reuven Frank, NBC's news chief, calls "the 'Catch 22' of politics." Although it is not guaranteed for accuracy, Frank insists he spotted a sign outside the Convention Hall which read: "No one can enter the hall without the following credentials which may be obtained inside the hall."

Occasionally, the confusion filters onto the tube. On NBC, for instance, Tom Pettit was interviewing Pierre Salinger. At the conclusion, Pettit turned and faced the camera and said, in a voice full of microphone authority: "We're talking here with Frank Mankiewicz."

At once, after the words tumbled out, puzzlement reigned on his face. "Did I say 'Mankiewicz'?" Pettit asked with a gulp.

"Yes," said Salinger. "You did."

Pettit sighed deeply. "And now," he said, "back to John Chancellor in the booth."

Chancellor was forgiving. "That'll happen from time to time," said Chancellor, hoping presumably that it would never happen to him.

Over on CBS, Mike Wallace, in his bulldog fashion, was quizzing Gloria Steinem about the intricacies of the challenge involving the South Carolina delegation. That's where the Civil War started, of course, in South Carolina, and the war between the sexes that James Thurber foresaw may well begin there, too.

The issue surrounding the South Carolina delegation centered on women — there weren't enough of them. At Wallace's request, Ms. Steinem began to clarify the problem besetting the South Carolina people. And she kept on clarifying. Boy, did she ever clarify! She may have set a new world record for free-style clarifying.

Finally, a dazed Mike Wallace smiled and nodded and broke in with: "Thank you very much." He turned up to Walter Cronkite in the booth.

"Walter, I don't know what she was talking about," he said. "Can you help me out?"

Cronkite shrugged, "No," he said. "I've been listening but I don't know what she said, either."

The nomenclature associated with Women's Liberation has obviously bestirred its own kind of confusion. David Brinkley mused at one point: "They don't seem to be sure here what the person occupying the 'chair' is to be called. Chairman? Chairwoman? Chairperson?"

In the ABC booth, Harry Reasoner was saying to Howard K. Smith as the long night neared its end: "I was surprised to hear a lady from South Carolina say she had been 'manning' the phones. A slip of the tongue, I'm sure. Maybe we'll have to refer to ourselves as co-anchor-persons."

Said Smith, ever the model of southern dignity: "You've seen the club here called Playperson?"

Playful humor from Howard K. Smith? As Walter would say, that's the way it is in Miami Beach.

Hickville-on-the-Hudson

With a touch of amiable perversity, ABC had acquired a fellow named Goldwater, well-known in Republican circles, to comment on whatever it is the Democrats were doing in New York in the summer of '76. He is, of course, the very same Barry Goldwater, from Arizona, who finished in the runner-up position in the '64 race.

They were talking, up in the ABC booth in the Garden, about the way we are affected by changes in perception and Harry Reasoner grew contemplative. "Tell me," Reasoner said to Goldwater, posing a light-hearted query, "do you think Lincoln would be nominated today by the Republicans?"

Goldwater smiled. "He'd have some trouble," the senator conceded. "But he'd get it."

"Times do change," Reasoner said. "Back at the start of the space program, I asked a psychiatrist at Wright Field, 'Could Columbus have been an astronaut?' The psychiatrist shook his head. 'Oh, no,' the psychiatrist said. 'We'd never pass Columbus. Far too independent-minded. Couldn't work with the group. He'd never do.'"

There was abundant laughter on all sides at Reasoner's yarn. But there was an awareness as well that the shrink had bespoken the truth. They're talking about a genuine individualist, this Columbus, who had the cooks serve garlic soup aboard the Santa Maria. He'd probably have garlic soup in his spaceship, too, which means, come to think of it, that he wouldn't have a group around to work with.

Reasoner may have had astronauts on his mind in the wake of John Glenn's keynote speech, which was aptly described by NBC's Douglas Kiker as "propelling platitudes in search of an idea." Glenn was followed by Rep. Barbara Jordan, who is black and from Texas and affectionately known as "The Voice."

Barbara really broke it up. She's a tremendous speaker, with emotion and bite, and there hasn't been such a wallop on TV since Archie Bunker erupted with "All in the Family" — and there is a slice of irony to mull over.

The times, they certainly do change — or do they? When the Democrats last convened in New York, in 1924 in the old, old Garden that Stanford White designed, the city responded with fervent small-town boosterism.

William Allen White, the great editor from Emporia, Kan., was there in 1924 and the small-town journalist slickly summed up New York in a phrase: "Hickville-on-the-Hudson."

For more history, on NBC's "Today Show," Dick Schaap summoned up ancient footage of New York as it was in 1924, which meant Babe Ruth swatting home runs in Yankee Stadium and someone named John W. Davis being nominated by the Democrats. Davis was thereafter knocked out of the box by a hard-hitting New Englander named Coolidge. Gabby fellow, it's said.

"John W. Davis is not a household word," said Schaap. "But ask the most avid fan who played second base and shortstop for the Yankees in 1924." (Pause.) "Aaron Ward and Everett Scott."

The camera turns to Yogi Berra, who is often mistaken for an Oxford don. "That I didn't know," Yogi said.

For Stassen a Morning After

Some of the people here in Kansas City are sporting "Stop Stassen!" buttons and they smile when they are noticed because Harold Stassen seems to be, in 1976, a faintly comic figure, the actor who refuses to leave the stage. There are collegians who carry placards that say, "Stassen Can Beat Carter" and when you ask them why they do this, the answer is accompanied by a smile.

"At first," says a fellow named Jay Glass, who is an 18-year-old sophomore at Central Missouri State University, "it was like nostalgia. Harold Stassen! It would be fun working for Harold Stassen. Some people think it's all a big joke but Gov. Stassen wouldn't be here if he weren't serious, would he?"

The name is mentioned to Eric Sevareid, the CBS pundit who went to the University of Minnesota in the '30s when Stassen was governor of the state — the "Boy Governor" is what they called him then. Stassen would go on to run for President in 1948, when he came closest to getting the Republicans' nomination, and in '52 and '60 and '64 and '68 and — is it possible? — in '76.

You say "Harold Stassen" to Eric Sevareid and he issues a rueful smile. "A remarkably able man," Sevareid says. "He was governor at age 31 and now to be in this position — perpetually running — but who can explain that virus?"

Now, for Harold Edward Stassen, it is another morning after. The Republican nominee had been selected and, once again, it was not Stassen. He sits alone in his tower suite at the Muehlebach Hotel and there is a trace of poignance here, a touch of wistful regret — but not too much. You might have expected more from a defeated candidate.

Nonetheless, for Harold Stassen, it was a candidacy with meaning. Stassen is a part of a big law firm in Philadelphia, he specializes in international business law. He is obviously well off. Altogether, his campaign cost $15,000 and there weren't too many contributions and no federal matching funds.

He is there at the door to his suite, a big man with a politician's handshake. He looks terrific and there is, still, a boyish quality about his face, a stubborn cast to the jaw — "Scandinavian stubborn," he calls it.

"How did the campaign go?" the defeated candidate is asked.

"I put my foot on the edge of the door," Stassen says with a broad smile.

How did he feel, this man who keeps losing and keeps coming back? He feels fine but this is, after all, '76 and not '48 when losing was painful.

"I remember how emotionally drained I was then, the morning after the nomination in '48," Stassen says. "I had been driving hard and then it was over and the energy was gone. Dewey had the delegate strength. I had the 'Students for Stassen'."

Stassen nods slowly. "All the polls indicated that I could have defeated Truman. I know I'd have put on a better campaign than Dewey did. I'd have gone in strong on the issues. I am not nor have I ever been a clever politician. And, in all my years of public life, my name has never, never been touched with scandal of any kind."

But now, in '76, was there really a goal for Harold Stassen here in Kansas City?

Well, these delegates had called him last June, Stassen says, and they were serious and he was serious, of course, and there were issues he was concerned with and he thought he could give them an effective airing. It narrows down to this — Harold Stassen was asked by these delgates if he wanted to run for President. You don't have to ask Harold Stassen twice.

"I tend not to dwell on what has been," Stassen says. "I'm always looking ahead. And by nature I've always been independent."

The presidential virus — could it go back to the days on the Stassen family farm in Dakota County, 17 miles out of Minneapolis, when the farm boy they called "Red" Stassen, this big kid with rust-red hair, had early dreams of the White House?

"I never had White House dreams," Stassen counters. "I've never had White House dreams."

The statement is followed by a smile. "I mean it," Stassen says. "I was never motivated by the desire for office merely for the sake of office. Issues — always it was the issues that interested me. My motivations were two-fold — to do everything possible for world peace and to achieve better conditions for people with low incomes. I asked myself what could I do? I could write, I could speak, I could teach but the only way to really accomplish anything was to get into the arena, to run for office."

He remembers, when he was 12, listening to Gov. Robert LaFollette and being deeply impressed by the Wisconsin populist known as "Fighting Bob." A brilliant student — straight A's in whatever class he ever set foot — Stassen went to the University of Minnesota when there were giants on the gridiron — the legendary Bronko Nagurski, for instance. To drive those 17 miles from the farm to the campus, Stassen bought an old crank-starter Ford for $13 at a sheriff's auction.

And he worked on the railroads as a parttime conductor. They called him the "Kid Conductor." He remembers those days with affection. He liked being a part of the railroads whose sound in the Minnesota nights, with the whistle echoing over the still prairie, had been by long tradition the siren call that lured the farm kids to the city.

His expression softens as he remembers those days on the railroads barreling over the northern plains and coming into places like Chicago and Milwaukee and Kansas City and Omaha, and seeing the bright lights.

"The way it worked," he says, "as a substitute conductor, I'd get a run if the regular conductor got sick and they all knew I was working my way through college. A conductor might say, 'Kid, you need to make some money?' I'd say, 'Yes sir.' And he'd say, 'Well, kid, I think I'll plan on being sick two days next week.'"

Stassen paused, reliving the moment. "When I ran for the nomination in 1948," he says, proudly, "I had the endorsement of the Railroad Brotherhood and the CIO and the AFL. No Republican ever had that before. The railroaders, the working people considered me one of them."

At 22, in 1930, he was out of law school, full of fire and ambition, and he ran for district attorney in Dakota County. He won once and then he won again. In 1936, he introduced Alf Landon, the Republican candidate for President, from the back platform of a train as it stopped at the Dakota County seat of Farmington. They were in agreement on everything except one issue — Landon was against Social Security, Stassen strongly for it.

"I remember the year very well — 1936, the year we swept Maine and Vermont," Stassen says, summing up an historic defeat in a phrase.

In 1938, he was 31 and governor of Minnesota, the youngest governor of any state ever, and they re-elected him twice. He was in the Pacific in World War II as a Navy commander under Halsey. He helped draft the original United Nations charter. There was 1948 and his first defeat for the Republican nomination. He was in Ike's administration. He was later the president of the University of Pennsylvania. And he kept running for President.

He was 69 in 1976 and was still running for President. He has been a vital part of the history of his time but that isn't what people think of when they hear his name. They don't think of Harold Stassen and his years of public service. They remember the man who never stopped running for President. He denies that he ever had that impossible dream. He denies it and so, perhaps, would Don Quixote.

How To Start a Rumor

As I was saying to Jerry and Ronnie the other day, there's nothing I hate worse than a name-dropper. Unless it's a rumormonger. And right here, at the 1976 Republican convention in Kansas City, as at every national convention that has ever preceded it, this is the place for names to be dropped and rumors to be mongered and then to grow as thick and abundant as the steaks they serve in these parts.

Actually, I hate only the run-of-the-mill, small-potatoes name-dropper and rumormonger. On the other hand, your big-time, top-drawer expert at these pursuits fills me with awe and envy. For the sad fact is that I, myself, am a run-of-the-mill, small-potatoes name-dropper and a bush league rumormonger.

I mentioned this at a cocktail party conversation with David Brinkley at NBC headquarters here and he nodded sympathetically. David is a congenial fellow with unstyled, straight-back hair and a distinctive manner of speaking. He has something to do with NBC News. Usually, he is based in New York or Washington, D.C., both being fertile areas for sending rumors into orbit and dropping names with casual and practiced ease.

"Well, you can't expect to be a big-time, top-drawer name-dropper or rumormonger first crack out of the box," Brinkley said, with a trace of a North Carolina accent. "You have got to get into shape first before going to a convention. To be a polished rumormonger, for example, you must polish your technique. A racetrack is an excellent place for this. Myself, I just spent some time at Saratoga.

"At the track, you start with rumors about claiming races and build up to bigger stakes. By the time one of your rumors can switch the odds on a horse, you are ready to tackle a big convention. But first, remember your basic rules."

"What's that?" I said, eagerly.

"The tone of voice is vital," Brinkley said. "You don't shout. You don't whisper. A true-blue rumormonger speaks so that his rumor is overheard clearly — but just barely. You keep your voice very well modulated — but make absolutely certain that it carries to your nearest eavesdropper who will in turn reveal himself as a first-class rumor-spreader by not letting on that he heard you at all. If he remains deadpan and looks away but doesn't move a muscle — you know he's hooked on your rumor."

"Tell me," I said, "where should rumors be started?"

"In places where they do the most good," Brinkley said. "You start rumors in hotel lobbies, in bars, in taxicabs, wherever people gather. But remember this — rumormongering isn't the same as name-dropping. To be a topflight rumormonger, you don't drop a name. You use pronouns.

"For example," Brinkley said, "you might say, 'My contact says it's definite that *he* plans to release his delegates.' No names, you see. But your victim — that is, your listener — can fill in the blanks.

"In a cab — it's best to pick a cab shared by a crowd from the Muehlebach Hotel going out to Kemper Arena — to get a good rumor going, you talk directly to the cabdriver and let the others listen in. They'll pretend not to listen but, of course, they will. Now, for rumor-mongering in a hotel lobby or a hotel elevator, it is not a bad idea to have an 'accomplice' — that is, a partner."

"Why would you need a partner?" I asked

"For effect, for pride of accomplishment," Brinkley said. "The partner's role is to listen and react as you announce your rumor. You say, 'I hear that *he* is making the big announcement today.' Your partner's eyebrows shoot up and he says, *'When* did you hear that?' That is a key word — 'when?' You fire back with, 'Two minutes ago!' The rumor then spreads like wildfire."

I said, "David, how do you know when you've really arrived as a big-time, top-drawer rumormonger and are no longer small potatoes?"

"Very simple," Brinkley said. "You're in the lobby of the Muehlebach and a man says to you, confidentially, 'I just heard this from an unimpeachable source who heard it from a guy who heard it from a cabdriver who took this group from the hotel out to the arena and he heard it from a guy in his cab — 'It's definite that *he* plans to release his delegation tonight.' By the time, the rumor gets back to you, it may be a bit distorted but you can still take pride in the fact that it's still your rumor.

"As for name-dropping," Brinkley said, "the first rule is, you only drop names that are known to others."

"At cocktail parties?"

"No," Brinkley said, firmly. "You drop names at cocktail parties after you've practiced and you've developed a technique. But you practice alone, in front of a mirror, preferably with a tape recorder. What you practice is inflections. Never stress the name itself. Take a sentence that begins, 'When I was talking to Howard Baker last night' — your amateur name-dropper would build up to the name, Howard Baker. The pro tosses the name away. Might even mumble it, so he'll be asked to repeat it more distinctly."

Brinkley paused. "Before I came out here to Kansas City, an odd thing happened," he said. "Now this is true. Someone called my secretary and said, 'Does David know Ronnie well?' My secretary turned to me and said, 'Do you know someone named Ronnie Well?' Well, obviously, the person on the phone was someone who didn't know how to drop a name. Probably couldn't spread a rumor, either."

The Barbecue at Bryant's

Only a few hours remained on this Friday afternoon after a week of the '76 Republican convention in Kansas City. Time for one more meal, a farewell lunch. There could be only one place to go. To Arthur Bryant's, of course, where they serve up ribs and barbecue beef of incomparable quality, and which Calvin Trillin, a Kansas City native writing in the New Yorker, has called — in capital letters — "THE SINGLE BEST RESTAURANT IN THE WORLD."

Is it possible that he exaggerates? Is Trillin, a professional eater of the type known in some parts of the country as a Big Hungry Boy, engaging in hometown hyperbole?

Andy Rooney had sniffed when I mentioned Bryant's to him a day earlier. "A sloppy place where they throw a lot of meat at you," summed up the man whose TV special, "Mr. Rooney Goes to Dinner," was a big hit.

"I couldn't get anything green there," Rooney grumbled.

Rooney, who is a restaurant buff, must have expected a salad with those fantastic ribs, which is like winning a 100-to-1 shot at the track and then complaining because you didn't get a ride home. Rooney can be, in a word, unreasonable.

Still, I was gripped with an overpowering compulsion to return to Bryant's. The first visit to Arthur Bryant's is a revelation, the second visit is a pilgrimage.

Outside the Muehlebach Hotel, there were two cabs and Bill Moyers of CBS was getting into the first one and the driver of the second one opened his door for me. "Where you going?" I asked Moyers.

"To the airport," he said. "Where you going?"

"To Bryant's," I said, as a surfer might announce that he is bound for storied Makaha on the shores of Oahu to test the 30-foot waves.

Bill Moyers is from Texas and he knows something about barbecue sauce and he is an admiring patron of Bryant's as well. He glanced at his watch and then he shook his head. "I would rather," he said, sadly, "be going with you."

To sum up Bryant's in a word, the place has character. There are two rooms at Bryant's and maybe 20 or 25 tables. The floor is cracked linoleum. One of the larger wall decorations is a temperature chart that advertises Muehlebach Beer, which the man in line in front of me says hasn't been in business for 20 years.

"Been coming here since I was in high school," says the man, who must be knocking at 50.

"Has it changed much?"

"No," the man says. "I've changed. The world's changed. But Bryant's stays the same."

The atmosphere is old, rural Southern and you can imagine Bryant's in a William Faulkner novel, somewhere in Yoknapatawpha County deep in Mississippi. They have soft drink machines that dispense Nehi and RC Cola. On the jukebox, you can hear the Detroit Emeralds romp through "If You Want It, You Got It."

And behind the counter, slicing beef at a frantic pace as the customers walk by with their aluminum plates and plastic cutlery in hand, is Arthur Bryant himself. He is black, a small man, plump and round, but his arms are as muscular as a steamfitter's. He is 74 but he could go for 10 to 15 years younger. He moves like a dervish.

Later, after I paid homage by devouring a mountainous barbecue beef and some burnt ends with a sauce that is smoky ambrosia, I talked with Mr. Bryant in his office. It is a cubicle with two chairs and a magnificently cluttered old rolltop desk. He showed me a recent guest register and pointed to some of the signatures: Howard Cosell, John Chancellor, Walter Cronkite, Sen. Edward Brooke.

"Harry Truman?" says Mr. Bryant. "Sure, I fed him, long ago when he was a county judge. That's how far back I go in the barbecue business. I fed everybody."

"What's your secret, Mr. Bryant?"

"My secret is that nobody can put it together but me," says Arthur Bryant. "Only but one other person knows the secret of my sauce and that's my niece. Doreeta Bryant. But she's a nurse and she's not interested."

It is no secret that he uses quality meat and that he prepares his fries in lard, which is expensive but to Arthur Bryant there is no other way. "I introduced fries with barbecue, don't you know? Oh, this is

back in 19-and-47 when they used to serve sweet potatoes with barbecue but that was so slow."

As you might expect, the franchising people have been after Arthur
Bryant to expand. But he would never do that.

"When I go," he says, "Bryant's goes."

And now I know exactly what Calvin Trillin was saying when he
wrote: "When I'm away from Kansas City and depressed, I try to envision someone walking up to the counterman at Bryant's and ordering
a beef sandwich to go — for me."

Make that two. With extra sauce.

The First Carter-Ford Debate

I thought Ford outpointed Carter, but just barely. I thought it was
a very close fight but rather a slow fight and I don't think the guys
at Kelsey's Bar stayed with it all the way. It was also a strange fight
in which the only knockout punch was delivered by technology which
should never, as the wise men keep telling us, be confused with
progress.

Technology failed us in the final round when the sound system went
off just as Jimmy Carter was answering one of the final questions. At
the Walnut Theater in Philadelphia, where the first of these debates
originated on Aug. 23, 1976, consternation must have enveloped
the control room. Not since "Heidi" was slipped in at the close of a
football game had technology so grievously erred.

Finally, we learned that a couple of amplifiers in the sound system
had misbehaved. In times of crisis, it is always reassuring to hear the
strong and able voice of Walter Cronkite and he didn't fail us this
time. "The fault has been dealt with," Walter proclaimed. And back
we went to NBC's Edwin Newman, the cool and learned moderator,
who instructed Carter to resume his remarks.

The political issues are not my business but you can't discuss style
and avoid substance altogether. I have no idea whether it was the de-
lay from those amplifiers that contributed to Carter's effectiveness in
his summation. But in those few minutes, on returning to the air,
Carter scored heavily as he had not done before.

Show people have a phrase for this. They would say that Carter
finally went into his "roll." His style turned warm and personal
and down-home, his words so flowingly lyrical you could have put them
to music.

The secretary of the state of Georgia, a man named Ben Fortson,
once said that Jimmy Carter can "charm the lard off a hog" — but
he added that Carter's "eyes can burn the buttons off your vest."

In his final remarks it was the charming Carter, the smooth and
effortlessly winning Carter who emerged. But by then the eyes had
already burned the buttons off a lot of vests.

Gerald Ford, by contrast, seemed to lose the momentum he had gained and he concluded on the note of uncertainty he had previously avoided. One thought of pitchers who lose their fast ball when they return to the mound after mid-inning rain delays a ball game.

On the previous night, Eric Sevareid had talked about what the American people — 100 million of them watching this first debate — would be looking for. And primarily it was something more than the specific answers to vexing issues.

"What they are looking for," Sevareid noted, "is that intangible but recognizable thing called 'size'."

Both men, to my eyes, possess more size than most. But while honest and perhaps informative arguments on the issues were skillfully articulated, there was almost no linguistic fire. Not a single great ringing phrase emanated from either candidate. I kept thinking what a Churchill or a Roosevelt or even a Truman would have done in these circumstances.

As the contemporary philosopher Michael Novak has written, "Each medium allows only certain surfaces of reality to be reflected through it. No medium carries all of reality." Certainly you won't find all of reality in the cool medium of television. What we are looking for instead of reality, I suppose, is a confirmation of our perceptions, a reinforcement of the image.

I don't think we learned too much that is new or startlingly revelatory about either man — except that Carter can confine his big, blockbuster smile to two in 90 minutes and that Ford does not stumble and that he can adapt his style of speech to television's curious demands that lie somewhere between ordinary conversation and oratory. Ford has learned. He has learned quickly and well.

"It was a lively debate," Walter Cronkite said.

I disagree. The direction was flat and uninspired. Few sparks were struck. But both combatants did speak to the issues and there were no low blows.

Round Two for the Candidates

As the morning of the second Great Debate dawned, Tom Brokaw and Ed Newman were exchanging thoughts on the "Today Show" on what might transpire. "Detente," said Newman, NBC's resident grammarian. "Nobody knows what the word really means. Nobody wants to mention the word. It's a bad word now and it always did sound — well, foreign to most people, anyway."

They talked about the cliches, the straight-faced stereotypes that might well emerge from both combatants as they met in San Francisco, the President and the soft-voiced challenger from Georgia. Brokaw gleefully issued this prophesy: "At one point, both men will look straight at the camera and say, 'We will have a defense capacity second to none.' "

As the debate unfolded, with President Gerald Ford and Gov. Jimmy Carter coming in at full strength for round two, the foregoing prediction proved to be right on the button. Less than a minute into the fray, Carter proclaimed that under his administration, we would have "a defense capability second to none." Good call, Brokaw.

In contrast to their first meeting, an exercise reminiscent of the ship in "Mister Roberts" going from Tedium to Apathy, this one was a pretty fair brawl. They came out swinging, two crowd-pleasing club-fighters going for a quick knockout.

This may or may not be good politics but it was certainly much better television. In their first encounter, both candidates were awfully cautious, as if they'd been warned that a mistake would cost them the whole prize. Caution never won any prizes, not in the back-alley scrap this one turned out to be.

Carter's people felt better, I think, after this second debate. Their tiger assumed the attack from the outset, his moves crisp and confident, attacking the President on what everyone assumed was his home turf, foreign policy.

Ford had more vigor than he had exhibited previously, with more snap to his punch. But he does ramble, his oral punctuation is distracting, and he needs roadwork on his syntax.

As I watched the two men fielding questions from the panel — fielding them, not necessarily answering them — I thought of Orson Welles' comments on the "Dinah Shore Show" in the wake of the first debate. Orson Welles is a man who knows something about stage presence, which is what we're talking about here — style not political substance, manner rather than matter.

What Carter does with his mouth, what others may perceive as a smile, strikes Welles as "shorthand for warmth." And Ford, says Welles, has a narrow range of expressions. "His face," said Welles, "looks almost like a knee."

And if the President and his challenger had to be characterized in terms of the animal world, Welles suggested that Ford would tend to be canine and Carter feline.

"The big villains," Welles said, "are the cosmetic advisers who counsel them on 'proper image.' "

But then, I guess the creation of a proper image is what these televised debates are all about. Instead of debate, Eric Sevareid prefers to say "group happening." By any name, and for all of the punches thrown, this second attempt to achieve a crystallization of the two candidates' philosophies, their visions of leadership and judgment, still showed a lack of genuine linguistic fire.

Not one ringing phrase emanated from either candidate. Language became compressed, flattened, oversimplified and graceless. Wit is a debater's device but wit was absent. There was no metaphor, no illustrative anecdote for the mind's eye to see. And so many answers seemed to be out of previous speeches, snippets from the stump.

The Long Election Night

Before the tide turned irrevocably on election night, 1976, one of Gerald Ford's aides told somebody from one of the networks: "It's still do-able." But of course it wasn't, as we would learn later. If it were, however, I suspect we might well have had a new turn of Washingtonese to add to the language.

In the wake of the long night, there are the impressions that remain from the flurry of images that confronted us on the screen. Perhaps the most vivid image is the family portrait of the Fords in defeat and it endures, I think, simply because it contained the most drama.

Is there a scriptwriter who would write such a finish to a campaign? In the old Jimmy Stewart movie, now gracing the late show, he is in Washington and his voice goes after the long, heroic filibuster. But he was a hero and therefore he was a winner. Reality takes only so many cues from old movies. Gerald Ford had lost his voice — "bruised by too many speeches," as John Chancellor observed — and he had lost the election as well.

As a consequence, Betty Ford read the President's words. She read them to the assembled press with grace and indomitability and with tears. The President stood nearby, mute and tearful. It seems to me a matter of significance, a President who is capable of yielding, without embarrassment, to tears.

A day or two earlier, in Grand Rapids, Gerald Ford had been moved to tears by a reception in his hometown. And in Plains, Ga., the President-elect, Jimmy Carter, had also been moved to tears — of triumph, of fatigue, of emotions spent.

And one remembered the vice presidential candidate, Bob Dole, shortly after being tapped for a place on the ticket, being welcomed in his hometown of Russell, Kan. — and he, too, was moved to tears.

Along such lines, I think back to the convention in Kansas City and the following description from the facile pen of the Kansas City Star's sports columnist, Joe McGuff:

"To me, the most moving scene of the convention developed ... when the loser, Ronald Reagan, sat in his box listening to a tumultuous ovation and tears welled up in his eyes. It is the sort of scene that television presents so effectively ...

"For reasons that I have never fully understood, Americans have the idea that grown men, especially politicians, should never cry in public no matter how emotional the occasion. Surely some day we will become mature enough to get over such silliness.

"I would be suspicious of any man who was so controlled, so devoid of emotion that he could sit though such a demonstration dry-eyed."

How many years ago was it that a man named Muskie cried in public? And with the tears went all his hopes for the Presidency — was it only four years earlier? Can four years have created such a difference in our response to emotion?

A Candidate Who Knows Television

Jimmy Carter is a cool candidate who, judging now from his acceptance speech, has a mystic affinity with the cool medium that is television. McLuhan has defined print as the hot medium, television as the cool. But it's a lesson that remains unlearned by the politicians who are, most of them, still making thunderous orations instead of talking for television.

Look at Mondale. When he talks, Fritz Mondale engages in oratory he might as well be speechifying for broadcast on an ancient Atwater Kent radio. This is a man who's younger than Jimmy Carter but Mondale is old-fashioned, an arm-waver, a thumper, a shouter. He has no perception of what this new medium is all about.

New medium? The thing has been with us, a part of our lives, for a quarter of a century and still it baffles the politicians who go on it. Some of them — Lyndon Johnson, for instance — it even terrified.

What we're talking about here is a tricky piece of electronic work that heightens every gesture, that magnifies every sound, that distorts with perplexing and defiant subtlety. When Dave Garroway came along, years ago, as the original host of the "Today Show," he was loose and casual and so soft-spoken you had to hug him to hear him. He beat the medium two falls out of three.

Garroway was an immediate success and people asked: "But what does he do?"

"Nothing," the reply went, "but he does it so well."

The trick is, of course, in doing almost nothing. But how do you hold the attention of the arena and do almost nothing for the cameras — and you and me at home, watching on our sets? How do you do this? Jimmy Carter, either by natural inclination or by intense study (or perhaps both), has acquired this rare — uncommonly rare — and profitable talent.

On the night before Carter's speech, Eric Sevareid was musing: "A few well-chosen words are worth a thousand pictures, despite what the Chinese philosopher said. I want to know what the man can do with the English language. Our great Presidents were able to write well.

I don't think a man can lead the nation without a grasp of the language."

"He must command the word," said Bill Moyers, who was running as an entry with Sevareid as a CBS pundit.

"Committee-written speeches don't become memorable," said Sevareid. "A speech should be the product of one man, one mind, locked up in his own solitude."

These are word people, of course, Eric and Bill, both of them former newspapermen. And like all of us word people, they may be overly concerned with felicity of expression. It is a failing of writers that they judge others, all too often, on the basis of their own literary standards.

In the wake of Carter's address — judged rather captiously by Sevareid, less severely by Moyers — the head man, Walter Cronkite, tossed in a recollection.

This one goes back to the Democratic convention in 1952. As Cronkite tells it, he and Sevareid were sitting in the anchor booth waiting for Gov. Adlai Stevenson to arrive and take the podium for his acceptance speech.

"We didn't get any advance text until Stevenson had arrived," Cronkite said. "The text was then rushed to us and Eric was thumbing through it and I was thumbing through my copy . . . I thought it was quite a speech and I assumed that Eric was thinking the same.

"Then Eric threw the speech down and kind of grumbled to himself. I said to him, 'What's the matter, Eric? Don't you like the speech?'

"And Sevareid looked up and said, 'I don't think I can care very much for a presidential candidate who writes better than I do!' "

As Walter recited the above, Sevareid assumed a slightly pained expression. "You'll never let me forget it," he said to Cronkite.

"Oh, I don't know," Walter said, merrily. "I only mention it once every four years."

Earlier, Cronkite and Carter's mother, Mrs. Lillian Carter, were visiting for a spell. "He favors me," said Mrs. Carter, which is pure down-home southern for noting a resemblance. "People say to me, 'I know you must be Jimmy Carter's mother. You look so much like him.' "

Cronkite inquired if Jimmy, as a boy, was interested in books. To which Mrs. Carter replied: "I think one main reason he's here is his love of reading."

His knowledge of the techniques of television did him no harm, either, Miz Lillian.

Frost Interviews Nixon

Human drama will always transcend politics. When the man from Whittier replied to the questions by the minister's son from Cambridge, what emerged was television drama of great intensity — not only for what was said but for the essence of the man that it revealed.

Richard Milhaus Nixon and David Paradine Frost — were ever two men more opposite? A one-time President and a one-time drama critic, a politician exiled to his Southern California Elba and a jet-setting entrepreneur of television. And the accents — one nondescript American, the other melodically British.

But in that accent lies a cutting edge. Frost's soothing cadences cloak a persistence that he exercised throughout the first of the four 90-minute sessions on May 4, 1977 — particularly in the early going — as the questions, tough and probing, popped out in rapid-fire bursts.

It was this unyielding persistence — and the intensive research that clearly preceded each question — that brought only in the end, a drained and cornered and seemingly defeated Nixon. "I screwed up terribly," Nixon says at one point. He admits to big mistakes in small matters but truth, he insists, was always in him in issues of significance.

He is, as the interview reaches its climax, apologetic and contrite but not altogether chastened. And there are those, as CBS' Fred Graham observed, who will contend that his demeanor could evoke a sympathetic response which "could propel him back into the mainstream of American life."

In that event, the amount that Nixon was paid for the interviews — $600,000 in front, with $1 million as a possibility — would be secondary.

In television terms, the drama was heightened by the simplicity of the setting — a comfortable, book-filled living room — and the economy of the direction, the use of the searing closeup. Occasionally sparks were struck. Nixon: "How many times do I have to tell you . . .?"

Always, as the colloquy touched various moods, there was a sense of moment, the heady tang of history riding tandem with journalism. And history always has its footnotes. For instance, two pictures graced the ad in which XETV, the only San Diego station to participate in the world-wide telecasts, trumpeted the opening program, and those two pictures are at sharp odds.

In one picture, Richard Nixon's standing alongside David Frost — it is a cool and presidential Nixon, a figure of dignity. It is the Nixon of positive achievements, the popular choice of '68 and '72. It is the Nixon who went to China.

From the other picture emerges a portrait that is almost, but not quite, of a piece with the Nixon that cartoonist Herblock so savagely caricatured in years past — the mouth is tight, the eyes furtive, the expression warily defensive. It is the Nixon of Watergate.

Were they, in those two pictures, trying to tell us something?

As another footnote, on "60 Minutes," Mike Wallace has posed a question to David Frost about his interview subject. "If you feel he is stonewalling or lying," Wallace said, "what'll you do?"

"I shall say so again and again," Frost said. "I should not want to give the impression that he is lying."

"Do you expect him to lie?" Wallace persisted.

"No," said Frost. "What I expect is a cascade of candor."

Wallace is amused and incredulous. "A cascade of candor? From Richard Nixon? Is that what you expect?"

Frost smiles. "No, it's just a phrase I thought would appeal to you," he says.

It is difficult to know precisely what Frost expected in his "television memoir," which is Frost's own description and a very apt one. Johnny Carson had cracked: "President Nixon has lied to us and is getting all this publicity and President Carter is telling the truth and nobody's paying any attention."

"It does seem strange," Mike Wallace had said on this "60 Minutes" segment, "that none of the three networks is carrying what could be an historic interview with the only President in the history of the United States who resigned in shame."

"I offered to carry it," says Richard C. Wald, who heads NBC News.

"And you just didn't have the money?" Wallace says.

"That's right," Wald says.

"NBC didn't have the money!" Wallace cries, mockingly. "Eighty million dollars for the Olympics and not half a million for Richard Nixon?"

Seems odd, doesn't it? The networks are supposed to be in the history business. It seems obvious now that the networks erred grievously. They let an outsider, a Briton, this carpetbagger from Cambridge, create a slice of American history.

The Range of Emotions

Now they are over, the originally scheduled quartet of interviews by David Frost, and we know that Richard Milhous Nixon still retains the capacity to bestir within us a perplexing range of emotions. Of all the emotional residues from these interviews, this strange public confessional by an intensely private man, perhaps the most curious one to emerge is the recurring echo of self-doubt from unexpected sources.

"Our footing is not quite as certain as we would like it to be," it says in the New Yorker, a magazine that has regarded Richard Nixon with cool loathing. "There is something unresolved in our attitude toward him. A major source of this anxiety is that we have never been able to answer the question of the extent to which Nixon, elected by us, is made in our image."

"Were We Fair To Nixon?" read the headline over a piece in Newsweek by columnist Meg Greenfield (also deputy editorial page director for the Washington Post.) She poses this one: "The question no longer is: 'Where was Richard Nixon on the night of June 16, 1972?' The question is: 'Did we — the nation — do the right thing?' "

And: "Typically, Nixon came to us as both the Wicked Witch of the East and the Good Witch of the North — conniving and hopeless on Watergate, plausible and impressive on foreign affairs. Did we let a minor matter get the better of our judgment, then? Were Nixon's offenses really all that distinctive in light of what we now know about his immediate predecessors?"

And Richard Nixon himself, let it be added, doesn't help his cause much as an interview subject, now caviling over flyspeck technicalities, now dismissing Woodward and Bernstein as "trashy people who wrote a trashy book," now uttering such oddities as "Call it paranoia, but paranoia for peace isn't that bad."

There was, in the interviews, the Nixon of international affairs, of China, of the delicate diplomacy with the Russians. But there was as well, in darker, murkier tones, the petty Nixon given to festering pique, the fancier of small slights still brooding with self-pity that he and Pat were never invited to dinner at the White House by the Kennedys. It is the Nixon once more of the "Checkers" speech, the perpetual self-designated victim, the Nixon who gives small comfort to his supporters.

It is this Nixon that one suspects Gerald Ford was thinking of when he rejected the request by NBC, his new employer, to go on the air with a three-minute analysis after each of the Nixon-Frost interviews. It is this Nixon that inspired the Oliphant cartoon in which Frost is pictured as the amiable quizmaster holding a long list of questions. Nixon, his expression mean and grasping, is wallowing in dollar bills.

And Frost is saying: "Correct! Contestant Nixon, you now have three hundred and sixty thousand dollars!! For another five hundred dollars, answer this question . . ."

Checkbook journalism is the phrase. And the networks, all of whom failed to recognize news in the making, are still loftily decrying the practice — even CBS, which shelled out $100,000 for the interview with H. R. (Bob) Haldeman. It's a slight case of hypocrisy, which is the wildflower that grows along the network corridors.

If any of the networks had had the prescience to know they could have sold time on the interviews — the agencies were apprehensive about this beforehand — they surely would have opened up their chaste airwaves, pocketed the loot and run for the bank.

Instead, they permitted David Frost to turn entrepreneur and hatch a million or two for himself and at least $600,000 for Nixon. (Said Johnny Carson one night: "I watched that second interview — you know, Frost looked guiltier than Nixon.")

Frost was a superb interviewer throughout. I can think of no one else who could have coaxed from Nixon the damning "I let down my friends, I let down the country" admission. In a cover yarn on Frost in People, the heading went: "Off TV, he's a driven man with millions, migraines and many women." Frost has since denied that he has migraines, but those two out of three aren't bad.

And now, with the interviews ended, the arguments are still aboil, including the view of a psychiatrist, Dr. David Abrahmsen, that Nixon "unconsciously sought failure," that he became "a self-absorbed paranoid," and so forth.

Maybe. But I think we are ahead of the shrink with his absolute judgments. For we know, in the wake of the interviews and their revelations, that there is much of mystery and of contradiction in Nixon the man. And that's the way it was and, perhaps, always will be.

The President Takes a Walk

As the helicopter lifted itself lazily into the wintry skies over Washington, carrying a former President who was leaving the trappings of power to his successor, David Brinkley summed up the occasion with an apt phrase. "There's the Constitution at work," Brinkley observed.

Earlier, much earlier on this chill morning, NBC's John Hart spotted a woman in the crowd that had gathered close to where Jimmy Carter would be sworn into office. She was heavily bundled, and she said she had been there, guarding her space, since 4 in the morning. "I wanted to see history," she explained.

There it was in two words — history and the Constitution. The inauguration of our Presidents, this orderly transfer of office, is a peculiarly American institution and it is also an absolutely corking television event, with the cameras and the commentators — and you and me in front of our sets — sharing a slice of history on the wing.

It was near the point of freezing, a typical January morning in Washington. With a shiver in his speech, Bob Schieffer, the CBS man, pointed out: "The Supreme Court justices have robes on but underneath they're wearing thermo-nuclear underwear."

"Thermo-nuclear?" said Walter Cronkite on a note of puzzlement. What Schieffer meant, of course, was thermal. But Walter's gaze was quickly distracted when Billy Carter, up from Plains, Ga., for the occasion, appeared on the screen.

"There's Billy Carter," Cronkite said with obvious delight. "Billy Carter, who is giving Pabst Blue Ribbon a new lease on life."

On the subject of the weather, another CBS correspondent, Charles Osgood, offered a smattering of philosophy. "Maybe nature wants to prove to Presidents that some things can't be controlled, no matter how powerful you are."

Thereafter, Osgood reached back into history for some nuggets. "The truth is, the weather man has not been kind to many of our Presidents. James Polk, according to one account, delivered his inaugural to a large assemblage of umbrellas.

"On his chilly inauguration day in 1909, William Howard Taft quipped to outgoing President Theodore Roosevelt, 'I always said it would be a cold day when I got to be President of the United States.'"

And: "Perhaps the coldest inaugural day was in 1873, the second inaugural of Ulysses S. Grant. There was sleet, snow, and a fierce, bitter wind. The President, however, rode in an open carriage, fortified by what antifreeze we can only surmise."

Billy Carter would probably know about such things.

But for Jimmy and Rosalynn Carter, warmed by the winter's sun, it was a grand day for a stroll — "a tradition-shattering walk," in Walter Cronkite's phrase.

In common with the rest of us, Cronkite was properly stunned and charmed by the sight of the Carters, hand-in-hand, walking down Pennsylvania Avenue from the inauguration platform a mile and a half to the White House. Down the center of this storied avenue, responding to the cheering populace, they walked, briskly, smiling, waving: A walk that was at once a dramatic gesture and an affirmation.

"By gosh, this is almost unbelievable," said Walter Cronkite, who once casually interviewed an astronaut who had stepped on the moon.

In the flurry of conjecture that followed, CBS' Bob Schieffer blurted: "If I were a betting man — no, I AM a betting man I'd almost bet you this is a spur-of-the-moment thing."

Later on, Lesley Stahl, also from CBS, offered her own theory on this extraordinary occurrence. "It may just be intuition on my part," she confided, "but I think this walk was Mrs. Carter's idea. She has a lot of good 'people' ideas."

Clockers tell us the stroll was negotiated in an elapsed time of 20 minutes. Since Howard Cosell wasn't on hand with an instant analysis, it is not known if the Carters' time equalled the world record for newly elected Presidents.

On ABC, the old hurdler from Louisiana State University, Howard K. Smith, observed in a voice tinged with the Deep South. "There is a statue of Gen. Sherman, who marched through Georgia with such destruction, and now Jimmy Carter will pass that statue as he marches through Washington."

One more vignette clings to the memory: A man named Ford said to a man named Mondale: "Can you sleep on a plane?"

"I'm going to find out," Mondale said.

And that's the way it was, to borrow the Cronkite phrase, on this day of history and the Constitution and thermo-nuclear underwear and a pleasant stroll by a President and his wife down a Washington avenue and into the future, theirs and ours.

-30-

In newspaper jargon, "30" means the end. Its derivation has been lost in the dark corridors of myth, but it is said that a telegrapher in the long ago, for obscure reasons, once tapped out "30" at the end of a reporter's story. It was his way of indicating that no more words were forthcoming.

With the advent of computerized printing known as photo-offset and the special typewriters — business machines, really — used to compose stories today, other notations designate what "30" once meant. And "30" itself, a legendary benchmark for generations, is now passed into journalistic history. Sic transit.

When certain performers of stature leave us, a columnist feels a tug of obligation to write more than a bare-boned obituary.

One Christmas, several years ago, I was reminded that W. C. Fields, the funniest man who ever lived, had died on another Christmas day four decades earlier. A Christmas column on a comic known for his churlishness, his fondness for the bottle, his distaste for children? It seemed, somehow, ironically appropriate.

For others on the following pages — for Jack Benny and Ernie Kovacs and Bing and Groucho and Ed Sullivan and Rod Serling and Elvis — the response to their passing was shared, I think, by writer and reader alike in a sharp mood of loss, the melancholy sense of "30."

W. C. Fields

More than three decades have passed, a generation has flowered, since that Christmas Day of 1948 when W. C. Fields slipped off from his hilltop home in Hollywood to be met by "that fellow in the bright nightgown." Such as the old vaudeville juggler's phrase of life's ultimate curtain. Likely (Fields often started a sentence with "likely") his last words on that Christmas Day were one final Edwardian expletive at the dismaying irony, the consuming futility of the human condition.

How improbable a coupling — W. C. Fields and Christmas, a wry mismatch of destiny. And yet, one remembers the movie version of Dickens' "David Copperfield" and there was Bill Fields rumbling on as the perfect Micawber, the definitive Dickens character. And who better than a character of Dickens to personify Christmas?

So Bill Fields died on Christmas Day, at an all too early and ravaged 68, this man with a face erected from Silly Putty, to the end vowing vengeance against the world. There was Bill Fields, forever plotting and scheming and jubilant in his small triumphs against society, rasping out his volcanic disdain for children and dogs — there was Bill Fields scoffing in real life, as in his films, at the soft caress of sentiment.

How ironic that Fields would be gone, his marvelous nasal trumpet of a voice stilled, at Christmas time when sentiment is at its warmest. It is an irony that Bill Fields likely would have rejoiced in, would have toasted as yet another example of life's essential and inexplicable folly.

Shortly before his death, Fields observed with characteristic wryness but not an ounce of self-pity: "I've drunk to so many friends' health that I've lost my own."

Well, this one is for you, Bill, a Christmas toast lifted high to the good health — the thriving, booming, astonishingly enduring good health — of the Fieldsian memory. "Godfrey Daniel!" Bill might have said as he glared a passing child into tears.

And so it was, on Christmas, that William Claude Dukinfield, also self-introduced at times and at various places as Prof. Eustace McGargle, Egbert Souse, T. Frothingell Bellows and Chester Snaveley, slipped silently from the world he had accused of deception at every turn.

It is beyond warmth of sentiment, however, that each year builds more life and substance to the Fields legend. There are Fields festivals in the theaters and, just as often, on television. Each year, Fields enjoys a rebirth and on the campuses there are dormitory walls adorned with his posters.

I remember Ray Bradbury, the best of the writers of fantasy, speaking on a college campus and recalling his first experience, at 14, as an autograph collector in Hollywood. He was standing, wide-eyed, at the gates of the Paramount Studios.

"There I stood," Bradbury related, "looking for stars. And then I saw three of them — celebrities! They were standing together, just talking, three stars. The first was Irvin S. Cobb, a writer of the time."

From the audience only blank stares.

"The second was Ben Bernie, a well-known orchestra leader of the time."

Still more blank stares.

"The third," Bradbury concluded, triumphantly, his voice rising, "was — W. C. Fields!"

An appreciative murmur ran like the wind through the youthful audience, Fields fans all. Bradbury recounted in rich detail how he thrust his autograph book and pen in Fields' hands. The Great Man scrawled out his name and as he returned the book he muttered a cheery obscenity at Bradbury, who still cherishes the moment. Who wouldn't?

The Fields buffs gather now and retell the old Fields yarns. They recall the time, for instance, that H. Allen Smith, the writer, paid a social call on Fields and found the comic standing by a lagoon, a martini in one hand, a whip in the other. He was, Smith saw to his horror, whipping a swan.

"Bill!" Smith cried. "What in heaven's name are you doing to that swan?"

Crack! Fields' whip lashed out once more. Malevolently, he explained: "The son-of-a-bitch hissed at me!"

They remember with fondness Bill Fields, punctuating his whine of mockery with a dandy's flick of his stick, reminiscing about a girl he had met once in his travels in some South Sea island. "She was tattooed all over with pictures of rattlesnakes," Fields confided. Then a pause, a rueful shake of his head and: "Yas, she was one of the prettiest girls in those parts!"

Fields used words as he juggled, with a fearless, colorful, casual quaintness of style. He had the words, he had the comic's face and he was blessed with a prodigious nose, a flaming beacon of a tribute to intemperance. He looked exactly the way he should.

As the end approached, on that Christmas Day in 1946, an old writer-friend named Gene Fowler entered the hospital room and there was Fields, a self-admitted agnostic, thumbing through a Bible.

"What are you doing, Bill?" asked the incredulous Fowler.

"I'm looking for loopholes," Fields whispered.

Louis

This one is for Louis Armstrong, a child of the century, the Yankee Doodle Dandy of the trumpet, who would have celebrated his 76th birthday on the Fourth of July, 1976. Here's one more chorus, one more refrain, for Satchmo Armstrong, a genuine American original whose influence on American music was beyond measure. There may be others who might serve better as a symbol of our Bicentennial but not many.

He was born July 4, 1900, into grinding poverty in a two-room shack in James Alley, just behind the stables of the Home of Detention in New Orleans. As a child, he was compelled to grovel in garbage cans for food. A judge called him a delinquent. And then, at Louisiana's Colored Waifs' Home, he learned to play the horn.

"Me and my horn," Louis once said. "We've come a long way together."

He became Ambassador Satch, a symbol of America wherever he traveled on foreign soil. ("This one's for you, Rex," he once called out to England's King George V as he began an encore.) It was singularly appropriate that his date of birth should coincide with that of his country.

Without Louis Armstrong, there would have been jazz but undoubtedly its course would have been markedly different. Without Louis, other artists from Bing Crosby to Dizzy Gillespie (and so many more) would have thrived but how different they would have been for not having Armstrong as the wellspring for their creativity.

"When you play jazz, you don't lie — you play from your heart," Louis always insisted.

"He can blow just one note," the late Bobby Hackett once observed, "and you know it's Louis."

You always knew it was Louis with his round, full, expansive, golden clarity of tone, the warmth, the exuberance, the soaring good humor. There was only one Louis, only one Armstrong sound, and he was aware of his distinction.

"A lot of cats copy the Mona Lisa," Louis would say, "but people still line up to see the original."

Once, after a concert I sat with Louis in his dressing room. He was 61 then and he was saying that he had been blowing his horn for 48 years. In another two years, he said, it would be an even 50 years of music — and then he would take a year off.

"Oh, I'll woodshed at home to keep my chops strong," Louis said. "But I won't play at all in public. I'll just sit and listen to tapes and albums and write incidents down in my typewriter. And my wife and I'll take trips, hither and yon. Then one day, I'll say to myself, 'Pops, the year's gone.'"

"And then?" I prompted.

"Then," Louis said, a half-moon grin lighting up his face, "I'll begin me another 50 years!"

It is pleasant to remember Louis then as he said: "The horn is my life, Pops. If I feel bad, I blow some fine, big notes and then right away I feel good. Maybe some day I'll feel bad and blow my horn and NOT feel good. That's the day I retire, Pops."

After a momentary reflection, he had an afterthought, a coda: "Maybe."

There was, of course, much more to the man than his trumpet and his singing, much more than the jovial, beloved performer. He had his own personal milestone in the history of social change. "I played in 9,900 hotels that I couldn't stay at," Louis once said. "Finally, I had it put in my contract that I wouldn't play no place I couldn't stay."

Once, he played with the New York Philharmonic, with Leonard Bernstein conducting. They played "St. Louis Blues" as its composer, W. C. Handy, 83 and blind, sat in the audience.

Louis was brilliant but the Philharmonic doesn't swing. Bernstein knew it, too. "Louis has said he is honored," Bernstein told the vast crowd. "But it is we who are honored. We are only doing a blown-up version of what he does. When he plays his horn, it is real and true and honest and simple and noble. No, it is we who are honored."

He honored all of us. And he never retired. His golden horn fell silent with his death on July 6, 1971, two days after his birthday on the Fourth of July.

Jack Benny

What a funny man he was! How irreplaceable, how beloved, how distinctive he was — nobody else ever looked like Jack Benny or talked like him or walked like him. He was an original, a towering figure in the most trying of professions, the pursuit of laughter. And at that trade, to which he brought the art of the vaudeville monologuist polished to a high gloss, he was the master.

Years ago, upon hearing of the death of George Gershwin, the novelist John O'Hara expressed his feelings with these words: "George Gershwin died on July 11, 1937, but I don't have to believe it if I don't want to."

They say that Jack Benny was 80 when he died but I don't have to believe that, either. He was, of course, forever 39.

There was a time, in the late '50s, that Jack Benny devoted one of his shows to the celebration of his "40th" birthday and it simply didn't work, that show and that absurd notion of Jack Benny ever surpassing 39.

Later, Benny admitted that the concept was a grave mistake. "I'm sorry I had that 'birthday,'" Jack said, solemnly. "It's a funny age — 39. But 40 is too serious. I don't look my age. Of course, I don't look 40, either. So I cheat. What's funny is that in being 39 I over-cheat."

Benny realized that once you start chipping away at the long-entrenched legend of Jack Benny being 39, you start nibbling at what was always, for all its durability, a rather fragile thing — the complete Jack Benny character. And what a skillfully wrought character that was, the most complete and fully realized character ever achieved by a comedian.

It is a part of show business history that Jack Benny, a successful comic in vaudeville and theaters, was introduced to radio in a show that Ed Sullivan had in New York back in 1932. What isn't so well known is the fact that five years of network radio exposure, by his own estimate, were required to establish the Jack Benny characterization firmly in the public consciousness.

I can remember listening to Jack, in an interview, reflecting on his style of comedy and saying, in truth: "There's a lot of everybody in Jack Benny."

But such a comic character, an archetype that is also inimitably original, can never be manufactured.

I remember Jack saying: "You can't plan a character. You can't say, 'Look, fellas, let's invent this cheap, vain guy who drives a Maxwell, keeps his money buried in a vault and has a sassy butler named Rochester and wears a toupee' — actually it would be funnier if I really wore a toupee, which I don't. But all of this adds up to 'Jack Benny.'"

It added up as well to more than a half-century of laughter and a special kind of humor that creates affection and warmth along with the laughs. The laughter always stemmed primarily from character. One of the longest laughs in Benny's career, for instance, flowed from the situation but even more from the many years of our acceptance of the Benny character.

In this one, a classic example of pure radio humor, Benny is confronted by a holdup man poking a gun in his ribs.

Holdup Man: "Your money or your life."

Benny: (Long pause).

Holdup Man: "Quit your stalling. I said your money or your life."

Benny: "I'M THINKING IT OVER!"

And only Jack Benny could have won 20 seconds of studio audience laughter — and that's a sizeable amount — with the following bit from an old TV show, with Mary Livingstone:

Mary: "Jack, why don't you stop being so stingy?"

Jack: "Mary, I'm not stingy and you know it."

Mary: "You're not, eh? Last year, when you were going to have your appendix removed, you wanted Rochester to do it."

Jack: "I DID NOT. I merely asked him if he knew how."

What Jack Benny created, along with his characterization of the lovable but petulant skinflint, was an enduring, irrepressibly fresh comic spirit. He was a rarity among the funnymen, a comic who never cracked a joke in public. But merely the sight of him, his walk, his stare, his manner, the skillfully honed way he had of mirroring our own petty failings, all of this made us feel good. Jokes don't necessarily do this.

It is a curious fact of show business that as actors grow older, they bow to age, accepting the gray hair and wrinkles and assume character roles. But the comedian, whatever his years, remains young forever. And so it was with Jack Benny.

As a comedian, as a human being, as a gentleman, Jack Benny was a matchless piece of work, incomparable and unique in our affections. His passing leaves us diminished but also, in another and perhaps bigger sense, nobly enriched by his legacy of laughter.

Groucho

It is best to remember him not as a frail octogenarian, the center of court squabbles, but as the rambunctious Capt. Spaulding the African explorer or the rollicking fraud of a lawyer or professor or hotel-keeper, wearing his swallow-tail coat, prancing around in his familiar loping stride, lightening the nation's mood in the Great Depression long before he was the acidulous quizmaster of radio and TV.

He was the one, the only — Groucho!

What made him so funny? Why this continuing and expanding Groucho Marx cult? "I believe there is a natural inborn greatness in Groucho that defies close analysis as it does with any genuine artist," Woody Allen once theorized. "He is simply unique in the same way that Picasso or Stravinsky are and I believe his outrageous unsentimental disregard for order will be equally funny a thousand years from now. In addition to all this, he makes me laugh."

Oh, how he made us laugh. Groucho — and the other Marx brothers, notably Chico and Harpo — embodied the spirit of anarchy in comedy. They were anti-establishment before there was such a word — none more so than Groucho himself with his impudent wave of the cigar, the waggle of the eyebrows and that raffish, bent-over walk, all adding up to an enduring personal trademark known the world over.

The funniest of the Marx brothers was also a master of insolent word play, a wry philosopher who once wrote to a friend: "My plans are still in embryo, a small town on the edge of wishful thinking."

Do you remember "A Night at the Opera?" This was the Marx brothers' movie with that classic crowded stateroom scene and Groucho, as Otis P. Driftwood, was in great form in one exchange with a waiter.

"Have you got any stewed prunes?" Groucho said.

"Yes," said the waiter.

"Well, give 'em some coffee. That'll sober 'em up."

It was Leo Rosten, the writer, who once observed that Groucho "hears with originality." The words, in short, would bounce off his ears in a special way, assuming a wackily personal coloration. Rosten was in a car one day with Groucho at the wheel when he, Rosten, realized that it was his father's birthday.

"Would you mind stopping at a Western Union office?" Rosten said. "I want to wire my father."

"What's the matter?" Groucho snapped. "Can't he stand by himself?"

Let the Groucho buffs assemble and the talk will flow about "Animal Crackers" and "A Day at the Races" and "Cocoanuts" — wasn't that the picture where Groucho's secret password to Harpo and Chico was "swordfish?" Your true Grouchophiles will recite in unison from the master: "One day I shot an elephant in my pajamas. How he got in my pajamas I'll never know. Getting his tusks off was quite a problem. In Alabama the Tuscaloosa."

And, as Groucho played a horse doctor posing as a neurologist: "Either this man is dead or my watch has stopped."

"Jennings has been waiting an hour and is waxing wroth," someone says to Groucho, who lifts his eyebrows and replies: "Tell Roth to wax Jennings for a while.

"Your eyes shine like my blue serge suit — but that's no reflection on you."

And, from one of Groucho's lawyer roles: "I suggest that we give him ten years in Leavenworth. Or eleven years in Twelve-worth — or five and ten in Woolworth's."

Did these movie lines stem originally from the pen of S. J. Perelman or Morrie Ryskind or George S. Kaufman or Harry Ruby? Some of these classic Groucho lines did and many of them didn't, either. A Groucho line goes beyond the words into the comic essence of the Groucho delivery, which he undoubtedly had since the day he was born. "And," as Groucho might have said, "the doctor's delivery wasn't bad, either."

Groucho never needed a script to be funny. Or to be Groucho. Once, seated at a restaurant, he was approached by a waiter, who asked: "What's your pleasure, sir?"

"Girls," Groucho snapped. "What's yours?"

And who but Groucho would have spurned an invitation to join the Friars with a haughty but crazily logical: "I wouldn't belong to any club that would have me for a member!"

"Say the secret word and the duck will come down," Groucho used to say on "You Bet Your Life." A generation that grew up with the Groucho of television flocked to Carnegie Hall five or six years ago for a one-man concert which attracted a huge following that included Dick Cavett, a Groucho buff, who introduced him onstage. Groucho sang all the old songs, such as "Lydia the Tattooed Lady," and he told the old stories and he puffed his cigar, and the hall was alive with merriment and laughter from the faithful.

The secret word was love.

An Innovator Named Kovacs

Sixteen years have passed since the night in 1962 that Ernie Kovacs was killed in an automobile crash on a rainswept street in Beverly Hills after leaving a party at Milton Berle's home. Ernie Kovacs was an asset beyond price, a brilliantly innovative comedian whose view of life was deliciously manic and wondrously off-tilt. He was a funny man, and just to think of him now brings on a wistful smile of remembrance.

Now Berle was hustling a book he had written, and we met for an interview. Berle was puffing on a cigar, a Cuban import roughly the size of a Nike missile.

Suddenly, in the middle of an anecdote, Berle paused. Then he said: "Do you know whose cigars these are?"

There was, at once, a mystical chill in the air, curious and inexplicable. We had been talking about vaudeville and nightclubs and the man's name had not entered the conversation. I have no reasonable explanation for what I heard myself say to Berle at that moment.

"Ernie's?" I said, very softly.

"Ernie's," said Berle, nodding slowly. "And I have so many more of Ernie's cigars that I may never smoke all of them in my lifetime."

Then Berle related how, after Ernie's death, he had paid something like $10,000 to Edie Adams, Ernie's widow, for the entire Kovacs cigar supply. "You must try one," Berle offered, and I did.

And so the interview turned into a session of reminiscences about Ernie Kovacs as we smoked our cigars — Ernie's cigars — and we laughed about Ernie and it was, somehow, a fitting toast to his memory. Some men you toast with wine. Ernie Kovacs you toasted with cigars.

It was typical of Ernie that they were the very best of cigars. The inscription on his tombstone at Forest Lawn reads: "Ernie Kovacs, 1919-1962 — Nothing in Moderation."

One reminiscence that I contributed to that conversation, I remember, dwelled on the first time I met Ernie Kovacs. Already a hit in New York, he had come to the coast for an NBC comedy show. One of the cast was another rising new comedian named Jonathan Winters.

During a break in rehearsal, the three of us went to a restaurant on Vine Street. And there, in a crowded restaurant, Jonnie Winters put on his own show and he was hilarious. Ernie, meanwhile, sat back and laughed with the rest of us. Not once did he try to team up with Winters or try to top his fellow comic. Ernie Kovacs was content to be an audience.

It struck me then that such a performer was a conspicuous rarity in show business and that, if only because of this, he was a very special human being.

The Kovacs characters remain terribly funny — Miklos Molnar, the Hungarian cook, Wolfgang von Sauerbraten, the German disc jockey; Auntie Gruesome, the bizarre children's story teller; Matzoh Hepplewhite, the drunken itinerant magician; Percy Dovetonsils, the effete, martini-guzzling poet.

What Kovacs was doing, years ago, was clearly the wellspring for what was to follow, from "Laugh-In" to the current "Saturday Night." An authentic original, Kovacs had an intuitive sense of the medium itself and its capabilities. He added sight to sound in a way that had never before been attempted — with his girl-in-the-bathtub routine or the Indian-shooting-the-arrow blackouts or that prize creation, the Nairobi Trio and on and on.

He was, in short, superbly visual — and he made television itself visual, shaping the medium to his own genius. Unlike his colleagues, Ernie Kovacs was not merely a comedian on television — he was, in the purest sense, a television comedian.

Ed Sullivan

He was part of all of our lives. For 23 years, Ed Sullivan reigned as the stone-faced symbol of Sunday night, a master showman who knew the medium of television better than anyone. It is difficult to think of him now in the past tense, for with his death there is a part of all of us, somehow linked to all those Sunday nights through all those many years, that has gone, too.

I saw him last, a few years ago in New York, on a St. Patrick's Day. But his Irish luck had turned. CBS had just brought an end to the "Ed Sullivan Show." In the wake of that announcement, Sullivan, typically, chose to give his first interview to an old friend. I was that friend.

"Twenty-three years," he mused then on a note of pride and regret. "A long time in this business. I didn't dream we'd last this long but we did. Must be my personality."

Then he grinned and if this went counter to his image it was also much more characteristic of the Ed Sullivan that I knew. Always warm-hearted, intensely loyal and generous, he could be very funny with a wry, self-deprecating glint to his humor.

Over the years, his awkward introductions had become legend. It was a part of his essential likability that warm laughter instead of irritation was the response when, for instance, he brought on a group of New Zealand natives and introduced them as "the fierce Maori tribe from New England."

But then, he never saw himself as the slick television host. Once, he was asked to describe himself in a single word. "Reporter," said Ed.

He was, always, a newspaper man, one of the very best of the Broadway columnists. A 15-letter athlete in high school in Port Chester,

N. Y., Ed began as a sportswriter and he delighted in talking about the champions of his time — Dempsey, Tunney, Bobby Jones. It was Ed, ironically, who gave Helen Wills, the tennis star, her nickname of "Little Miss Poker Face."

Before that, at 15, he ran off to Chicago to enlist in the Marines during World War I. Lacking a birth certificate, he was rejected and returned home. "I thought my father would beat the hell out of me, but he didn't," Ed recalled. "He just threw his arms around me and cried. It was the first time I'd ever seen my father cry."

Sullivan's people came from Bantry Bay in County Cork, Ireland. Once, he returned there and, aglow with nostalgia, he said proudly to the Irish woman serving tea, "I'm the first of the clan to get back here."

"Is that so?" the woman said. "Well, it took ye a damned long time!"

Ed Sullivan would recall that moment and laugh from his toes. Not the show, not the poker-face, but that laugh is what I choose to remember most about him.

Rod Serling

For Rod Serling, a writer who was obsessed with the phenomenon of time, the ultimate and surpassingly tragic irony is that he was granted so little of it. "There are no third acts in American lives," Scott Fitzgerald once said, meaning in particular the lives of American writers. What might have unfolded from the typewriter of Rod Serling, dead at 50, if he had been given those added years, his own third act?

As a playwright — perhaps the dominant literary figure spawned by television — Serling was moving into trickier waters, deeper, more profound emotions. From the very outset, entering TV's upper ranks with an explosive drama about big business called "Patterns," Serling etched his reputation as an exponent of the trip-hammer school.

There was, in a Serling script, always that trademark of cracking buckshot for dialogue in which the colloquial and the literate were somehow deftly fused. His work, as someone once remarked about Fitzgerald's writing, invariably had bones in it, along with a very special pungent imprint, distinctly Serling.

A subtle transformation occurred, however, in one of his last major works, "A Storm in Summer." In "A Storm in Summer," Serling cast his gaze on the conflict of youth and age as personified by an elderly delicatessen proprietor and a black lad of 10, a product of the Harlem ghetto with terribly old, angry eyes that told of hate and suspicion.

This was Serling expanding his horizons. Here was Serling edging out with compassion in another, warmer dimension, stretching his vast gifts as dramatist, and we could share his searching glimpse into the truth of the human condition as he perceived it.

It was, moreover, characteristic of Rod Serling in its absorption with time. In "Requiem for a Heavyweight," his best-known play for television, it was again the passage of time that gave the yarn its substance as Serling dwelled on an old prizefighter at the end of his rope.

Even before "The Twilight Zone," which was indisputably concerned with time, Serling wrote a science-fiction item called "The Time Element," wherein a horse-player (played by William Bendix) is transplanted in his dreams to Dec. 6, 1941. And there, given his prior knowledge of events past, he scatters bets on the Joe Louis-Buddy Baer fight, on the next World Series, on the Kentucky Derby.

If time was a theme of persistent fascination to Serling as a writer, the inexorable march of the years he found both distressing and, in a curious sense, challenging. A paratrooper in World War II with 60 combat leaps to his credit, Serling elected to celebrate his 40th birthday by hitting the silk at Ft. Bragg in North Carolina with 120 other jumpers.

Serling made the leap from 2,000 feet with 35 other men aboard a C-124 Globemaster. He was the second man out.

There was Rod Serling: self-deprecatory, good-natured, candid, tough-minded. Rod Serling — you thought of him always as a guy who smiled and laughed more than most of us, a very likable man who took sharp bites out of life and who, sitting quietly at a table, created the odd tension of a boxer in his corner, a wound-up welterweight about to enter the ring.

It was one of life's ironies that Rod Serling's voice, the voice of a writer, would become so recognizable. You could hear Rod's voice in narration of the Jacques Costeau specials on ocean life and you could also hear his voice over commercials, a lucrative venture.

Once, in the spirit of banter, I asked Rod why he wasn't hammering at his typewriter instead of talking into a microphone.

I remember his shrug and his smile. "It's not easy to turn down," Serling said then. "For one aspirin commercial they pay me a fast $4,000 up front and it'll bring in maybe $15,000 over a year — all this for 20 minutes work in an afternoon. On the other hand, I can work months on a script and it may not satisfy me or a producer and that's time down the tube."

Time down the tube. And then the time ran out.

Elvis

How long ago was it that this wiggling rocker named Presley with the unruly sideburns and the sleek black mop of carefully undisciplined hair, this earthy truck driver from the Deep South with the raw sensuality, how long ago was it that he suddenly and so explosively erupted into our consciousness — was it really 20 years ago? Only yesterday, it seems.

All of those yesterdays go back to the mid-1950's and in that time of innocence there were the farsighted people — me, for instance — who looked and listened and even talked with this fellow and we all figured, well, Elvis Presley is a nice, polite, modestly gifted young chap, a novelty act that would soon fade away like hula hoops in the sunset. In fact, I remember nodding in agreement to that very prophecy from a guy who was all set to make a bundle selling Stassen buttons.

As we all know now, Elvis Presley not only lasted, he endured. He endured and he thrived and he became, in time, what the late Bobby Darin had always said that he, Bobby Darin, would become — a legend.

Now the legend is gone, at 42, his life spent all too early, and as Bing Crosby remarked on the ABC special dedicated to Presley's memory: "He'll leave so many bereaved — deeply bereaved." Hastily stitched together and, in that regard, necessarily superficial, this ABC special was narrated by Geraldo Rivera and its title was fitting: "Elvis — Love Me Tender."

"So he's dead, the king of rock 'n' roll," said Rivera at the conclusion. "Long live the memory. Long live the music."

Both the music and the memory were served, on the special, with a plenitude of clips from his movies, all of them hugely successful and all interchangeable. "These are Presley pictures," an MGM publicist once said with an amiable shrug. "They don't need titles. They could be numbered and they'd still sell."

Perhaps of all the comments that flowed from every side, the most telling came from ABC's resident purveyor of gossip, Rona Barrett, who observed: "The private man, the insecure Elvis could never be alone. The good ol' boys — the Memphis Mafia as we called them — were always with him . . . Sometimes he would walk onstage with a Derringer in his boot . . . Still lonely and insecure, Elvis Presley died an enigma."

Earlier in the evening, I had watched Henry Winkler on "Happy Days," strutting through his role of The Fonz, which is, at some remove, a pasteurized extension of the Elvis of the '50s. And I thought of Mae West, who shocked the populace in her day, and it seemed to me that both of them, Mae West and Elvis, were instinctive performers at once aware of the great sensuality they shared and of how this commodity could be spoofed with rich, good humor.

And both were authentic originals. Presley always gave due credit to his musical roots, to the black gospel singers and the rhythm-and-blues artists such as Chuck Berry. But Presley was an original, none-theless, an authentic American primitive talent in full flower.

I thought of another phenomenon — Frank Sinatra, who was, in his first burst of fame, so very thin and emaciated but still tough and wiry. Presley was big and rangy and he was also soft and pasty. Both men were gifted, in short, with a similarly delicate blend of strength and vulnerability.

What Elvis did, with his gyrations and his guttural sounds and mocking humor, was lash out at the last remaining vestiges of Victorianism in this country. When Presley went on Milton Berle's TV show somewhere in the 1950's, he put people in shock.

"Execrable taste, bordering on obscenity," a high school music teacher wrote to Berle.

A police officer, after watching Presley's writhings on the stage, commented grimly: "If he did that on the street, we'd arrest him!"

Presley, in that placid time, bestirred a storm of complaint by parents, teachers, sociologists. And about five or six years later, all of these same people were doing the Twist.

How quaint it seems now that Steve Allen, who had a Sunday night variety show then, refused to have Presley appear on moral grounds. And Ed Sullivan, whose own show was in mortal combat with Allen's, signed Presley for three appearances — but ordered the cameras kept scrupulously above Presley's waist. Thus were the morals of the nation safeguarded.

I interviewed Presley once, when he was first on the rise, and I asked about his singing style. "It came natural," Presley said in his languid drawl. "It's like I feel all this wild emotion down deep and I express it. If I didn't feel it deep, I just couldn't sing it."

Those down-deep wild emotions expressed in song and movement brought him fame and adulation and a mountain of money. But in the end, for the lonely country boy, that may not have been enough.

Bing

The name itself had such a leisurely lilt about it, a casual, light-hearted and appealing grace. Bing Crosby.

I remember once asking Bing Crosby if the name "Bing" had proved to be an asset in his career. Bing nodded and puffed slowly on one of the pipes he used to buy on his trips to Ireland. "Absolutely," Bing said. "Made all the difference in the world. The appellation was right for a wandering minstrel of my stripe. People kind of remembered the name. There just aren't many Bings in public life."

Many Bings? There was only one Bing Crosby and he is gone now and there is a perplexing sense of loss and finality. Death was not a word one could ever associate with this symbol of good times who had been a part of our lives for so long. He was always there, a national asset, and for me personally, a hero and model going back to college days. My man was Crosby. Strolling the campus, I wanted to be Bing Crosby. I sought the easy insouciance that was Bing. I learned to smoke a pipe, like Bing. I tried to talk like Bing and move like Bing, in his ingratiatingly effortless style. I went about crooning "Pennies From Heaven."

Small matter that I did all of this so badly that people, unaware of my wellspring, merely thought I was talking funny. And I couldn't keep the pipe lit.

Once, I mentioned this to Crosby. He was amused. "Tell you what," Bing said to me a year or two ago, "if you ever get a bit thin on top, I've got an old toupee you can have."

One remembers warmly these touches reflective of a man embraced for decades by worldwide fame but who seemed, in a curious way, to be one of us. Some months ago, working closely with Bing, I had written a piece for one of the travel magazines on his favorite golf holes around the world. Later, he phoned me. "Hi, Don," he said, "this is Bing Crosby."

It was typical, I think, of Bing, that self-effacing salutation on the phone. "Bing Crosby," he had said, not simply "Bing," which would surely have been sufficient. How many Bings are there? How many voices so easily recognized, so ingrained in the public consciousness, so rich and individual?

I think now of a chilly morning up in the stately San Francisco suburb of Hillsborough, and Bing Crosby greeting me at the door to his home. I had come for an interview. "Come on in," Bing said then. "It's a little fresh out there."

Then he glanced up at the darkening clouds. "May get ourselves something of a soak later on."

I had brought him a can of English tobacco and we sat in his den, with the blazing fire in the fireplace and the walls alive with original Russells and Remingtons and Wieghorsts, and we smoked our pipes and Bing talked.

There was much pleasure in listening to Bing, with his special feel for words and how they sound, the well-burnished phrases tumbling out like musical notes. He talked about his early inspiration, the Irish tenor John McCormick — "a hero in our house" — and how he studied law at Gonzaga University in his native Spokane, Wash. He talked about going out in the 1920s as a singer with the Three Rhythm Boys and working with Paul Whiteman.

"We killed 'em all over the country," Bing remembered, "but we laid an omelet in New York."

There was always, in Bing's language, the flair for the droll touch, the appealing spin of original phrase. As Fred Russell, the sports-writer from Nashville, has suggested, some words are wallflowers and others dance the night away. Bing's words had feet like Fred Astaire.

When the television camera first came to the Crosby Clambake, Bing's annual golf tournament at Monterey, Crosby put aside his clubs and took to the microphone as a commentator. Let others remember the scenic glories of Pebble Beach and the celebrity hackers in the rain and the crackerjack pros. Bing's descriptions, his playful thrusts of language, cling to the memory.

Bing would talk about a "whisper of a wind" and a golfer using a "quiet six-iron to best a heartless pin placement." In Bing's eyes, the ball didn't roll close to the hole — "it snuggled up to the aperture." He would refer to the 18th at Pebble as "a stern finishing hole, very testing." An indecisive swing he would describe as "a bit girlish," and a powerhouse swing he might sum up as "very athletic." One year, as Jack Lemmon delighted the crowd with the game's most ungainly swing off the tee, Bing merrily offered this apt description: "He looks like he's basting a turkey!"

"Loose as ashes" is another phrase that Bing once contributed to the language, referring to someone else. But the words might well have applied to Harry Lillis Crosby. He was, assuredly, an American original. It was once said that to an American living abroad, no other voice would sound so American as Bing Crosby's. It seems appropriate that his favorite historical character, his own personal hero, was one of the architects of the American Revolution, Benjamin Franklin.

"Anything written about Ben I've got it in my library," I remember Bing saying one day. "This goes back to, oh, 1939, when a doctor friend of mine loaned me a biography. I ate it up. Been a Franklin buff ever since. People think of Ben as a bit of a roisterer with a bawdy side. But he was a great negotiator. Nobody outsmarted him. He was an all-round fellow, a great bibbler known to accept a friendly glass, a great scientist, a great statesman. Ben had a few amours, too. A wanderin' eye, y'know."

There was such a tang and style about Bing, a singularity of voice and manner. Once having seen or heard Bing Crosby, you would never confuse him with anyone else. I make no pretense of having known Bing other than professionally, as a writer in pursuit of an interview. Bing Crosby was a complex blend of the public figure and the private man. There were those who would attempt to march uninvited past that wall of privacy and at once the Crosby blue eyes would turn to ice. It was a side of the man that I never witnessed.

When I saw Bing, he was always rich with good humor, the breezy raconteur spinning tales. Once, at a restaurant in San Francisco a few weeks before the Crosby golf tournament one year, Bing dropped by to hoist a few with the gentlemen of the press.

For Bing, there had been a pleasant morning of duck hunting and he arrived still dressed for the shoot. He put a light to his pipe and a sip to his wine and there was talk soon thereafter of the breezes that whip around the Monterey Peninsula, site of his tournament.

"Listen, they have a few breezes in Ireland, too," Bing informed the group at the table. "They're mighty keen on golf over there, all very knowledgable. One day I'm playing at Killarney and I'm having trouble hitting my drive into a stiff breeze and this little old Irish lady, bundled to the nines, pipes up from the gallery: 'Bing, slip it UNDER the wind!'"

Then Bing was reminded of another incident during one of his many visits to Ireland. "I was supposed to give a little talk," Bing said, "and I'd been introduced by the master of ceremonies and I was just starting my remarks. Before I could finish a sentence, this big Irishman way back in the hall yells out in a brogue as thick as bog: 'We can't see you, Bing. Would you ever stand on your wallet?'"

The last time I saw Bing Crosby was at Lakeside Golf Club in North Hollywood as we did an interview sitting in a golf cart at the first tee. I wish he were there still, starting out all over again.

THE END